MYTH OF MONEY

MYTH OF MONEY

Breaking Out of the Failing Financial System

TATIANA KOFFMAN

WILEY

For general information on our other products and services or for technical support, please contact our Customer Care Department within the United States at (800) 762-2974, outside the United States at (317) 572-3993 or fax (317) 572-4002.

Wiley also publishes its books in a variety of electronic formats. Some content that appears in print may not be available in electronic formats. For more information about Wiley products, visit our web site at www.wiley.com.

Library of Congress Cataloging-in-Publication Data is Available:

ISBN 9781394226863 (Cloth)
ISBN 9781394226870 (ePub)
ISBN 9781394226887 (ePDF)

Cover Artwork: Denisa Zaionciuc | Cryptopunks © 2017 Yuga Labs
Cover Design: Wiley

SKY10081528_081424

Contents

Acknowledgments

Writing a book has proven to be far more challenging than I ever imagined. Choosing to write is choosing to bring a piece of yourself into the world, something that will stand the test of time and reflect who you are in that moment. It demands attention to countless details, each capable of derailing the project. Moreover, it requires daily introspection, questioning whether you have what it takes and whether anyone will care to read it once it's finished. It's a self-imposed existential crisis that lasts the entirety of the journey.

The creation of this book would not have been possible without the support of incredible people along the way, each playing a pivotal role in this journey.

First, I extend my sincere appreciation to everyone who helped bring this project to life: Bill Falloon and the entire Wiley team, Molly Pisani and Katherine MacLellan for their exceptional editing support, and my team at Moonwalker Capital, Saif Shaikh and Axel Broks, who made space for this project and helped refine it along the way.

This journey of my life and career would not have been possible without many friends who have supported me and brought joy to every occasion. While including a full list is nearly impossible, I wish to mention a few names that come to mind. A heartfelt thank you to Eyal Baumel and Corey McGuire for keeping me inspired and motivated, Trevor Koverko and Q Dhalla for always inviting me on new adventures, many of which were content for the stories I share, Nataliya Kotlyarova, Lauren Bissel, Teodora Atanasova, and Kate Kallot for being my real-life "Charlie's Angels" as we explored the world, Sir Richard Branson for helping me discover my hidden talent for backgammon, Rob Rhinehart for pushing me to write, Chris Pan and Brett Leve for believing in my potential, Ben Zion and Loro Masnah for rekindling my passion for art, and my dear friends Analise Roland and Ebeneezer Bond for showing up with kindness during the toughest moments of this journey.

Additionally, I extend my gratitude to the great mentors in my life: Professor Jim Crimmins, who taught me about philosophy and the workings of the world, Senator Jerry Grafstein, who taught me to believe in myself, Jay Rosenzweig for his loyal support and encouragement in all my endeavors, and Rabbi Lori Shapiro for always leading with light.

Finally, a deep thank-you to my parents and my family for giving me a story worth telling.

Myth, n:
/miTH/

1. a traditional story, especially one concerning the early history of a people or explaining some natural or social phenomenon.
2. a widely held but false belief or idea.

Adapted from Oxford Languages

Money, n:
/ˈmə-nē/

1. any item or medium of exchange that symbolizes perceived value.
2. the assets, property, and resources owned by someone or something; wealth.

Investopedia

Introduction: My Journey to Freedom

The only true wisdom is in knowing you know nothing.

—Socrates

I started writing this book in April 2020, amid the beginnings of the COVID-19 pandemic. By that point, it was dawning on me that money might be a myth, in either or both of the common senses of the term. Was money anything more than a story we tell ourselves, and had been telling ourselves since we first traded cowrie shells on the beaches of prehistory? And was the story based on anything inherently true, real, or within our power or control?

It has been a personal four-year odyssey as the world changed around me. Countries and economies closed down for weeks, months, years. Social upheaval spread throughout the West as police brutality sparked mass demonstrations and riots that led to further police brutality. Wars in Ukraine and the Middle East—and armed conflicts in dozens of other places—ignited, reminding us that humanity has a long way to go when it comes to achieving equality, justice, and peace.

At the time this journey started, I was 32 years old and residing in Los Angeles. My life looked perfect on the outside, but everything was quietly, or not so quietly, falling apart. As a highly educated professional holding degrees in political science, law, and business, I had spent the previous decade working in the finance industry, from stuffy trading floors of banks to the penthouses and closed-door parties of Los Angeles, California.

1

My career encompassed investment banking, derivatives trading, and venture capital investments for celebrities such as the iconic band Linkin Park, and the Chainsmokers, ranked among the top five highest-paid DJ acts in the world. This line of work took me to glamorous destinations such as New York, London, Dubai, and Monaco, offering Instagram-worthy experiences that were far from my humble origins in Ukraine and the financial instability of most of my early days. I felt a sense of pride in my life.

Yet by early 2020, as the pandemic appeared on the horizon, I was also feeling consistent pangs of anxiety and dissatisfaction. I realized that despite the seemingly glamorous exterior, my career in finance had left me empty-handed—I couldn't afford to buy a home or a car and was living paycheck to paycheck, struggling under the burden of over $50,000 in credit card debt. I was surrounded by wealth, I created it for others, and yet I felt unmistakably (for lack of a better word) broke.

I share this information upfront because our worldview is inherently subjective and shaped by our life experiences, and it is important to be honest about our circumstances when we present our stories and opinions. The views expressed in this book are no exception, encompassing elements of history, analysis, and innate biases. If our minds were a blender, the resulting mixture would consist of childhood memories, education, media exposure, and dinner table discussions with friends and family, as well as a healthy dose of fear presented by our current life circumstances. My mind is no exception. Had I been writing from another part of the world, or with a different set of experiences, my story might have been vastly different.

Nevertheless, this book is a collection of knowledge told from my perspective: knowledge of the financial world I was forced to reckon with and market catastrophes that shaped my path. It recounts everything I've learned about money over a lifetime, detailing my journey to achieve financial independence and become the first self-made millionaire in my family, and to no longer feel blindsided by the daily effects of the financial system that governs our lives.

I started working on this book during the pandemic, and thus, at times, I try to answer a somewhat existential question: How did we get here?

On March 11, 2020, United States President Donald Trump made a late-night announcement during a press conference. In an unprecedented move, he declared that the American border would be closed to travelers from Europe. Within a week, the travel ban was extended to Canada, Mexico, and the rest of the world. Panic filled the air—fear, uncertainty, and doubt. Many people wondered: Could we trust the information presented to us by those in power?

Returning to Los Angeles on the last flight from JFK, I went to the store and stocked up on a six-month supply of nonperishable items—rice, buckwheat, ramen, and canned corn—still without fully grasping the scope of this emerging crisis. I couldn't help but wonder whether this situation mirrored what my Jewish great-grandparents experienced during World War II, or what my mother experienced while anxiously waiting for hours in line, clutching her food coupons in the Soviet Union. To this day, I believe my reflex to hoard supplies was a genetic memory encoded in me by the traumas of my ancestors. After all, I was the only one among my friends with enough sanitizer to last the season.

In the following weeks, businesses in major cities closed their doors, schools and universities sent students home, and cruise ships and planes were grounded indefinitely. To curb the virus's spread, people refrained from going to restaurants, shopping in stores, and taking vacations. Concerns over paying rent and other expenses escalated as money became a top priority for everyone.

The US wasn't alone in its self-imposed isolation, as countries worldwide implemented their own lockdown measures. Russia threatened to imprison those leaving their homes without permission, while China employed sophisticated tracking technology to monitor citizens' movements. With a population of 1.3 billion, India mandated that all residents stay at home for 21 days, leading to millions cramped in tight living spaces with poor sanitation and limited access to supplies. After decades of globalization and free trade, the world was abruptly silenced.

The 2020 pandemic had a significant impact on the US economy, plunging it into a state of panic. On March 12, the Dow Jones saw its steepest one-day drop since 1987, falling by over 10%, while oil prices plummeted by 34%. By May, over 30 million Americans had filed for unemployment, and all new jobs created since the 2008 financial crisis had vanished, with unemployment rates reaching levels akin to those of the Great Depression. Tens of thousands of Americans began dying each week, and morgues in some places were filling so quickly that hospitals were forced to resort to storing bodies in refrigerated trucks.

And then, just when we thought 2020 couldn't get any worse, the world was rocked by the wrongful death of George Floyd at the hands of police on May 25. Outrage surged across the globe, leading to protests in more than 140 cities around the world. Peaceful demonstrators, children among them, were maced, beaten, shot at, and even driven at by police vehicles, all of which was captured on video and shared on social media platforms such as Instagram. Small business owners saw their storefronts looted by opportunists who exploited the political unrest during violent riots in Minneapolis, Atlanta, Chicago, Los Angeles, and New York, among other places.

My heart ached.

Although I am an outsider in American life in some ways—Jewish, an immigrant, a non-native English speaker—over time, I have become more integrated; new friends don't always realize I was born abroad. And being white, I never had to worry about being mistreated by teachers or the police, nor did I have to fear being denied a job because of my skin color. Most significantly, I never understood what it was like to live in a system designed to hurt me rather than protect me. I had yet to witness firsthand a society turning on itself.

The ongoing economic and racial crises in our society reminded me of the philosophical principles I had studied in my college days. In his 1651 book *The Leviathan*, English philosopher Thomas Hobbes posited that every democratic society is founded on a social contract—an agreement we all implicitly enter into to cooperate with state regulations in return for social benefits. Simply put, citizens consent to follow the rules and express their opinions through peaceful means in exchange for services such as roads, hospitals, security, education, economic welfare, and more. Naturally, there are those who opt not to participate—they avoid taxes, live off the land in remote areas, or emigrate elsewhere. However, for most of us, the benefits of being part of an organized, democratic society outweigh the sacrifices.

In 2020, the American government fell short in three key areas of its obligation under the social contract. The first and most obvious area was that of security, as evidenced by the growing discontent over police brutality. We rely on our government and police to protect us and to be on the side of the innocent. What happens when communities no longer trust law enforcement and start self-policing? Do we still agree to a social contract with a state whose law enforcement we no longer trust?

The second notable area of governmental failure was health care. Health care should be a basic human right, yet America is the only developed country in the world that does not offer public health care to its citizens. Instead, it requires citizens to buy into an overpriced insurance system that makes health care unaffordable for the majority. Meanwhile, not only does the US have the lowest life expectancy among developed countries, but we also have the highest rate of avoidable deaths. While the pandemic may not have cared about borders or differences in economic status, it revealed that our system definitely does: those in lower socioeconomic brackets—who more often relied on communal transportation, lived in close quarters, and had preexisting health conditions—suffered the most from COVID-19. Of course, they were also the exact people who were less likely to be able to afford health care in the first place.

The third and most significant government failure during the pandemic was economic, and this is the failure that takes precedence in this book.

As hard experiences have taught me, there is light at the end of the tunnel, but only for those who seek it out and persevere in their quest. In this book, I offer a ray of hope for anyone tangled in financial confusion or disillusioned by the financial system that so often seems rigged against us. I unfold my personal odyssey—a journey that spans the political spheres of the East and West, ventures through the high-stakes world of traditional finance, and dives into the realms of entertainment and venture capital in the heart of Los Angeles. I recount my deep plunge into the Bitcoin vortex, my ringside seat at a colossal cryptocurrency scheme in Dubai, and my explorative sojourns across the diverse landscapes of Africa. Alongside, I bring to light the firsthand experiences of others through the financial upheavals and breakthroughs in Lebanon and El Salvador. In the wake of it all, I am left with one overarching belief: if money is a myth, it is a story you had better write for yourself.

Throughout this book, you'll find a recurrent theme emphasizing Bitcoin and decentralized financial systems. This isn't by accident. I aim to offer a comprehensive perspective on our financial ecosystem and its historical pitfalls, as well as a glimpse into our potential future trajectory. Bitcoin, in my eyes, is not just a digital asset; it's our strongest economic safeguard against what lies ahead.

This is not a personal finance book.

What lies within these pages is a mosaic of stories and hard-earned lessons from the past decade, a period that saw me outmaneuver the financial system, carve out my own version of success, and navigate the amusing, sometimes painful detours life threw my way. My aspiration is that as you turn these pages, you'll experience eye-opening revelations and, at the very least, find some entertainment in the recounting of my journey.

But this book is more than a memoir; it's a critical analysis of the world's shifting economic currents, a candid look at the challenges America grapples with globally due to its economic strategies, and, most crucially, a guide on how to navigate the financial storm of the coming decade. This book is crafted not only for my contemporaries, but also for a new generation eager to learn, as well as the generation of my parents, who find themselves struggling to keep pace with the ever-shifting financial landscape.

I hope that as you make your way through the following chapters, you forge your own journey to demystifying the myth of money, and gain a little inspiration to join me on a path less travelled.

1

Drawing Back the Iron Curtain

Happiness and freedom begin with a clear understanding of one principle: Some things are within our control, and some things are not.
—Epictetus

In the summer of 2023, as I pieced together this chapter, an invitation arrived to deliver a guest lecture at Pepperdine University, nestled in the tranquil mountains of Malibu, California. Pepperdine, a prestigious Christian institution renowned for its rigorous academics and spiritual ethos, draws students from affluent American families and international elites, all shelling out upwards of $60,000 per year for tuition.

Though it wasn't my first lecture, this particular engagement carved a lasting impression on me. Fresh from riding the tumultuous yet rewarding wave of the latest cryptocurrency bull cycle, I arrived on campus with an air of newfound status. A string of astute investments and strategic deals had catapulted me into a life I once only dreamed of: living in a serene oceanfront home in Malibu, driving the sleek, quiet hum of a brand-new Tesla, and wearing the subtle gleam of a presidential Rolex. I moved through the world with a sense of poise, as if I'd deciphered life's most cryptic codes, especially those concerning wealth.

Yet, I was mindful of never giving off that "new money" stench. Those who come from very little, like me, experience substantial psychological changes when they first step into wealth. It's part of the myth of money. Most times, the feelings are a mix of imposter syndrome wrapped up with guilt. *Why do I have the fancy new car and the expensive watch, while others have so little by comparison? I'm no better than my sweet cleaning lady from Venezuela, who cleans my house for $20 an hour, and yet she earns her living through physical labor, while I get to travel the world and work on multimillion-dollar deals.* I'd worked hard to achieve my newfound success, yet the pointed feelings of guilt continued to bubble up as queasiness in my weak stomach.

These feelings accompanied me as I prepared for my lecture on cryptocurrency, facing a hundred or so guests and students, most of whom hailed from established, wealthy families—families unlikely to have experienced the brink of poverty like mine or the imposter syndrome that accompanies newfound success. I wondered: *Will they see right through me? Will they think I'm a fraud?*

Still, being invited to impart wisdom to the bright, eager minds at Pepperdine was not just an honor; it was an affirmation of my journey, a tangible marker of having "made it." As I stood before those students, I felt a sense of completion, a moment of reflection and recognition that what I had achieved was truly mine, a testament to the journey, the decisions, and the relentless pursuit of success that had brought me to that moment. It was a poignant reminder that some milestones in life are not just about arriving but about understanding and embracing the path that led us there.

Roots of Resilience

A few years ago, I explored my ancestry through 23 and Me, uncovering a kaleidoscope of European roots that span Ukrainian, Hungarian, Polish, Russian, and Ashkenazi Jewish heritage, with a surprising hint of 1% East Asian descent. I was born on February 9, 1988, in the Ukrainian city of Cherkasy, of not quite 300,000 people, or at least it was before Vladimir Putin invaded Ukraine in 2022. My birthplace was not entirely a matter of choice but rather a last-minute decision. My mother, ever resourceful, opted for Cherkasy because her father lived there; with her due date fast approaching, she sought familiar surroundings and some semblance of support as she embarked on her labor solo.

There's a term for children like me: "wedding night babies." My parents' love story was a whirlwind romance—a courtship of just five dates—culminating in my father, a soon-to-be-deployed captain on a

Soviet ship, proposing marriage. They had mere days to make things official before he was set to sail from Severomorsk, a port high above the Arctic Circle, home to the Russian Northern Fleet. He would be at sea for nine months.

To this day, my father laughs about how, on their wedding day, every cosmic sign urged him to flee. First, the taxi was late, making them late for the ceremony. Second, both witnesses came down with an inexplicable virus and couldn't attend. Third, my father received an urgent call that his ship had disappeared—a false alarm, it turned out, as the ship had been moved for maintenance without proper reporting. All in all, their wedding day was a fiasco. The details of the wedding night remain a mystery, except for one undeniable fact: it was the night I was conceived.

Years later, in my 20s, my father handed me an album. It wasn't filled with baby pictures or mementos from family outings—those couldn't exist, as my father wasn't part of my childhood. Instead, the album chronicled my parents' relationship during his post-wedding deployment. Within its pages were the letters exchanged between the young newlyweds. Initially, their correspondence was filled with love and the excitement of building a life together. The joy of impending parenthood brightened their exchanges, as my mother shared her first inklings of my existence.

However, the tone of the letters soon shifted. Financial strain crept in, emotional commitment wavered, and the dream of a cohesive family began to unravel. By the time my father's ship docked, I had already been born, and my mother wanted nothing to do with him. When he arrived at the hospital, he was served with divorce papers and asked to exit my life until my 21st birthday.

Yet, genetics had its own sense of humor. Despite my mother's dominant blue-eyed, blonde lineage, I emerged a stark contrast: my father's brown eyes, a mop of dark, curly hair, and porcelain skin—a nod to my paternal Ashkenazi heritage. Throughout my childhood, my mother and I often drew quizzical looks from strangers; we made an odd-looking pair.

The Fall of the Soviet Empire

In 1989, when I was one and a half years old, my mother remarried, and we moved to Moscow. Two years later, on December 25, 1991, Mikhail Gorbachev delivered his final speech as the leader of the USSR, explaining his decision to resign. "The reason was evident—society was suffocating in the grip of the command-bureaucratic system. Doomed to serve ideology and to bear the terrible burden of the arms race, it had been pushed to the limit of what was possible," Gorbachev asserted. "All attempts at partial reforms—and there were many—failed, one after the other. The country had lost direction. It was impossible to go on living that way. Everything had to be changed fundamentally."

That New Year's Eve, the atmosphere in our Moscow living room was charged with more than the usual suspense and anticipation. Every television set across the vast expanse of the Soviet Union was tuned to the same channel. Boris Yeltsin—the newly elected president of the Russian Soviet Federative Socialist Republic (RSFSR) and the first popularly elected head of state in Russian history—was about to announce the beginning of a new era for Russia, and its satellite republics, as an independent state. Yeltsin also promised to transform Russia's command economy into a capitalist market economy; in other words, he planned to finish the job that Gorbachev began. And indeed, Yeltsin's presidency was marked by significant political and economic reforms in Russia. He would soon implement economic shock therapy, floating the ruble on the free market, instituting nationwide privatization, and lifting price controls.

With a gravity that matched the historical weight of the moment, as the clock struck midnight that New Year's Eve, Yeltsin declared the USSR, a behemoth that had stood unyielding for decades, dissolved. Yeltsin finished his speech with the following words: "We, the multinational people of Russia, united by a common fate on our land ... declare our sovereignty."

I was on the cusp of turning four. While children my age in the West took the stability of their governments for granted or didn't think about government at all, I witnessed firsthand the disintegration of the structure that formed the very basis of our lives. For most people, governments are seen as eternal, their permanence as certain as the rising sun. As my earliest memories formed, my eyes were opened to a profound truth: even the mightiest of structures can crumble. Perhaps the only Americans who would have similar memories from childhood are those who lived through the assassination of JFK in 1963.

The realization that governments and their leaders are fallible left a permanent scar on my psyche. While the world around me continued, and continues to this day, to evolve, this new understanding of impermanence became a cornerstone of my worldview. The knowledge that foundations can shift, and that the familiar can become unfamiliar seemingly overnight, shaped my perspective in profound and lasting ways. I questioned everything and everyone, including the adults around me. After all, if the leader of one of the greatest super-powers on Earth couldn't hold it together, what gave anyone else any authority?

Contrary to how it seemed to me then, the downfall of the Soviet Union was not an abrupt event but a culmination of several critical factors. Foremost was the escalating cost of the Cold War, a draining, decades-long contest of military and ideological supremacy with America that stretched both nations' resources thin. Mounting interna-tional pressures, with other global actors prodding at the superpower's stability, exacerbated the situation. Additionally, an internal ideological crisis simmered within the heart of the Soviet Union; there was growing disillusionment and skepticism among its people and leaders about the sustainability and morality of communism. Doubts about whether the nation's economic system could continue to provide for its people and compete on the world stage led to a weakening of belief in the com-munist path. Collectively, these elements eroded the foundations of the Soviet giant, leading to its eventual, historic dissolution.

At the heart of Soviet disillusionment was the age-old debate between communism and capitalism, ideologies that have shaped the course of nations and economies throughout modern history. Most nations navigate a middle path, integrating elements of socialism and communism with the principles of capitalism to various degrees. The United States, for instance, is often seen as the bastion of capital-ism, a system underpinned by market-driven economics and individual entrepreneurship, yet these are interspersed with certain social safety nets and programs. In contrast, China functions under a nominally socialist system that has, over recent decades, largely embraced state sponsored capitalism, characterized by robust state intervention and guidance, including the implementation of "five-year plans" (a concept reminis-cent of the central planning so essential to communist ideology).

Experiencing both systems firsthand, I've come to be a proponent for less government and more individual freedoms and opportunities. But living through Russia's transition from rations to riches was an incredibly bumpy ride.

Systems of Government

There are several main political systems of government, each with its own structure and principles for governing a country. Here are some of the most common political systems:

1. **Democracy:** In a democracy, power is vested in the people. Citizens have the right to participate in the decision-making process, often through free and fair elections. Representative democracies, such as those of the United States and many Western countries, involve elected officials who make decisions on behalf of the people, while in direct democracies people make those decisions themselves. Democracies can vary in structure from republics to parliamentary systems. Examples of democracies include the United States, Canada, France, and Israel.

2. **Monarchy:** In a monarchy, a single individual, the monarch, holds supreme authority; the position is typically inherited. There are two main types of monarchy:

   - **Absolute monarchy:** The monarch has virtually unchecked power. Examples include Saudi Arabia and the United Arab Emirates.

   - **Constitutional monarchy:** The monarch's powers are limited by a constitution or laws, and there may be an elected legislature alongside the monarchy (e.g. the United Kingdom, Sweden, and Spain).

3. **Authoritarianism:** In authoritarian systems, power is concentrated in the hands of a single leader or a small group. Political opposition is suppressed, and civil liberties may be limited. Authoritarian governments have little or no accountability to the people, with limited political competition and restrictions on free speech. Examples include modern-day Russia and Syria.

4. **Totalitarianism:** Totalitarian regimes exert extreme control over all aspects of society, including politics, the economy, culture, and even personal life. These governments often use propaganda and censorship to maintain their grip on power. North Korea is a frequently cited example of a totalitarian regime.

5. **Theocracy:** In a theocracy, religious leaders or religious institutions hold political power, and government decisions are heavily influenced by religious doctrine or principles. Iran is an example of a modern-day theocracy.

6. **Communism:** In a communist system, the government controls all aspects of the economy, and property is commonly owned. The aim is to create a classless society where wealth and resources are distributed equally. In practice, communist regimes have often resulted in authoritarian rule; the People's Republic of China and Cuba are examples.

★★

The 1990s ushered in a period of profound transformation in Russia, marking a departure from the Soviet era's centralized control to an emerging landscape of fledgling capitalism. This was a time of stark dichotomies, as the remnants of a rationed economy lingered amid the nascent signs of market-driven change. My recollections of those early post-Soviet years are etched with the stark realities of scarcity. I remember the empty aisles in grocery stores, the limited variety of cars that dotted the roads, and a collective resignation to the fact that desires most often remained unfulfilled.

Under the USSR—composed of fifteen republics, spanning 11 time zones, including Russia, Ukraine, Georgia, Latvia, and Estonia—citizens had been viewed more as functional components of the greater state than as individuals with personal aspirations. There were some benefits to this system: believe it or not, gender equality was more advanced under the Soviet system than here in the West; fully subsidized university education was available and encouraged for anyone who wanted it, regardless of gender. Indeed, women were a strong component of productivity for the Soviet collective; the state couldn't afford to forgo the use of their human inventory.

Yet, there were evident drawbacks to the collectivist approach. Each autumn, for example, it was customary for professionals from various sectors to be mobilized to the agricultural fields, assisting in the harvest. I have tried to imagine myself finishing a round of fundraising for a technology start-up one day, and then being forced to pick grapes in the

Sonoma Valley for wine harvest season the next. I can't really see how this arrangement would make either practical or economic sense.

As capitalism began to infuse the Russian spirit, a transformation occurred. Choice, a concept previously foreign to most Russians, now took center stage. Businesses emerged, entrepreneurs flourished, and competition spurred innovation. Our streets, once lined with homogeneous Soviet-era Ladas, now showcased a parade of foreign cars. The monochrome fabric of our society was slowly being interwoven with vibrant new threads of diversity and opportunity.

The pent-up demand for the hallmark capitalist goods and luxuries among ordinary Russians became evident during the final years of the Soviet Union. It took 16 years of negotiations, but on January 31, 1990, George Cohon, a Canadian McDonald's executive, finally opened Russia's first McDonald's in Moscow. In the bitter cold, people started lining up outside the restaurant at 4:00 a.m. According to the *Washington Post*, when the restaurant opened at 10:00 a.m., there was already a five-hundred-yard-long line of customers waiting to get in; an incredible 38,000 people got their first taste of Big Macs that day. I tasted my first McDonald's Happy Meal a few years later, as a reward for earning all A's on my report card—one of the happiest days of my childhood.

The Birth of Property Rights in the East

The drastic shift from communism to capitalism heralded the emergence of property rights. A well-known cornerstone of economic development, this concept was a game changer in Russia. Homes were no longer just assigned dwellings based on professional and societal contribution; they transformed into assets, a potential source of financial leverage.

Our family was fortuitously positioned when this shift occurred. My stepfather's dad—whom I have always considered my grandfather— was a well-established engineering professor at Moscow State University during the Soviet era. Due to his contributions to the collective, he had the use of a lavish penthouse in the heart of Moscow. Under the new regime, we became the owners of that apartment seemingly overnight. This windfall to our family was a pivotal step in securing our financial future, or so we thought.

Ownership Laws: The Cornerstone of Economic Development

Property rights refer to socially recognized and legally protected claims or entitlements over assets, be they land, buildings, inventions, or other forms of property. They are crucial for economic development because they incentivize individuals to invest in, innovate on, and take care of their property, knowing they will benefit from any future returns.

For most families, their largest asset is their home, against which they can borrow to accomplish goals such as starting a business. The stronger the property rights in a country, the more likely it is that entrepreneurs will start businesses and foreign companies will be inclined to invest. This leads to job creation, increased economic activity, and overall GDP growth.

In his book *The Mystery of Capital: Why Capitalism Triumphs in the West and Fails Everywhere Else*, Peruvian economist Hernando de Soto argues that the lack of clear property rights is a primary factor hindering the economic development of many countries. In Lima, Peru, for example, there are vast squatter communities, or shantytowns, where people built their homes on land they didn't legally own. Meanwhile, just around the corner are homes built on land that is legally owned. Consequences arose from the discrepancy between informal and formal ownership.

1. **Effects on Development and Investment:** Without formal property titles, people couldn't use their homes as collateral for loans. This made it difficult for them to secure capital, hindering small business development and home improvement efforts. As a result, these homes often lacked basic services and infrastructure. On the other hand, those with legal title to their homes could access credit, leading to increased economic activity in their neighborhoods. Their ability to leverage their property meant they could invest in their homes, their businesses, and their children's education.

2. **Effects on Economic Growth:** Areas characterized by informal ownership often lag in economic growth because businesses are wary of investing where property rights aren't

secure. Additionally, the residents of these areas contribute less to the formal economy, reducing potential tax revenues. When property rights are secured in an area, it draws more investment and increases property values, aiding in the integration of these areas into the city's broader economic life.

The countries of the former USSR experienced a seismic transition from informal to formal property ownership, with individuals enjoying property rights and their corresponding economic benefits for the first time in their lifetimes.

Childhood Lessons: It's a Hard-Knock Life

For many children, early mathematical encounters revolve around counting toys, sharing candies, or maybe solving simple arithmetic problems in school. But growing up in a transitional economy, I was receiving firsthand the type of economic education that most PhDs read about only in textbooks. I vividly remember one morning, at the age of six, I experienced a math problem that no classroom had prepared me for. Since the start of first grade, my daily allowance for lunch money had been 5,000 rubles, a consistent figure that I had grown accustomed to. But on this particular day, my mother handed me a paper note that read, simply, "5." The zeros had mysteriously vanished.

My mother tried to explain it away, hastily brushing over the subject: "Prices were skyrocketing, and there were too many zeros, so the government divided it by a thousand. Don't worry, five is the same as five thousand." But as a child with a keen eye for details, I couldn't shake off my confusion. Why should the price suddenly change when the value of my lunch remained the same? The notion that money could be so easily altered bewildered me.

It wasn't until my university years that I truly grasped the significance of what had happened to my lunch allowance. With the collapse of the Soviet Union, Russia plunged headfirst into a free market economy. Prices of goods and services soared practically overnight. In the early 1990s, hyperinflation gripped the nation, with annual rates surpassing 2,000%. This devastating inflation eroded the purchasing power of the ruble, devastating the savings of countless Russians. In response, the government redefined the currency's value, slashing off three zeros. New notes were introduced, effectively scaling down the currency by a factor of 1,000.

Understanding inflation, a crucial thread throughout this book, is crucial to understanding economics, because it affects everything from the prices of everyday goods to strategic decisions made by governments and corporations. It's a key metric that central banks monitor when setting monetary policy, and it plays an influential role in the health of any economy. Inflation is also often referred to as a "hidden taxation" on the people, as regular consumers are the ones who usually pay the price for inflation-management policies gone wrong.

What Is Inflation?

Inflation is the rate at which the general level of prices for goods and services rises, causing purchasing power—the ability to buy these goods and services—to fall. Essentially, as inflation rises, each unit of currency buys fewer items and services.

There are several causes of inflation:

1. **Demand-pull inflation:** Occurs when the demand for goods and services exceeds supply, for instance, when expansionary fiscal policies such as tax cuts boost aggregate demand—a classic case of too much money chasing too few goods.

2. **Cost-push inflation:** Arises due to increased costs of production, causing producers to raise their prices in order to maintain profit margins. Cost-push inflation could be due to rising prices of raw materials, currency devaluation, or supply disruptions.

3. **Built-in inflation:** Often termed "wage-price inflation," it occurs when workers demand wage increases, and, if they get those pay raises, businesses then raise their prices to cover the higher wage costs they must pay.

4. **Monetary inflation:** Caused by an oversupply of money, usually printed by a central bank.

The impacts of inflation can be both positive and negative.

Positive: Encourages spending and investment; reduces the real burden of debt.

(*continued*)

Negative: Reduces the purchasing power of money, creates uncertainty in the economy, potentially leading to reduced economic growth, negatively affecting interest rates and international competitiveness.

Central banks and governments often use monetary and fiscal policies to manage inflation. Monetary policy includes manipulating interest rates, conducting open-market operations, and setting reserve requirements for how much cash financial institutions must hold at any given time. Fiscal policy involves adjusting government spending and tax rates.

What about Deflation?

The opposite of inflation, deflation is a decline in prices for goods and services. Prolonged deflation can be detrimental to an economy, as it increases the real value of debt and may lead to reduced spending and investment.

Russian Run on the Banks

Amid the shifting tides of Russia's economy, my family astutely navigated the evolving terrain. Benefiting from the nation's freshly instituted property rights, we now had ownership of a luxurious four-bedroom penthouse, which we decided to sell, moving our family into a cozier two-bedroom apartment. The returns from this sale were notable, particularly against the backdrop of the rapid inflation of the time.

Given the precarious financial landscape, my parents chose to shield our gains. They converted a significant portion of our profit to US dollars and entrusted it to a Russian bank, favoring a US dollar–denominated account. But as fate would have it, the impending Asian financial crisis cast its shadow on Russia. To our surprise and disappointment, when we sought to withdraw our funds, the bank notified us that the funds were "not available at this time."

Our story was not unique. Similar economic turbulence has rippled through continents periodically, from the shores of Asia and the heartlands of Eastern Europe to the vast landscapes of South America and, in more recent times, the coast of Lebanon. Countless families have faced the twin specters of soaring inflation and locked bank accounts.

The Asian Financial Crisis

The Asian financial crisis began in July 1997 and was characterized by the devaluation of currencies, the collapse of financial institutions, and sharp declines in stock markets across several Asian economies, most notably in Thailand, Indonesia, South Korea, and Malaysia. The crisis started in Thailand with the collapse of the Thai baht after the government was forced to float the currency due to a lack of foreign currency on hand to support its peg to the US dollar. The economic turbulence was caused by **overreliance on foreign capital, overinvestment in the speculative real estate sectors,** and **weak financial institutions.**

When investors began to lose confidence and the speculative bubbles burst, capital started to flee these economies. As the crisis spread, it also affected other economies that had initially seemed more robust.

Impact on Russia and other Eastern European countries:

Russia, though geographically distant from the Asian economies most directly affected, was not immune to the repercussions of the Asian financial crisis due to several factors:

1. **Commodity prices:** The Asian crisis dampened global demand, leading to a decline in commodity prices. Russia, being a major exporter of oil and other commodities, saw a drop in its export revenues.

2. **Capital flight:** The crisis led to reduced investor confidence in emerging markets, resulting in capital flight from countries such as Russia. This put added pressure on the Russian ruble, as the exodus of money from a country leads to sharp drops in its exchange rate.

3. **Debt and default:** In August 1998, Russia devalued the ruble and defaulted on its domestic debt, leading to the Russian financial crisis.

4. **Foreign aid and the IMF:** Russia sought aid from the International Monetary Fund (IMF) and other international institutions to stabilize its economy.

In 1998, my mother made a momentous decision to part ways with my stepfather, marking the beginning of a new chapter in our lives. With a steadfast resolve, she set her sights on Canada, envisioning a brighter future for both of us in a land of opportunity. I remember vividly how she dedicated herself to English lessons during this period, tirelessly honing her fluency.

Meanwhile, I got a TV pass, albeit with a condition: all my viewing choices had to be American. It was her way of preparing me, ensuring that I would acclimate more seamlessly to the Western environment awaiting us and that my transition to English would be a tad smoother. Within that same year, her perseverance bore fruit as she was granted a "skilled worker" immigration visa to Canada—a testament to her resilience and the sacrifices she was willing to make for our future.

Go West: Starting a New Life in North America

October 31, 1998. We left Sheremetyevo International Airport in Moscow, bound for Toronto. Our past lives, keepsakes, and memories— all condensed into two measly suitcases. I clung to my Barbie, a relic of the capitalism I once knew. Mom wore the weight of our move like a cloak of concern. Her distant gaze mirrored the uncertainty in her heart. As the plane touched down in North America, her grip on our documents tightened, hoping they'd pass customs scrutiny.

Emerging from the maze, we were met with a surreal sight: Halloween in full swing. Witches, vampires, and mystical creatures roamed the terminal. It was a quirky intro to our new home.

Upon our arrival, a representative from an immigrant aid organization awaited us, our names scribbled on a placard he held. Gratefully, we followed him to what would become our first Canadian home, a modest one-bedroom apartment in a somewhat timeworn high-rise on Marlee Avenue. This street, served as a melting pot for immigrants from Eastern Europe, the Caribbean, and other parts of the world. I would later learn that Marlee Avenue stood as a bridge between two starkly contrasting worlds: the gritty and vibrant Little Jamaica and the opulent enclave of Forest Hill, where many wealthy Jews lived because for years they had been kept out of Rosedale, a tony downtown neighborhood populated by Toronto WASPs (White Anglo-Saxon Protestants).

In the initial weeks in our Toronto apartment, the echoes of our conversations bounced off the bare walls, filling the otherwise empty space. Our sole possession was a queen-sized mattress that became my mother's and my shared sanctuary every night. As we scoured the city for affordable furniture and essentials, my mother's gaze often betrayed her worries about my transition to this foreign land.

While I was generally adept at grasping new skills quickly, English was not among them. One evening, my mother presented a Harvard research paper she'd stumbled upon. It emphasized that children could attain fluency in a new language if immersed in it completely before turning eleven. I was on the brink—just four months shy of that pivotal age. So my mother made a challenging decision: I would speak English, and only English, even at home. The initial weeks were fraught with frustration, as I struggled to express myself in the most basic of ways. But soon enough, I could form coherent sentences, and things developed from there.

The following year, I transitioned to a middle school nestled in posh Forest Hill. Here, an evaluation for their gifted program yielded a conundrum: my math results were impeccable, but my English scores, although vastly improved, still narrowly missed the mark. Distressed, my mother made an impassioned plea to the principal: "You must let her in. She deserves this." Moved by her earnestness, the principal conceded.

Being inducted into this elite program was a watershed moment for me. My classmates were not just bright minds; they also hailed from affluent backgrounds, providing me with a window into a world of privilege. Friendships blossomed—some of which endured through high school, college, and beyond. The parents of these new acquaintances, often unknowingly, offered glimpses of a lifestyle that I would come to desire, shaping my aspirations in profound ways.

It was also my first introduction to Jewish culture. Though my biological father is Jewish, I never felt that I had permission to identify as Jewish until I became a part of the Forest Hill community. Today, I go to temple regularly, observe Shabbat, and identify most closely as a Reform Jew, a perspective that emphasizes the evolving nature of Judaism, the superiority of its spiritual aspects to its religious ones.

★★

To ease the financial strain of our new life in Canada, I followed my mother's example and threw myself relentlessly into hard work. At 11, I found a job through the classifieds, a setup that would politely be termed part of the "informal economy" and that involved immigrant children being handed buckets of flowers to sell in front of malls and liquor stores. The only problem was that the minimum required age for the job was 13. So I fibbed about my age and thereby garnered a summer hustle for the next three years.

By 14, a friend introduced me to another gig. Her sister, also an immigrant, sold newspaper subscriptions for the *Toronto Star* door-to-door. The game plan was simple: hit a street during dinner and convince households to subscribe. The age requirement? Fifteen. I stretched the truth and dove into my next hustle. High school saw countless doors slammed in my face, literally. But against the odds, I consistently out-earned my peers. While they scraped by on hourly wages, I raked in over $200 in just a couple of hours. That financial independence defined my teenage years.

With every rejection, I earned essentials, paid my way, squirreled away for education, and at 18, scored my first car—a slightly battered Mazda Protégé. That car and I shared countless memories, especially after I moved away for college.

College Years: A Philosopher's Chair

In the fall of 2006, I landed at Huron College, a cozy corner within the University of Western Ontario. While the main campus bustled with 30,000 students, Huron offered an intimate vibe akin to Wesleyan or Colgate. High school ended with me treading dangerous waters. Sure, my grades sparkled, and I ruled the track as the MVP. But beneath the surface lurked trouble. Teenage antics and defiance became my signature moves. Looking back, I cringe at the time wasted. University was my reset button. A tidy dorm room, sorority sisters, and a good boyfriend from a good family—it felt like stepping into a different life. I chased normalcy, shedding the chaos of my past.

University life helped lessen the traumatic memories of my childhood. My favorite classes were those rooted in political philosophy, and I soon decided to work toward my undergraduate degree in political science. What I learned in those years would help shape my worldview and, later, my investment thesis as a venture capitalist.

From an early age, I had been curious about economic and political systems. Perhaps due to having lived under both communism and capitalism as a child, I was always trying to puzzle out how a small group of people could decide what was best for an entire population. In college, I read Plato, Thomas Hobbes, John Stuart Mill, and Marx, always with an eye toward contemplating what exactly it was that made a society work. How do we make sure people are happy and fulfilled? How do we encourage innovation and productivity? How do we guarantee the health and safety of millions of citizens? Is freedom necessary? Equality? Justice? What makes a society successful?

In addition to living in Ukraine, Russia, and Canada, over the following decade, I would live in Europe and the United Arab Emirates and, eventually, become a permanent resident of the United States. Everywhere I went, I would use the lens of the philosophies and struc-tures I had studied in college to analyze and absorb the world around me. Over time, after reading countless books, I became more and more sure that the current liberal system of the Western world is perhaps imperfect, but it's the best we as humanity have come up with so far. As Winston Churchill famously said: "No one pretends that democracy is perfect or all-wise. Indeed it has been said that democracy is the worst form of Government except for all those other forms that have been tried from time to time."

One political philosopher who addressed these issues in a way that really resonated with me is John Rawls (1921–2002). This truly great American's work was recognized by President Bill Clinton for having helped "a whole generation of learned Americans revive their faith in democracy itself." Rawls proposed that we should make societal and moral decisions behind a so-called "veil of ignorance." Imagine if we, as the founding fathers (or mothers) of a society, stepped into a room together to design the rule book. We do not know what place we will take in this society, which cards life will deal to us: whether we'll be intelligent or not so intelligent, white or black, rich or poor, male or female, qualified or still learning, etc. Under these circumstances, what rules might we then create that we would all agree on? What might we change about the current rule book? In such a scenario, it would likely serve us best to raise the living standard of the least well-off in our society to the highest possible level, acknowledging the risk that we ourselves might be among them.

Rawls would argue that once you give everyone the same oppor-tunities, it is entirely up to them to build their life the way they want. And I'd say that's an integral part of the definition of freedom. The #BlackLivesMatter and #MeToo movements, in my opinion, boiled down to this very premise. Do you feel that opportunities for happiness and success are fairly distributed throughout our society? Does the law protect you equally to how it protects your neighbor? If not, how would you adjust the system to address this inequity?

Rawls also introduced the principle of "justice as fairness," in which he argued that the talents and dispositions we are born with are mere happenstance and that, therefore, we should not feel that the wealth that follows from the exercise of those talents is properly and fully ours. Therefore, it is our duty to give back to those who are less fortunate. For example, if you are smart enough to be a doctor, it would be just for you to donate some of your time to those who cannot afford health care. In the same vein, if you are a wealthy businessman, it is your duty to not only create jobs for others but to support young and rising talent. Each of us gets to decide what we owe to our community, but being part of a society means we should all contribute something.

Equipped with the lessons and principles instilled in me by my education, I was ready to embark on a decade-long journey that ultimately led to a career as an investor in technologies aimed at creating a better future for humanity. Aside from my education, I was psychologically armed for the journey: I was hungry, eager, and an immigrant.

Immigration is and always has been fundamental to the growth and prosperity of America. Today, 55% of billion-dollar companies in the US have at least one immigrant founder, and several Fortune 500 companies are led by immigrant CEOs, including Google, IBM, and Intel. Some of the most famous immigrants in American business include Elon Musk (CEO of Tesla and SpaceX, born in South Africa), Sergey Brin (cofounder of Google, born in Russia), and Satya Nadella (CEO of Microsoft, born in India).

Growing up, I did all I could to fit in and hide where I came from. Today, I'm proud to acknowledge I'm an immigrant and also proud to reside in America.

As we continue on the journey of this book, I aim to highlight some of the life and financial lessons I have learned along the way. We call them the "money myths."

MONEY MYTH #1: Your past defines your future.

The further I go in my career, the more I realize that the world is made up of two types of people: those who believe in themselves and those who don't. Sure, there will always be circumstances that might prevent you from accomplishing something. But the truth is, the world is full of people who started with almost nothing and accomplished everything they wanted.

The notion that your past determines your future is a limiting belief that can stifle potential and hinder personal growth. In reality, there are countless stories of people achieving success despite modest beginnings, underscoring the idea that where you start does not dictate where you will end up. Life is dynamic and offers each individual multiple opportunities to redefine their path, learn from past experiences, and make choices that lead to success. The critical elements in this journey are resilience, determination, and willingness to pursue your goals relentlessly.

This ability to transcend one's background is rooted in the human capacity for change and adaptation. The willingness to learn from past mistakes and challenges is a foundational tool for achieving wealth and success. Every setback can teach valuable lessons that will help you refine strategies and strengthen your resolve. Moreover, embracing a mindset that views the past as a series of learning moments, rather than an embarrassing and permanent shadow, can be liberating and empowering. With the right attitude, support, and work ethic, individuals from even the most humble beginnings can achieve great heights.

The old school of thinking will tell you that no matter how hard you work, your success is dependent on factors such as privilege, connections, timing, and plain old chance. (This same school of thinking will lay out a predefined path you should follow to achieve what others determine as your presupposed level of success.) And although these elements do play a role in our success, we now live in a time of unlimited possibilities. The Internet has significantly leveled the playing field, allowing anyone from anywhere to seek success in innovative ways, whether it be through content creation, entrepreneurship, or even playing the financial markets. I didn't follow a traditional career path to get to where I am, and I am living proof that you can take all sorts of paths to get to where you want to be in life.

2

The Modern Boiler Room

The only thing standing between you and your goal is the bullshit
story you keep telling yourself as to why you can't achieve it.
                                                      —Jordan Belfort

It's 7:35 a.m. My head is throbbing.

I'm only three months into my first job at TD Bank, as a junior
on the derivatives desk, but benders such as the this one have become
a nightly occurrence. I sleep an average of two to three hours a night,
usually stumbling into my walk-up apartment well after midnight following a night out with colleagues from the trading floor. Bonding with
bourbon shots is part of the culture—and leaving early is seen as a sign
of weakness.

Unfortunately for me, arriving to work late is also seen as a sign of
weakness. The hazing culture of the trading floor permeates the air with
the familiar smell of the food court. Arrived after 7:30 a.m.? You're on
the hook to buy everyone breakfast. Arrived after 8:00 a.m.? Better
make that lunch, too.

This particular morning, my head was pounding more than usual.
The phones were ringing incessantly, and the Bloomberg terminals were
blinking an extra bright orange. I was only 25, but I already had worked
for years to get to this place—and yet it somehow felt empty, devoid of
anything that gave me joy. Though I was just in the door, I already had

a sense of what many in my field come to feel about their jobs: 67% of finance professionals would choose a different career if they could start over, primarily due to stress. Numerous reports indicate that early on, young bankers begin suffering from severe health issues due to the demanding work culture, and things don't get much better as they rise through the ranks.

I had arrived, yet I was nowhere near where I needed to be.

I reflect fondly on my undergraduate years at Western University. Those were the days I reveled in literature, exploring philosophy, economics, and history. Dreams of authoring a book of my own one day danced in my mind. Yet, the realities of immigrant life held sway. Fueled by the classic immigrant success narrative, my mother envisioned me as either a doctor or a lawyer; investment banking was also an acceptable career path if all else failed. Over time, recognizing my aversion to blood but my propensity for arguing pretty much anything—at age six she earmarked me for the legal profession.

Yielding to my mother's aspirations, I took the LSATs in my junior year at Western, applied to law school, and was accepted into a JD-MBA program at York University, back in Toronto. Having completed my undergrad a year ahead of schedule, in true overachiever fashion, I immediately returned to Toronto and embarked on the four-year JD/MBA program, studying through the summers in order to complete both postgraduate degrees in three years.

I was 24 years old when I started my professional career. I may have been prepared academically, but emotionally and mentally I was still a child, craving life and adventure outside of school, something I never got to experience in my formulaic march toward a traditional path of "success."

Girl on the Trading Floor: The Lows of High Finance

Despite my craving for adventure, after graduating from Western, heading to grad school right away seemed like a saving grace at the time. My last year in university was also the year of the 2008–2009 financial crisis that wreaked havoc on economies worldwide. The economic events I read about in the news seemed to manifest directly from the knowledge I had acquired throughout my studies, a real-life postgraduate master class in the consequences of backroom dealing, the negligence of unsophisticated borrowers, and the negligent permissiveness of the financial industry and the government entities charged with regulating it.

The 2008 financial crisis will be recorded in financial textbooks as a pivotal moment in recent economic history. During my final undergraduate year, its immediate effects were palpable: the subprime mortgage crisis led to the burst of the housing bubble that began in the 1990s, causing a liquidity contraction that threatened to destroy the global financial system. Several major investment and commercial banks faced failure or near failure; mortgage lenders, insurance companies, and savings and loan associations were also severely affected. Great titans of the investment world began dropping like flies: Bear Sterns collapsed; Lehman Brothers declared bankruptcy. The chain reactions of financial failure that followed revealed the high-risk interconnectedness of global economic and financial systems, precipitating the worst global economic downturn since the 1930s. From 2007 to 2009, *all* major developed economies experienced negative growth rates. Between January 1 and October 11, 2008, holders of US stocks suffered approximately $8 trillion in losses. Many families' savings evaporated overnight.

It was not, needless to say, a good time to be looking for a job. Countless university graduates found themselves grappling with an uncertain future and moving back in with their families, their job prospects having evaporated almost overnight. Some offers of corporate employment were deferred, others were outright rescinded, plunging many into a period of disillusionment and anxiety.

But for me, the 2008 debacle wasn't my introduction to financial calamities or the realization that my government might not be reliable when it came to protecting the financial well-being of individual citizens. Memories of the 1998 Russian financial crisis, which severely affected my family, still lingered. The sharp devaluation of the ruble and Russia's default on its debt had spillover effects all over the region. The losses we and millions of other families incurred were a harsh lesson about the vulnerabilities of economies and the ripple effects present in global financial systems. And when our financial system collapsed on our heads, the government did nothing to dig us out.

The crisis of 2008 not only reshaped global finance, but it also instigated profound introspection among many, forcing us to question the very foundations on which we had built our aspirations. Amid the financial chaos, a burning sense of betrayal spread like wildfire among ordinary citizens. The fallout from the crisis was not limited to distant boardrooms or trading floors; it penetrated deep into the fabric of everyday lives. For many of my peers, the future that once brimmed with promise had become unsettlingly uncertain. Families who had spent decades building modest nests of savings watched in helpless despair as those investments became worthless. Heart-wrenching tales of hardworking individuals losing their homes, often ones their families had lived in for generations, became tragically commonplace.

Yet, as the dust began to settle, what further intensified the public's disillusionment was the glaring absence of accountability from those who had caused the mess. While countless ordinary citizens faced severe repercussions from the crisis, the architects of the meltdown seemed to emerge largely unscathed. In fact, only one (*one!*) Wall Street executive was sent to jail for his role in the conflagration. Kareem Serageldin, a trader at Credit Suisse, received a 30-month prison sentence for approving the concealment of hundreds of millions of dollars in losses in Credit Suisse's mortgage-backed securities portfolio—a practice that was, many believe, industry-wide.

The stark contrast between the swift government bailouts of major financial institutions and the lack of aid or relief for average families was not lost on the public. Few, if any, high-flying executives and decision-makers faced prosecution, let alone jail time, for their roles in the crisis. Some didn't even lose their jobs. The shield for many of the institutions complicit in the crisis was government designation as a "systemically important financial institution" ("SIFI"); in common parlance, these banks were deemed "too big to fail." This palpable lack of justice only deepened the wound felt by average citizens, fostering a profound mistrust in the very institutions that had once been regarded as pillars of wealth generation, stability, and reliability.

Amid the chaos of the financial crisis and its aftermath, my three years at law school flew by. My time was marked by learning about Western judicial systems and diving deep into concepts of morality in criminal and family law. (Admittedly, contracts and securities law did make me doze off.) Completing my education at the age of 24 with both a law degree and an MBA meant diving into the world of Bay Street, Canada's version of Wall Street, earlier than most. Eager to make my mark, I joined a well-reputed midsized Jewish law firm, almost humorously named Minden Gross Grafstein and Greenstein. I cherished the firm's culture, particularly the aspect of being the only one among my recently graduated law school peers who had the privilege of a 24-hour phone-free break during Shabbat. Every Friday at 4:00 p.m., the firm's doors would shut, gifting the juniors a rare peaceful day to rejuvenate.

What Caused the 2008 Financial Crisis? An In-Depth Look

Michael Lewis, in his bestseller *The Big Short*, meticulously chronicled the nuances of the crisis, later immortalized in the film of the same name with the memorable scene of Margot Robbie explaining the complexities of derivatives from a bubble-filled bathtub. While I'm no Margot Robbie in a bathtub, here's a brief technical explainer:

The 2008 crisis was a perfect storm, shaped by the convergence of multiple factors. High-risk lending and borrowing practices, excessive securitization of mortgages, lax regulatory oversight, flawed credit rating agency assessments, and an unsustainable housing bubble coalesced, leading to the catastrophic failure of key financial institutions, bailout measures, and a global recession. The repercussions were profound and long-lasting, reshaping the financial landscape and prompting calls for more stringent regulations and oversight.

The derivatives (financial products that derive their value from that of an underlying asset, or from the value of a rate or index) that played a central role in causing the 2008 financial crisis were primarily mortgage-backed securities and credit default swaps.

1. **Mortgage-backed securities (MBS)** are financial instruments that represent ownership in a pool of mortgage loans. These loans are typically residential mortgages, such as home loans.

   • To create MBS, financial institutions pool together thousands of individual mortgage loans and transfer them to a special purpose vehicle (SPV). The SPV then issues securities backed by these pooled loans.

   • MBS are structured with multiple tranches (segments), each with varying levels of risk. The cash flows from the underlying mortgage loans, including principal and interest payments made by homeowners, are used to make payments to MBS holders.

(continued)

- The risk in MBS arises from the potential for homeowners to default on their mortgage payments. If a large number of borrowers default, the value of the MBS can decline significantly, leading to losses for investors.

2. **Credit default swaps (CDS)** are financial contracts that act as insurance against the default of a particular debt instrument or entity, such as a corporate bond or a mortgage-backed security.

   - In a CDS, one party, often referred to as the "protection buyer," pays a periodic premium to another party, the "protection seller." In return, the protection seller agrees to compensate the protection buyer in the event of a default on the underlying debt instrument.

   - CDS can be used for both hedging and speculative purposes. For example, investors holding MBS may purchase CDS as a hedge against a potential default on those MBS. Speculators may buy CDS without holding the underlying assets, effectively betting on the likelihood of defaults.

   - One critical issue with CDS leading up to the crisis was a lack of transparency. The market for CDS was largely unregulated and decentralized, making it difficult for anyone to assess the total exposure to default risk that was present in the financial system.

Impact of MBS and CDS on the 2008 Financial Crisis:

- *The housing bubble and mortgage defaults:* Like all price bubbles, the housing bubble that began in the 1990s, characterized by soaring home prices and excessive issuance of mortgages to buyers who couldn't really afford them ("subprime mortgages"), eventually burst. Many homeowners, particularly those with subprime mortgages, began to default on their payments, leading to a significant drop in MBS values.

- *Contagion effect:* Numerous financial institutions worldwide held large portfolios of MBS and CDS, often with highly leveraged positions—meaning they had borrowed money from other institutions to purchase these derivatives in the first place, expecting to repay the loan from their resulting profits. As MBS values declined due to mortgage defaults, these institutions incurred massive losses, as a toxic web of lending obligations and CDS began to be called in across the system. The interconnectedness of financial institutions through these derivatives resulted in a contagion effect, causing a crisis of confidence in the global financial system.

- *Credit freeze:* The widespread losses and uncertainty over the extent of any one institution's exposure to bad loans led to a credit freeze. Banks became reluctant to lend to each other or to consumers and businesses, exacerbating the crisis.

- *Government interventions:* To prevent a complete collapse of the financial system, governments and central banks implemented massive bailouts and stimulus packages, including the Troubled Asset Relief Program (TARP) in the United States, which ultimately purchased approximately $426 billion in distressed assets.

The 2008 financial crisis was driven by the risky interconnectedness of financial institutions holding complex derivatives such as mortgage-backed securities and credit default swaps, which were based on a housing market bubble and mortgages at high risk of non-repayment. The crisis underscored the need for greater transparency, careful risk management, and strong regulation in the financial industry.

One memorable Friday stands out: As juniors, we were summoned to the boardroom, expecting a reprimand. Instead, senior partners spent the time showcasing their private collections of scotches and whiskeys. We were educated on the nuances of different recipes—bourbon, single malt, double malt—and encouraged to master the art of savoring each sip. To balance the strong flavors, delightful squares of homemade chocolate fudge were distributed. The afternoon was a lesson in both work and pleasure and established a skill that would serve me well when wining and dining with clients in the future.

During my tenure at the law firm, I encountered Jerry Grafstein, a retired Canadian senator and one of the firm's founding partners.

Despite being in his mid-70s, Jerry's zest for life and entrepreneurial spirit remained palpable. At some point, news of my proficiency in Russian, a language I had all but abandoned after my mother prohibited its use upon our arrival to Canada, had reached him. An art aficionado, Jerry beckoned me to his office one day to decipher inscriptions on artworks from Ukraine. As he smoked a forbidden cigar in his glass tower office, sharing with me tales of his adventures in Cuba, I felt that I was privy to another world.

That afternoon, Jerry gifted me my first Havana cigar, a memento I still treasure. Our bond grew stronger over time, with him mentoring me on etiquette at high-profile gatherings and the art of strategic thinking. As my inaugural year at the law firm concluded, I confided in Jerry about a deferred job offer from TD Bank I had received upon graduation, an invitation to join their trading floor. Although my stint at the law firm had yielded much insight, I lacked passion for the profession, feeling a stronger pull instead toward the entrepreneurial endeavors of my business school peers.

Jerry's response provided the clarity I needed. Urging me to recognize my potential, he candidly expressed that the confines of the firm would stifle my growth. Observing my colleagues, I had to acknowledge that while the respectable, balanced, yet monotonous rhythm of their lives was a commendable path, it wasn't one I envisioned for myself. Heeding Jerry's advice, I mustered the courage to embark on a new journey, eager to pen the next chapter of my life.

David and Goliath: Navigating the Investment Banking World

August 2013 was a turning point for me. As I stepped onto the trading floor at TD Bank, it felt like a scene straight out of movies such as *Boiler Room* and *Wall Street*. The fixed-income floor buzzed with energy, and testosterone—out of the six hundred traders there, only three other women shared the floor with me.

The vastness of the room, with its ceilings that seemed to stretch away forever and rows of desks, was awe-inspiring. Each desk was a flurry of activity, with Bloomberg terminals flashing continuously updated numbers and phones ringing nonstop. The deliberate cold of the room, designed to counteract the heat from the countless computers, was always challenging. Notoriously, investment banks' offices are kept to a temperature meant to accommodate men's corporate fashion of wool suits. Not only are women expected to wear chillier, feminized attire, but we are expected to do it in four-inch heels we could barely walk to lunch in, let alone evacuate the building in if there were an emergency. To combat this, I and the few other women on the floor hid personal heaters and UGG boots under our desks.

The trading floor of an investment bank is a high-octane environment, with countless transactions taking place every second. In 2013, financial markets were still recovering from the 2008 financial crisis, but there was increasing investor confidence that the worst of the crisis was past. Bond trading, in particular, saw substantial activity, since central banks around the world had slashed interest rates to stimulate economic growth. Global debt markets hovered around $100 trillion in investment in mid-2013, up from $70 trillion in 2007. This led to increased demand for corporate bonds, as investors sought better yields than those available from government securities.

While my hazy memory cannot provide an exact number of bonds or the precise volume that went through TD's trading floor in 2013, it is safe to say that the figure would have been substantial, given the bank's prominent position as one of the major financial institutions in North America. A single mistake, such as an incorrect bond curve, could potentially affect transactions worth billions of dollars—a daunting reality that served to emphasize the importance of accuracy and attention to detail in roles such as the one I now held.

The trading floor had its own set of unwritten rules and rites of passage. A significant portion of these rituals extended beyond working hours. After wrapping up our work each night, usually between 6 and 7 p.m., there was an unspoken expectation that all junior workers would head out with colleagues for drinks. Many of those nights are a haze in my memory now; countless evenings that ended with me stumbling into bed in the wee hours, having drowned in one whiskey too many, only to jolt awake a few hours later, having to rush to make it to work on time.

Amid this whirlwind of work and post-work rituals, my personal life was undergoing its own turbulence. I had recently taken a significant relationship step, moving in with a boyfriend, someone I'd known since childhood, with whom I envisioned a shared future. But the combined pressures of our respective demanding jobs took a toll on our relationship. Before we realized it, the bond we had was crumbling, and our dreams for a life together dissipated as quickly as they had formed. This was perhaps the first time I truly experienced a broken heart. I often refer to this breakup as my "sliding door" moment, referring to the famous movie starring Gwyneth Paltrow. It was the moment I said goodbye to living a calm, predictable life in Canada, with a family and kids, and opened the door to a much bigger future that the universe had in store for me.

Although investment bankers often get glamorized in books and movies, the reality of working in an investment bank can be anything but. Sure, there are fancy clothes, fancy dinners, and overpriced drinks. But there is also a lot of very dull work that can numb the senses and freeze the brain, even more than your favorite post-work poison.

Banks are complex organizations, with various divisions ranging from retail banking, the arm of the bank that serves mom-and-pop savers, to wholesale, the division that services institutional clients, such as pension funds and universities. When folks refer to "investment banks," often they're referring to either the investment banking division, sales and trading, or research, the entirety of which is known in the industry as "the front office." (The rest of the bank consists of branches such as asset management, private banking, and retail products.)

Typical Investment Bank Structure: Who's Who in the Front Office

1. **Investment banking division (IB):** The investment banking division is responsible for helping companies figure out how best to access the public markets (and, in so doing, generate advisory fees that provide income to the bank).
   - Mergers and acquisitions (M&A) professionals advise companies on buying, selling, or merging with other businesses. They conduct due diligence to assess the financial health and potential risks of target companies. Valuation experts determine the fair market value of the businesses involved. Negotiation teams handle discussions between buyers and sellers, striving to achieve favorable terms for their clients.
   - Capital markets teams assist companies in raising capital by issuing securities, such as stocks and bonds. In initial public

offerings (IPOs), they help companies go public by under-
writing and marketing the offering. In secondary offerings,
they facilitate the sale of additional shares in a company to
the public. Debt capital markets professionals help companies
issue bonds and other debt instruments to raise funds.

- Corporate finance specialists work on various financial
transactions beyond M&A and capital markets. These may
include financial restructuring to improve a company's financial position, leveraged finance for transactions involving high
levels of debt, and private placements of securities. Finance
specialists often work closely with corporate clients to address
specific financial challenges or opportunities.

2. **Sales and trading:** These employees advise institutional clients
in managing their assets by providing investment opportunities
and the services necessary to execute those opportunities.

- Sales professionals establish and maintain relationships with
institutional clients, such as asset managers, hedge funds, and
pension funds. Sales teams aim to understand clients' investment objectives and offer financial products that align with
their strategies.

- Trading desks execute buy and sell orders on behalf of the
bank's clients for various financial instruments, including
stocks, bonds, commodities, and derivatives. Traders make
split-second decisions to achieve the best execution for their
clients or the bank's own trading portfolios. There are specialized trading desks for different asset classes, such as equity
trading, fixed-income trading, and foreign exchange trading.

3. **Research:** The bank's research arm is responsible for the
analytical legwork required to rank the investability of financial
opportunities.

- Equity research analysts study individual companies, industries,
and sectors to provide detailed insights and recommendations
on specific stocks. They analyze financial statements, market
trends, and competitive dynamics. Equity research reports
often include price targets, buy/sell recommendations, and
earnings forecasts, helping investors make informed decisions.

(continued)

- Fixed-income researchers focus on debt securities, such as bonds and credit derivatives. They assess credit risk, interest rate trends, and macroeconomic factors that affect fixed-income markets. Research in this area assists both internal trading desks and external clients in making investment choices within the bond and debt markets.

These divisions and functions within the front office of an investment bank work closely together to serve the needs of corporate clients, institutional investors, and high-net-worth individuals while generating revenue through various financial transactions and advisory service fees.

Sweating the Swap Desk: Fixed Income

My first-quarter rotation at TD was on the swap desk. Here, I was introduced to the world of fixed-income and currency swaps. I quickly realized the real-world impact of our work when companies such as Apple would contact our desk to hedge against currency fluctuations in various countries where they did business. The outdated teaching philosophy of my superiors with regard to these very modern-day business problems was evident in my initial tasks: I was handed a textbook and commanded to manually construct a swap using just a pencil, paper, and a calculator. This painstaking work stretched over pages of intricate mathematical calculations, teaching me the fundamentals of the job in the most hands-on way possible.

My daily routine began aggressively at 7:00 a.m. when, sober and rested or not, I was entrusted with tasks crucial to the functioning of the trading floor. Each morning, I sat before two screens; the left-hand one displayed the Bloomberg window, with both short-term and long-term interest rates, while the one on the right reminded me of a bygone era with an MS-DOS window. My job was to meticulously transfer data from the Bloomberg terminal to construct the bond curve, a foundational tool for pricing bonds and swaps for the entire floor. The weight of this responsibility was not lost on me—one error could have monumental repercussions. The smooth functioning of such a behemoth rested on the shoulders of tortured junior individuals like me, necessitating precision and accuracy in every task.

What Is a Bond?

A bond is a financial instrument that represents a debt obligation. When an entity (usually a corporation, government, or municipality) issues a bond, it is essentially borrowing money from investors. In return, the issuer promises to pay periodic interest (coupon payments) to bondholders and return the principal amount (face value, or par value) at the bond's maturity date.

Here's an outline of how bonds work:

- The issuer of a bond is the entity (corporation, government, or municipality) that needs to raise capital. These entities issue bonds as a way to borrow money from investors to fund various projects or operations. The face value or par value of a bond is the amount the issuer agrees to repay to bondholders when the bond matures. It is typically set at $1,000 per bond, but it can vary.

- The **coupon rate** is the fixed annual interest rate that the bond pays to its holders. It is expressed as a percentage of the bond's face value. For example, a bond with a face value of $1,000 and a coupon rate of 5% will pay $50 in interest annually ($1,000 × 0.05). Bondholders receive periodic **coupon payments**, typically semiannually, based on the bond's coupon rate. These payments provide a predictable income stream to bondholders.

- The **maturity date** is the date on which the issuer is obligated to repay the bond's face value to bondholders. Bonds can have various maturity dates, ranging from a few months to several decades. The **yield to maturity (YTM)** is the total return an investor can expect to receive from a bond if it is held until the maturity date. It takes into account the bond's current market price, coupon payments, and the face value at maturity. YTM can differ from the bond's coupon rate if the bond is bought or sold at a price other than its face value.

Bonds serve multiple purposes, such as raising capital, funding projects, managing debt, and providing investors with income and diversification in their investment portfolios. Independent

(continued)

credit rating agencies—the three largest globally being Moody's, Standard & Poor's, and Fitch—provide reassurance to investors by assessing the creditworthiness of bond issuers and assigning them credit ratings. Higher-rated bonds (e.g. AAA) are considered less risky and usually offer lower interest rates, while lower-rated bonds (e.g. junk bonds) offer higher yields to compensate for the higher risk of default.

Bonds are bought and sold in the bond market. Bond prices can fluctuate in response to changes in interest rates and market conditions. When bond prices rise, their yields (the effective interest rates) fall, and vice versa. In 2023, the size of the global bond market was estimated by the Bank for International Settlements to be around $133 trillion. The total size of the US bond market is over $51 trillion, making it the largest bond market globally, followed distantly by China's.

Bonds are a key component of the financial markets and offer a means for both issuers and investors to achieve their financial goals while managing risk. Investors receive both regular interest payments and the return of their principal at maturity, making bonds an attractive investment for income and capital preservation.

During my tenure at TD Bank, a few deals stand out as reflecting the massive impacts, good and bad, that the financial industry can have on the society that surrounds it. One that remains particularly vivid in my memory was the monumental multibillion bond issuance for a Maritime infrastructure project. This deal, co-orchestrated with J.P. Morgan, wasn't just any ordinary transaction—it was the largest government-backed bond issuance in North American history. Our desk was responsible for the interest-rate swaps associated with this deal, and the enormity of our success was palpable. Upon the deal's completion, the entire trading floor was in a festive spirit, with celebrations stretching on for two weeks. Colleagues who'd received fat bonuses splurged on luxury cars, dream homes, and extravagant jewelry for their spouses. There was a light at the end of the tunnel of mind-numbing work, and that light gleamed gold.

Another memorable assignment was a collateralization deal I worked on during my rotation at the asset-backed securities desk. The complexity and scope of this task felt eerily reminiscent of the intricate financial maneuvers detailed in accounts of the 2008 financial crisis. Despite everything the industry had supposedly learned in those dark times, there I was, right in the thick of things, tranching a diverse array of loans—everything from auto loans and credit-card receivables to something as seemingly trivial as iPhone payment plans—through a process dubbed "asset-backed securitization." Many of these asset-backed securities may not have been underpinned by subprime residential mortgages, but the dance was made up of the same old steps from the heady days before the Great Recession.

Big, Smart Money: Stocks and Equities

Although in my tenure in TD's front office, I never worked on the other, more fabled, side of the banking industry—namely stocks and equities—I would be remiss if I didn't touch on their basic workings here. After all, the total market capitalization of publicly traded corporate equities, represented by the combined value of all publicly traded stocks on US stock exchanges, is approximately $50.8 trillion as of January 1, 2024—about 42% of the global equity market capitalization.

A Primer on Equities

Equities, also known as stocks or shares, represent ownership in a company. When you own equities, you hold a stake in that company, and you become a shareholder. Equities are a type of equity security, which is one of the two main classes of securities, the other being debt securities (bonds). Equity securities represent an ownership interest in the issuing company, while debt securities represent a loan that the issuer must repay.

There are two primary types of equities:

1. Holders of **common stock** have voting rights in the company and may receive dividends if the company distributes profits. They also have a claim on the company's assets in the event of liquidation, but they are subordinate to bondholders and preferred stockholders.

(continued)

2. Holders of **preferred stock** typically do not have voting rights, but they have a higher claim on the company's assets and earnings than common shareholders. They often receive fixed dividends, paid on a routine basis regardless of the company's financial position.

The price of equities is determined by supply and demand in the stock market. Factors such as company performance, financial metrics, market sentiment, and economic conditions influence stock prices. Equities are traded on stock exchanges, which are organized markets where buyers and sellers transact shares. Major stock exchanges in the United States include the New York Stock Exchange (NYSE) and NASDAQ. Equities are generally highly liquid, meaning they can be bought or sold relatively quickly, with minimal impact on their market price. Even so, liquidity can vary among different stocks.

Investing in equities carries both risks and potential rewards. Stock prices can be volatile, and investors can lose money if the value of their holdings declines. However, equities historically have the potential for long-term capital appreciation and dividends, which can provide a return on investment. To spread risk, investors often aim to build diversified portfolios of equities. By holding shares in various companies across different industries, investors seek to reduce the impact of poor performance by one company on their overall portfolio.

Stock indices, such as the Standard & Poor's (S&P) 500 and the Dow Jones Industrial Average (DJIA), track the performance of a group of stocks. These indices serve as benchmarks to gauge the overall health of the stock market. Some retail investors find it helpful to lessen the amount of research required to enter the equities markets by investing in index funds—funds whose value tracks the overall value of a stock index as it rises and falls—rather than individual companies.

Equities play a crucial role in financial markets, providing companies with capital for growth and offering investors opportunities to participate in the success of businesses. But participating in the success of businesses also means participating in their failure, and outperforming the overall stock market as an individual investor is a feat few can achieve.

In today's media, stocks frequently get all of the attention. For example, the stock for the automotive and clean-energy company Tesla (TSLA) has a cult following, largely due to the clickbait antics of CEO Elon Musk, with thousands listening to the company's earnings calls. Stocks represent all companies whose shares are traded publicly on stock exchanges. Usually, these companies will have gone through a start-up or venture capital stage, before going through a process known as the initial public offering, or IPO. Once a company IPOs, its shares can be bought and sold by the public on exchanges where the company has listed its shares. In venture-capital-funded enterprises, which I touch on in the next chapter, the shares in a company are sold privately and are valued based on the trajectory and perceived revenue potential of the company, but the above principles of governance remain intact.

"I Like This Stock": A GameStop Saga

The 2008 financial crisis created an inherent distrust in the Western financial system. The fruits of this distrust would ripen a little more than a decade later in the form of the GameStop saga of 2021, as recounted in the movie *Dumb Money*. A David vs. Goliath story that unfolded in the financial markets, spotlighting the rising influence of retail investors against institutional Wall Street dominance, this remarkable event centered on the stock in GameStop (GME), a struggling video game retailer, which became the focal point of an epic short squeeze in the equities market, primarily fueled by retail investors coordinating through social media platforms such as Reddit's r/wallstreetbets. Instead of taking to the streets (like they did during the Occupy Movement), for the first time, disgruntled and disenfranchised citizens coordinated using social media to directly take on the "smart money" of large banks and hedge funds.

In January 2021, GameStop's stock price saw an unprecedented surge, rising over 1,500% within two weeks. The stock, which had been trading below $20 a share in early January, skyrocketed to a peak of nearly $350 by January 27. This dramatic increase was due not to any fundamental improvement in GameStop's business but rather to a concerted effort by retail investors to buy shares and call options, thereby driving up the price. These investors were keenly aware that GameStop was one of the most shorted stocks on the market, with short interest exceeding 100% of the available shares at certain points.

Hedge funds and other institutional investors had shorted GameStop so heavily due to the company's failing business fundamentals—until the 2021 conflict began, the idea that the company's share price would continue to fall seemed a safe bet. Retail investors, rallying through forums such as Reddit, sought to initiate a short squeeze by driving up GameStop's price, thereby forcing short sellers to buy shares at much higher prices to cover their positions. This additional buying pressure, in turn, pushed the stock even higher, creating a feedback loop that led to massive losses for short sellers. Notably, Melvin Capital, a prominent hedge fund, required a capital infusion of nearly $3 billion from other hedge funds to cover losses from its short positions in the stock.

The volatility in GameStop's stock price caused significant market turbulence and led to trading restrictions by several brokerage firms, most notably Robinhood, a stock trading and investing app that many investors in the GameStop squeeze were using to access equities markets. Finally, on January 28, Robinhood and other brokers limited the buying of GameStop and other heavily shorted stocks, citing liquidity and regulatory requirements. This decision to "de-platform and silence individual investors," as one member of Congress would later put it, sparked widespread outrage among retail investors and prompted Congressional hearings questioning the brokers' motives and the overall fairness of the market. It seemed that the rules of the game could be bent, but only when the big players were losing.

Amid the chaos of the global pandemic and the attendant financial actions of governments that seemed, once again, to favor the interests of corporations over the suffering of individuals, institutional investors learned they could no longer ignore individual investors, who have now discovered they have the power to act as one. Not only did the means by which the short squeezers accomplished what they did challenge the status quo, but the philosophy behind WallStreetBets introduced a new way of thinking about investing in equities: part hail-mary bet, part rebellion, and part activism, a strong antithesis to the conservative, long-term, slow-and-steady traditional approach to investing. The following is a snippet from an anonymous Reddit post from the time that encapsulates the psychology of the short squeezers:

I was in my early teens during the '08 crisis. I vividly remember the enormous repercussions that the reckless actions by those on Wall Street had in my personal life, and the lives of those close to me.... Do you know what tomato soup made out of school cafeteria ketchup packets taste like? My friends got to find out....

To Melvin Capital: you stand for everything that I hated during that time. You're a firm who makes money off of exploiting a company and manipulating markets and media to your advantage. Your continued existence is a sharp reminder that the ones in charge of so much hardship during the '08 crisis were not punished.... I bought shares a few days ago. I dumped my savings into GME, paid my rent for this month with my credit card, and dumped my rent money into more GME (which for the people here at WSB, I would not recommend).... I'm making this as painful as I can for you.

To WSB: you all are amazing. I imagine that I'm not the only one that this is personal for. I've read myself so many posts on what you guys went through during the '08 crash. Whether you're here for the gains, to stick it to the man as I am, or just to be part of a potentially market changing movement—thank you. Each and every one of you are the reason that we have this chance.

The GameStop episode has been hailed as a watershed moment for retail investing, demonstrating the collective power of individual investors to affect the stock market significantly. It also sparked discussions about market regulation, the role of social media in investing (especially in so-called "meme stocks," of which GameStop was the first but by no means the last), and the practices of brokerage firms, especially concerning payment for order flow. The gamification of investing would become a widespread trend in cryptocurrency markets, as will be seen in later chapters.

Stepping Off the Merry-Go-Round

My time at TD Bank was a tale of perseverance amid tumult. Navigating the trading floor was a double-edged sword. On one side were the allure of complex mathematical challenges, the thrill of sealing a deal, and the intellectual satisfaction derived from analyzing fresh market trends or crafting intricate models. But always shadowing these victories was an inescapable dark cloud: a toxic culture that I found hard to breathe in.

Being among the few women in that sea of men was taxing. I felt men's eyes on me each time I made the dreaded walk across the trading floor to the bathroom. The loneliness was exacerbated by the underlying sentiment that as women, we *shouldn't* bolster each other, that somehow the hellfire of our individual journeys should become the next woman's crucible too. Among my colleagues, Abby stood out as a

beacon of intelligence and hustle on the swap desk. Her grit was both
awe-inspiring and heart-wrenching: pregnant with her first child, she
powered through each day from the early hours to well after the markets
closed, with her signature Starbucks Americano in tow. (My naive query
about the level of her caffeine intake during pregnancy, driven by sheer
youthful curiosity, was met with a curt response; in retrospect, I can see
the pressures weighing on her.) She barely took a hiatus after childbirth,
driven by whispers that her absence would cost her clients.

And these issues weren't confined to the trading desk. The broader
bank culture was marred with excuses for hedonism masquerading
as work events, infidelities whispered about in hushed tones, and an
entrenched tradition of hazing. A particularly jarring episode saw me
cornered by a senior manager, who pressed me to profess my love for
the job. Failure to acquiesce would result in the punishment of having
to pick up his dry cleaning for a week. His aggressive demand left me
shaking, but as a novice in the corporate world with looming student
debts to repay, my response was a meek affirmation.

The crescendo of my time there coincided with the bank's ostentatious summer charity gala. Amid the glitz and glamour, the size of donations made being tacitly assessed as a measure of one's value, the night
blurred into an after-party in the upscale enclaves of Toronto's Hazelton
Hotel, in the ultra-rich district of Yorkville. The euphoria I was chasing
through the supply of free-flowing alcohol, however, finally took a sinis-
ter turn. An innocuous chat with a managing director, whose name now
eludes my memory, veered into territory I hadn't foreseen. He offered to
walk me home from the party, and before I knew it, he was in my apartment, unzipping my dress. In my drunken haze, I briefly came to clarity
and pushed him out the door with all my might.

The following workday dawned with a mask of normalcy, as the
"Me Too" tidal wave was still years away, and my financial insecurity
tethered me to the heavy anchor of silence. However, the universe (and
perhaps this managing director) had other plans for me. Within days,
I was handed a pink slip, under the guise of a "cultural mismatch," as my
exit ticket, sweetened with a handsome severance. A brief negotiation
later, I bid adieu to my apartment, boarded a flight to Los Angeles, and
left that chapter of my life behind, never to revisit it again.

MONEY MYTH #2: Banks exist for our benefit.

Part of the trappings of the banking industry is a farce so pervasive that we rarely dare to question it: the idea that banks exist for our benefit. This misconception is rooted in the idealized image of financial institutions as benevolent entities rooted in communities, working tirelessly to enhance the wealth of everyday people. Reality contrasts starkly with this rosy picture. The people who run these institutions, despite projecting an aura of competence and infallibility, are often driven by self-interest and, just like all humans, are prone to significant errors. Their mistakes, compounded by everyday greed and a steadfast belief in their own superior ability to time and even manipulate markets, can lead to disastrous outcomes that ripple through the economy.

Financial institutions operate on a zero-sum principle: for one party to gain, another must lose. And for the massive corporate banks of today, the party who must gain is *always* the retail investor. The focus of banks is not on ensuring that the average person becomes wealthy but on maximizing their own bottom line. Banks thrive on fees, interest rates, and financial products that all come at a cost to the consumer. The financial game they play is rigged from the start—no matter who else wins or loses, the bank invariably comes out better for it (and that's before we even consider government bailouts).

The government, despite its role as a supposed guardian of the public interest, is a better friend to banks than it is to account holders. Even well-intentioned governments will prioritize the stability of financial institutions over the welfare of individual citizens, believing that the collapse of a bank could have catastrophic effects on the broader economy. This preference for institutional stability over individual protection highlights the need for everyday investors to remain vigilant and skeptical.

Think critically about the idea that an investment bank is there to serve you, and approach traditional financial products with caution. Understanding that banks prioritize their own interests means having a personal financial safety plan, as relying solely on banks or government protection can lead to significant losses. Recognizing the true nature of financial institutions and preparing accordingly will allow you to better navigate the complex financial landscape of today and protect your own wealth.

3

The Culture of Money

Twenty years from now you will be more disappointed by the things you didn't do than by the ones you did do.

—Mark Twain

On June 20, 2014, as I sat at a gate at Pearson International Airport awaiting my boarding call, the weight of my departure from the investment bank pressed heavily on my spirit. My sense of worth had always been intertwined with excelling at everything. I was a perfect example of a type A individual: straight A's, three university degrees by the age of 24, and several jobs at coveted roles in top-tier firms. Yet, here I was, freshly fired, the circumstances of my ejection a blurred mess shadowed by the haze of alcohol that clouded my final days at the bank and the weeks of despair and recrimination that followed. Los Angeles beckoned to me not just as a change in location but with a promise of rebirth. My ties to the City of Angels were slender—three acquaintances from my law school years. But it was a leap I felt compelled to take, visa or no visa, plan or no plan.

The warmth of California would be a welcome respite from the frosty embrace of Canadian winters, but it was LA's bold culture of dreamers, more than anything, that truly captivated me. There, it seemed each soiree bubbled with tales of aspiration: a screenplay here, a start-up there, a novel in the making, an acting debut. The city pulsed with an energy that felt both overwhelming and intoxicating, especially when juxtaposed against the predictable rhythms of my peers back home, who were engrossed in discussions of housing prices, insurance rates, and settling down with children. I was still only in my 20s—surely life had more to offer?

So, at the crossroads of my life, jobless, fresh off a breakup, and amid a chorus of naysayers suggesting I was having a breakdown and would soon change my mind, I clutched a one-way ticket to LA, ready to cast my lot with fate. I nestled into a quaint guesthouse in West Hollywood, tucked away behind a mid-century craftsman home inhabited by a vibrant lesbian couple in their 50s with two teenage boys. This petite haven, accentuated by a personal hot tub, became my sanctuary for my first few months in the city. Assessing my financial reserves and account-ing for lingering debts from law school and business school, I calculated that I had a cushion of roughly six months before the necessity of employment would beckon. This was the most uninhibited period I had ever known, and my gratitude for this financial freedom was palpable. For once in my life, instead of a trail already blazed for me, ahead lay an abyss of potential, and I was ready to dive in deep.

Embracing my newfound liberty, I pledged to befriend as many souls as I could. Isaac and Gracie, a couple I'd encountered years before on an exchange program in Amsterdam, quickly became my LA anchors. Isaac, a fiery half-Jew with a penchant for impassioned tirades, was a discontented Tulane law grad harboring writing aspirations. His debut self-published book, aptly titled *Philosophy and F*cking in Vietnam*, explored his journey doing exactly that through southeast Asia. Gracie, in contrast, was a gentle, artistic spirit, always seeking harmony in her relationship with Isaac and with those around them. Evan, another of Isaac's acquaintances and a fellow law school grad disillusioned by his current role in the mail room of the Creative Artists Agency (CAA), one of the city's preeminent talent agencies, became an unexpected confi-dant. Evan was tall, Black, handsome, and beyond cool. To me, he looked as if he had walked straight out of a Supreme hoodie ad.

Those initial months in LA, filled with revelries and escapades, are etched deeply into my memories. Guided by Isaac, my social circle blossomed. I adhered to a strict regimen of embracing every invitation, seeing each one as an opportunity to mold this novel chapter of my life. With that mentality, my inaugural year in Los Angeles was a carousel of unprecedented experiences. On one memorable evening, my three com-panions and I found ourselves meandering through the Hollywood Hills to celebrate the birthday of a top CAA agent's six-year-old daughter. We pulled up to a mansion of grandeur, where the valet ushered us past gourmet food trucks and through a lavishly decorated living room. (Indeed, you read that correctly: it was a celebration to the tune of a million bucks—ostensibly, for a child.) The party, with a Parisian twist, featured a miniature Eiffel Tower and a designated area, almost regal in its setup, for the young birthday girl and her equally young entourage.

As we made our way to the backyard, the scene transformed dramatically. There, amid cascading champagne towers and sushi platters paraded by scarcely clad burlesque dancers, was a spectacle that seemed straight out of a Hollywood movie. Live music filled the air, creating a surreal ambiance. As I glanced around, absorbing the extravagance, it felt as though a scene from my TV screen had spilled into reality. Actors whom I frequently watched on prime time mingled before me. Isaac, sensing my astonishment, nudged me: "Don't stare."

Despite the mischief of my teenage years, drugs were a line I had never crossed, a boundary firmly etched by stern warnings from my mother. Yet, in this world of lavish excess, they seemed almost common-place. As the party's intensity grew, one thing led to another, and soon the four of us found ourselves secluded in one of the mansion's opulent bathrooms. There, on the sink counter, lay meticulously arranged lines of cocaine, a stark contrast to the innocence of the party's initial facade. We exchanged glances, a mix of excitement and disbelief in our eyes until, in unspoken agreement, we collectively shrugged off our reserva-tions. There was a moment of daring defiance as we all seemed to think, "Why the fuck not?"

Drugs never became a significant part of my life, despite my frequent presence in the LA party scene. That single experience, however, sym-bolized a new and fearless chapter in my life—a leap into the unknown.

My days often culminated on Evan's Venice rooftop, staring at the Pacific Ocean sunset through the palm trees and engulfed in a marijuana haze. It was Evan who first candidly broached with me the topic of American racism—a concept I'd only fleetingly encountered growing up in the multicultural embrace of Toronto. Evan's Louisiana upbring-ing profoundly influenced his view of American society, making him acutely aware of the psychological and physical threats posed by racial prejudices.

One evening, I got to see firsthand what it could be like to be Black in America. At the Brig on Abbot Kinney Boulevard, a favored Venice dive bar known for its Thursday hip-hop nights, we struck up a friendship with another couple over a game of pool. Later, the four of us stepped outside. I was in a good mood, finding a sense of coolness in the fact that a dorky white girl like me could blend in relatively seamlessly with three African Americans, all of us sharing a joint and vibing to 90s hip-hop blaring from the car speakers nearby. But our tranquil night was abruptly interrupted by the harsh glare of flashlights and a stern, authoritative command: "Put your hands where I can see them." Suddenly, I found myself in an unexpected standoff with American law enforcement.

With a cautious turn, moonlight illuminating my curly hair, I faced the police officers. Their initial hostility waned, replaced by visible surprise at my ethnicity, and their demeanor softened from aggression to something milder. "Maybe you should head elsewhere," they suggested, the edge in their tone now blunted. The confrontation dissolved as quickly as it had escalated, leaving us to retreat into the shadows of the night. Once we were safely away from the scene, I remained motionless, stunned, for what felt like an eternity, processing the encounter. That moment often replays in my mind, a stark reminder of how in certain places and times, the color of one's skin can alter the course of an evening. "Welcome to America," Evan said with a half-crooked smile.

Coming face-to-face with overt racial discrimination by the police made me think deeply about how economic systems reflect the same prejudices as legal and social ones. A 2015 study by the Federal Reserve Bank of Boston and Duke University reported a staggering generational racial wealth gap between white and Black families. The median net worth for white households in Greater Boston was $247,500; for Black households, it was just $8.

The gender wage gap is a different chapter of the same story. US Census data from 2020 reveals that women who are employed full-time and year-round earn only 83 percent of what their male counterparts make. The gap is much larger for women of color, who take home only 63 cents for every dollar earned by a non-Hispanic white man. The intersection of race, ethnicity, and gender has compounding effects on the wage gap, often deepening the divide. One can't help but wonder if systemic racism and sexism that is represented by official sources is just the tip of the iceberg. Discrimination so explicit and pronounced in public suggests its prevalence in less official corners of the economy. Once we accept that this system is skewed in the favor of some, it becomes easier to step around the landmines.

From Linkin Park to The Chainsmokers: Music and the Art of Venture Capital

My first work opportunity in Los Angeles came to me through a complete stroke of luck. Evan had invited me to join him as his plus-one to an entertainment industry jazz night at the Hammer Museum. We settled into a table in the museum's courtyard courtesy of CAA, Evan having generously secured the last two seats for us. Looking around, I felt a tad underdressed; I had not yet fully acclimated to LA's signature cool dress code. I worried the whole night would be tainted by this awkward feeling. But, as serendipity would have it, I was seated next to Kevin, who had recently left CAA to work for none other than Linkin Park.

"Like the rock band?" I queried, in confusion.

I was awed. Songs such as "Numb" and "In the End" had been the soundtrack to my angsty teenage years, with the crossover Jay-Z album *Collision Course* holding a special place in my heart. Kevin shared his insights about the band's recent decision to expand their business interests into a family-office format, housing a collection of brands, a creative studio, and even a venture capital department. At the time, I had never really pictured celebrities as venture capitalists or even business moguls. Still, emboldened by my new "try anything once" philosophy, I pitched myself as Kevin's right-hand person. I told him all about my work at the law firm and on the trading floor, assuring him of my analytical prowess. But above all, I'm sure, I conveyed that most LA of qualities: a raw, unyielding hunger to make something of myself.

Kevin summoned me to his office the following week. Amid my palpable nerves, I navigated the interview with poise, showcasing my keenness to explore this uncharted terrain. Sure, the idea of working for a rock band seemed alluring. But more than that, I yearned for this reinvention—an opportunity to use the skills I already had in a job where I could be fueled by passion and creativity, away from the predictable confines of the corporate world. I wanted to build a new life in a city I had come to love. The interview process culminated with an unexpected lunch with Linkin Park legends Mike Shinoda and Brad Delson. As the brainpower behind the venture capital side of their organization, they probed my readiness and aptitude. Struggling to mask my awe, I hoped my enthusiasm did not overshadow my credentials. Driving home, the blaring notes of "Numb/Encore (Remix)" became my anthem for celebrating a job well done.

A week later, the call came. The universe had heard my plea, and I was the new investment director at Machine Shop Ventures.

★★

In 2014 and 2015, LA's show-business glitz at last collided head-on with the more unassuming world of Silicon Valley's venture capital. An emerging trend, wherein stardom transitioned from the Billboard charts and Hollywood screen to the adrenaline-filled world of investment, began making waves. It all seemed to begin with Jared Leto, known now not only as an Oscar winner but as an early believer in future corporate behemoths such as Uber and Airbnb. Quickly on the heels of Leto's success, the dynamic duo of Troy Carter and Lady Gaga moved into the spotlight, placing their bets on Spotify, Uber, and Dropbox.

The team at Machine Shop Ventures followed shortly after and made their mark with investments in Lyft, Robinhood, Blue Bottle Coffee, and other notable ventures. Ashton Kutcher wasn't far behind. Parlaying previously successful investments into his own VC firm, Sound Ventures (launched in 2015 with the backing of Live Nation), he arguably became the poster child for celebrity venture capitalism. By 2023, his clout in the industry was undeniable, with a newly announced AI fund of a whopping $240M and a portfolio boasting early stakes in Airbnb, Bird, Nest, Robinhood, Uber, Pinterest, and Square. These investments delivered returns that left many traditional VCs in awe.

These luminaries of entertainment realized the potency of their platforms. Their fan bases could be tapped for more than just your regular revenue streams; rather, such loyal followings provided celebrity investors with ultimate leverage over brands in which they held an ownership stake. Instead of pocketing a $20,000 endorsement check from one of the start-ups looking to do a little marketing, they could play the long game. If they invested in companies directly and used their media reach to amplify a brand, their potential returns could skyrocket, sometimes by a multiple of 50 to even 100. These new celebrity moguls weren't just passive investors, either—they entered the fray, rubbing shoulders and competing for deals with Silicon Valley titans such as A16Z and Sequoia Capital.

Today, the intersection of entertainment and investment extends far beyond the realm of venture capital, embracing a universe where celebrities are not just faces of brands but are also founders, investors, and financial moguls in their own right. In my view, the quintessential example of this trend is the incomparable Kim Kardashian. As we increasingly watched celebrities monetize their brands and go from taking endorsement checks to investing in companies, Kim went a step further. She took control of the company-building process itself and began to create venture capital–worthy brands within her empire. Her portfolio includes KKW Beauty (her cosmetics brand worth more than $1 billion, making it a "unicorn" company), Skims (an underwear and apparel brand in which her stake is estimated to be worth an impressive $225 million), and now her very own private equity firm, SKKY Partners (cofounded with Jay Sammons, a former partner at the Carlyle Group) that focuses on direct-to-consumer brands.

Aside from the admirable financial success of her ventures, Kim Kardashian's involvement in the world of business and finance stands out for another reason. The venture capital world is significantly skewed toward male founders; in 2020, only about 2.3% of the total capital raised through VC went to women-led start-ups. Overall, Kardashian's path illustrates the evolving paradigm of what it means to be both a celebrity and a mogul, setting a new standard for women in business and beyond venture capital. With a net worth now estimated at a staggering $1.8 billion, Kardashian's checkered past (peppered with headline-grabbing moments, from a scandalous sex tape to a short-lived marriage) now echoes as a distant backdrop to her present achievements. A lawyer, an investor, and a founder, she is a woman on a mission.

But back in 2014, much of this discovery of opportunities for celebrities to shape the world of business was still in the future. And in the backdrop of this growing star-studded investment surge, amplifying the allure of the space where showbiz met start-ups, was the zenith of Y Combinator.

Y Combinator and the Venture Capital Framework

In the mid-2000s, the existing venture capital landscape experienced a seismic shift with the advent of Y Combinator (YC). Launched in March 2005, YC wasn't just another VC firm—it pioneered the start-up accelerator model, a structured program wherein start-ups, in exchange for a sizable 7% of equity, would receive approximately $300,000 in seed money, as well as crucial training and industry connections. Over an intense three-month period, these budding companies honed their pitches and products, culminating in the much-anticipated Demo Day, a rite of passage during which they showcased their innovations to an eager crowd of investors.

The YC effect was palpable. As start-ups such as Dropbox, Airbnb, Stripe, Coinbase, Instacart, and Reddit emerged from its stables, YC's clout in the industry surged. It wasn't just the success stories, though there were plenty of those; it was also the way YC fundamentally altered the dynamic between investors and founders. Start-ups bearing the YC badge suddenly found doors opening more effortlessly, leveling the playing field and giving founders more leverage in future funding negotiations. Additionally, YC streamlined early-stage investing with the introduction of the SAFE (Simple Agreement for Future Equity), offering a straightforward alternative to traditional convertible notes. (An overview of modern-day venture capital investment instruments is provided further on in this chapter.)

What further set YC apart from its competitors was its commitment to democratizing access to capital. Unlike the closed doors of traditional VC firms, YC's doors were open to all, ushering in a wave of innovation. This wasn't a Silicon Valley—exclusive club; start-ups from all corners of the globe flocked to YC, drawn by its promise of mentorship and opportunity. And while YC's heart was undeniably in tech, its arms reached out to diverse sectors, from biotech to hardware.

Beyond funding, YC became synonymous with start-up education. With initiatives such as Startup School, a plethora of insightful essays published on its blog, and invaluable advice shared freely on its platforms, YC was as much a mentor as it was an investor. The firm's mantra of "make something people want," emphasizing the pivotal importance of product-market fit, became the gospel for start-ups worldwide.

As the years rolled on, YC's influence only deepened. It introduced the Continuity Fund, ensuring its involvement in the success stories it helped write well beyond the early stages. Throughout its evolution, YC remained a beacon, a testament to the power of mentorship, innovation, and the relentless pursuit of building something people truly want. Notably, Sam Altman, the father of ChatGPT, was one of the founding partners of Y Combinator at the age of 26, and served as president of the organization from 2014 to 2019, before he went on to focus on the creation of OpenAI full-time.

Y Combinator, along with other leading Bay Area funds such as Sequoia and A16Z, pioneered the rinse-and-repeat venture capital framework of the early 21st century.

The venture capital industry operates within a structured framework similar to that seen in investment banks, designed to ensure that potential investments align with the firm's objectives and have a reasonable chance of success. While each VC firm might have a unique industry or investment horizon on which it prefers to focus, the general VC investment process can be broken down into several steps.

Stages of the Venture Capital Process

1. **Deal sourcing:** This is where potential investment opportunities are identified. VCs often rely on their networks, industry events, other investors, or inbound pitches to find promising start-ups, sometimes via data providers. Referrals from trusted sources are especially valued.

2. **Screening:** Given the volume of start-ups seeking capital, VCs have to screen opportunities to determine which ones are worth a closer look. They'll consider the startup's market, technology, team, and other factors to decide whether it fits their investment thesis.

3. **Initial due diligence:** For start-ups that make it past the initial screening, VCs will dive deeper into understanding the business. This might involve analyzing financials, understanding the product and technology, meeting the team, and assessing market size and competition.

4. **Term sheet:** If a VC decides to move forward, they will offer the start-up a term sheet. This nonbinding document outlines the basic terms and conditions of the investment. It includes details about the investment amount, equity stake, valuation, governance terms, and other key considerations.

5. **Detailed due diligence:** After the term sheet is agreed upon, the VC conducts a more exhaustive examination. This can involve deeper financial analyses, technical evaluations, customer and supplier interviews, and even background checks on the founders.

(continued)

6. **Final approval/investment decision:** Once due diligence is complete, the investment team will often need to get approval from a committee or the partnership to proceed with the investment. This is typically a formal process wherein the merits and risks of the deal are debated.

7. **Closing:** With the approval secured, legal documents are drawn up and signed, and funds are transferred. This step includes the creation of the share purchase agreement (SPA), shareholders' agreement, and other related documents.

8. **Post-investment management:** After the investment is made, VCs often take a board seat or have some form of governance role in the company. They'll work with the start-up, providing guidance, connections, and support. The aim is to help the company grow and eventually reach an exit through either an acquisition or an initial public offering (IPO).

9. **Exit:** This is the final stage of the process, where the VC aims to realize a return on their investment. Common exit strategies include selling their stake after an IPO, a trade sale (sale to another company), or a buyback by the company itself.

In the venture capital process, the assessment of risk versus reward takes center stage. Venture capitalists are tasked with weighing a start-up's potential for growth against the inherent risks and the possibility of failure. Their goal is to identify opportunities that promise significant returns on their investment.

One of the most challenging aspects of a VC's role is to place a value on an idea, often in the nascent stages, before a tangible product or technology exists. Valuing start-ups is more akin to an art form than a strict science, primarily due to these companies often having little to no operating history and, in many cases, lacking profitability. Nonetheless, VCs employ a variety of methods and considerations in their valuation process. One common approach is a comparables analysis, where VCs examine companies they deem similar to the one they're screening to understand the prices paid by other investors for comparable ventures. They may also use the discounted cash flow method to project the start-up's future cash flows and determine its present value. However, more often than not, VCs base their valuation of a company on the potential exit value of the investment, which is significantly influenced by the start-up's market buzz and hype. This approach underlines the speculative nature of venture capital, a world where the perception and potential of a company often weigh as heavily as its tangible assets or current revenues.

Generally, start-ups seek funding from venture capital firms and other investors in structured "rounds" that reflect the stage of the company's development. Funds provided at the earliest life stages are, logically, much less than the amount that must be sought as a company takes on more employees and more expenses of research and development to bring its product or service to market.

Stages of Venture Capital Funding

1. **Pre-Seed/Seed:** The earliest stage of funding, often used to develop a prototype or conduct market research. Typically sourced from angel investors, friends, and family.
2. **Series A:** After the seed phase, start-ups may go for a Series A round. At this point, they have a working business model and may have early traction in the market, but they need funds to optimize their product or scale their business model.
3. **Series B:** Used to scale the business further, often for purposes of wider market expansion, hiring, or even acquisition of other businesses.
4. **Series C and beyond:** At this stage, the start-up is more mature and may be looking at expansion into new markets, diversifying product ranges, or preparing for an IPO.
5. **Bridge rounds/mezzanine financing:** These refer to short-term loans or equity sales occurring between other funding rounds, often in anticipation of an IPO.

Most VCs will specialize in a particular stage of company funding based on their experience and the size of the check they're able to write. Smaller funds will often take high-risk, but small, bets at the pre-seed and seed stages, while large firms will take bigger and more concentrated bets in later rounds.

Except for venture debt lenders (a different approach that we'll be skipping over here), most VCs will invest in the equity of a start-up through a handful of common investment instruments.

The selection of the right instrument and valuation method for each investment often depends on the negotiation between the investor and the startup, the stage of the startup, market conditions, and the specific nature and prospects of the business.

Investment Instruments in Venture Capital

Common stock: Represents ownership in a company and entitles the shareholder to a portion of the company's earnings and assets.

Preferred stock: Similar to common stock, but holders have a higher claim on the company's assets and earnings. Preferred stockholders are paid dividends before common stockholders. The purchase of preferred stock is common in VC deals because it may offer dividends and/or preference during exits, or be convertible to common stock.

Convertible note: A short-term debt that converts into equity, typically in conjunction with a future financing round. A convertible note is a loan that becomes equity.

SAFE (Simple Agreement for Future Equity): Pioneered by Y Combinator, this is an agreement that grants the investor the right to purchase stock in a future equity round, without determining a specific price per share at the time of the initial investment. SAFE notes aren't debt, so they don't accrue interest.

Warrants: Similar to options, these allow the holder to buy the stock of the issuer at a specific price within a certain time frame.

Unicorns, Kardashians, and the NFT Revolution

My work with Machine Shop Ventures was my first experience at the nexus of entertainment and finance, but the meeting of these two passions would be a theme of my career throughout my time living in LA. In 2015, I would be connected to a now-longtime friend, Corey McGuire, who lived in a loft on Electric Avenue. Hosting Thursday night music shows for neighborhood friends, the loft became a local hang-out for young artists such as Justin Bieber, Cody Simpson, Corey Harper, Adrian Cota, and Miley Cyrus. Artists such as Billie Eilish would play some of their first shows on the loosely built stage. Performing at the house became somewhat of a status symbol among young musicians seeking to jump-start their careers. Beers, joints, and laughter would flow among partygoers late into the night as folks jammed on their guitars or sang their hearts out.

One night, Corey pulled me aside quietly to share some dreaded news: "We're out of money. I can't make rent next month. But I can't let the magic die. What do we do?" Together, we hatched a plan: we would form a company in which I would receive advisory shares for making introductions to wealthy individuals looking to support the arts with an investment ... a risky investment that they might not ever see again. Under this new model, Winston House survived and thrived on Electric Avenue until 2020, when it moved to a new building, under the historic Venice Sign, reopening as a full-fledged music venue. To this day, the magic lives on, bringing exciting new live music to the shore of the Pacific.

A few years later, in 2019, I would be given the opportunity to work on another entertainer-backed venture capital fund, this time for the award-winning DJ duo the Chainsmokers, composed of Alex Pall and Drew Taggart. I was brought in by some of the managers who helped put together a fund called MANTIS VC, which focused on early-stage investments in blockchain technology.

The day I interviewed for the gig with the Chainsmokers remains one of the funnier stories I tell about my journey. Already at the height of their career at this point, the duo played gigs at the Encore Beach Club in Las Vegas every Saturday. Accordingly, on one such day, I found myself on a flight to Vegas to catch up with them over lunch. Our meeting point was the grandest suite in the Wynn Hotel, where the overwhelming opulence of the golden decor was almost blinding.

Having lived in LA for almost five years at the time, the allure of celebrity had largely lost its sheen for me, but the Chainsmokers were an exception. I admired their journey, from tinkering with remixes in their dorm rooms to becoming the most-streamed DJs in the world, reportedly commanding a staggering $250,000 per show. My nervousness at our lunch wasn't due to their star power, though; it was the weight of what this meeting represented. Rather than asking probing professional questions, they seemed more interested in gauging the person behind the résumé, sizing up whether I could fit into their world. They wanted to see if I could "hang."

After lunch, we made our way to the pulsating Encore Beach Club, right below our suite. The ambiance was electric. With a buzzing crowd both indoors and out, the duo took center stage while I, along with their crew, stood behind the DJ booth. As the opening notes of their hit "Closer" filled the air, Drew hopped onto the stage, encouraging the audience to sing along by passing the mic around. Amid this charged atmosphere, Alex, who had recently invested in the tequila brand Jaja, grabbed the spotlight. Holding a row of tequila shots, he called my name on the mic to take a shot. Challenge accepted: we started matching each other shot for shot, the setting around me growing fuzzier with each face-off. The scene was wild, surreal even—something I can't quite remember but will never forget.

The debauchery continued well into the night, culminating in an impromptu trip back to LA on a private jet. Drinks flowed, music blared, and amid this partying atmosphere, I recall one of my fund partners sprawled out, unconscious, at the back of the jet. I caught myself wondering if this was real life. I'd done my share of hard partying with finance bros in my day, yet in this moment I still felt far from the sea of black suits on the trading floor. The music kept playing. Somehow, in the early hours, I at last found myself crawling into my Venice Beach home, only to be met with the most excruciating 48-hour hangover.

But as the fog of my hangover began to lift, my phone buzzed with the message I had been waiting for: "You got the job."

My stint with the Chainsmokers was a fun journey of hard work counteracted with fancy dinners, backstage passes, and private jets. It was truly a once-in-a-lifetime experience, working with two entertainment icons of our time. The thing that always stood out to me about Drew and Alex, even as they were surrounded by a sea of adoring fans (and girls) everywhere we went, is how they treated each other, their family, and everyone on their team.

Making people feel seen and appreciated is a quality that Dale Carnegie discusses in his famous book *How to Win Friends and Influence*

People. Carnegie also encourages us to show genuine interest in others, give honest and sincere appreciation, and make others feel important. Alex and Drew were exceptional at these skills, and as a result their entire team, including myself, loved them and went to bat for them. As Maya Angelou and others have observed, people don't remember what you do, but they do remember how you made them feel. There were many reasons for my eventual departure from the Chainsmokers team, compensation and team dynamics being among them. But in hindsight, the true reason I left was that I was ready to make a bet on myself. And, as the world began to fall apart around me during the pandemic the following year, I realized that I had very little to lose.

Looking back now, this era of celebrity venture capital was responsible for minting billions of dollars for many who seemingly got lucky overnight, giving rise to an entire culture of making fun of these so-called professionals. Social media influencer accounts such as "Praying for Exits" and "VC Brags," where the VC world's lavish ski and yacht trips, as well as unrealistic morning routines, would routinely be made fun of grew in popularity. Some VCs became celebrities in their own right, garnering large followings on social media, throwing lavish parties, and living opulent lifestyles, all while the founders they backed grinded night after night in hopes of one day achieving similar levels of wealth and renown.

In retrospect, the sudden ubiquity and meteoric rise of VC culture in this period may also have contributed to the backlash against it. It is almost like VC egos inflated overnight with matching Teslas and Patagonia vests. Below is just a sample of the hysterical and very real tweets by popular venture capitalists featured on @VCBrags, also known as "VCs Congratulating Themselves":

> *"Got off a call with a Y Combinator-backed co-founder creating a tool for cold email. Once again, I'm reminded of how world-class I am at this game. There might be just a small handful that can outperform me."* (@pontivlex)

> *"Before you make fun of a kid for believing in Santa, just remember many believe venture capitalists actually add value."* (@VCBrags)

> *"If you're questioning whether it's too early to ship your product, just remember that Boeing shipped 737 Max airplanes without fully tightening down all the bolts."* (@anothercohen)

Some investors went a step further, creating brands that went on to far eclipse their investing careers. One such example is the team behind the *All-In Podcast*, which has emerged as a significant voice in the realms of tech, finance, and politics, gaining a dedicated following for its insightful and often candid discussions. The podcast is hosted by a quartet of renowned investors and entrepreneurs known colloquially as the "Besties:" Chamath Palihapitiya, a former Facebook executive and the founder of Social Capital, celebrated for his sharp insights and out-spoken views on venture capital and societal issues; Jason Calacanis, a serial entrepreneur and angel investor known for a wealth of experience in the start-up ecosystem, including early investments in companies such as Uber and Robinhood; David Sacks, a PayPal alum and founder of Yammer with a blend of operational expertise and investment acumen; and David Friedberg, CEO of the Production Board and a former Google executive with deep knowledge of climate science and biotechnology.

Together, these four investors-cum-media-personalities provide a blend of expertise, opinion, and analysis, making the *All-In Podcast* a go-to resource for anyone interested in the intersection of technology, business, and current affairs. The four-pack has accumulated millions of Twitter followers and even started their own summit, featuring venture capital icons such as Bill Gurley (the VC behind Uber's success) and entrepreneurs including Elon Musk. Did they have successful investing careers? Sure. But what is becoming more evident each day is that their ability to create a brand together and garner the attention of large audi-ences is much more powerful than their ability to manage capital. They have truly taken venture capital and made it a celebrity sport.

Is Venture Capital Sustainable?

The scale of venture capital investments has grown exponentially in recent years. In the United States alone, annual venture capital invest-ment grew from $30 billion in 2009 to over $130 billion by 2020. With the growing glitz and glamour of venture capital, however, what few talk or post about is that the venture capital model has started to become unsustainable. With high overheads, a long-term return horizon (typi-cally eight to ten years), and a largely illiquid model, many VCs have been obliged, and able, to hide their overall lack of performance behind the success of their marquee investments.

One key argument against the long-term viability of the VC model is its inherent focus on high growth and high returns in a relatively short period. This relentless pursuit of "unicorn" start-ups often leads to an unsustainable growth trajectory along which nascent companies are pressured to scale rapidly, sometimes at the cost of developing a solid, long-term business foundation. Such an approach can encourage a culture of risk-taking that prioritizes short-term gains over sustainable, long-term value creation. Additionally, the VC model's success is often measured by the frequency of high-profile exits, such as IPOs or acquisitions. This exit-driven mentality can risk sidelining the building of fundamentally strong companies in favor of strategies more likely to lead to a lucrative exit. In the long run, such an approach may not be sustainable, as it may encourage short-term strategies rather than the creation of businesses with enduring value and impact.

Even more importantly, as we face the end of a 13-year near-zero-interest-rate policy in the US, increasing inflation and interest rates, and a potential recession, many in 2024 are asking whether the VC model is no longer viable, or whether profits can be created more sustainably with other methods.

Overall, venture capital developed over four distinct eras:

1. **Silicon Valley's genesis:** The innovation of the silicon junction transistor in 1954 catalyzed the rise of the semiconductor industry. Though Shockley Semiconductor faltered, its offshoot, Fairchild Semiconductor, thrived and eventually gave birth to giants such as Intel that made the valley what it is today.

2. **The PC revolution:** The 1970s and '80s saw the rise of the personal computer, marking a transition from computers as exclusive hobbyist devices to their current role as mainstream consumer electronics. Pioneering software companies such as Microsoft and Oracle also emerged during this time.

3. **Dot-com era:** The 1990s ushered in the rise of the Internet, giving birth to companies such as Amazon and Google. However, rapid growth in this sector ultimately led to the dot-com bubble, with many companies facing post-burst oblivion.

4. **Mobile era:** With the iPhone's launch, 2007 marked the birth of mobile apps, cultivating today's dominant technology companies such as Airbnb, Uber, and Snapchat.

As we look toward the future of venture capital, three distinct trends stand out, each signaling a transformative shift in the landscape of investment and innovation:

1. **Artificial intelligence proliferation:** AI is poised to redefine a multitude of industries, from health care to finance. Its increasing integration into our lives suggests a landscape where decision-making, operational efficiency, and customer interactions are revolutionized. As AI technology becomes more sophisticated, venture capital is increasingly flowing into start-ups that leverage AI for innovative solutions and disruptive business models.

2. **Energy revolution:** The energy sector is on the cusp of a major transformation. Driven by the rapid advancement and adoption of renewable energy sources, the cost of energy is projected to fall dramatically in the coming years, potentially reaching near-zero levels. This shift not only opens the door to more environmentally sustainable practices but also heralds a new era of energy independence and innovation. Venture capital is expected to play a crucial role in funding start-ups that are at the forefront of this energy revolution, particularly those exploring new forms of renewable energy, energy storage, and smart grid technologies.

3. **Computing leap:** We are currently witnessing a pivotal computing shift from traditional central processing units (CPUs) to graphics processing units (GPUs), which offer superior capabilities for parallel processing. This shift goes hand in hand with the diminishing application of Moore's law (an observation prevalent in computer science that the number of transistors in an integrated circuit doubles about every two years). The transition to GPUs is particularly significant for fields that require immense computational power, such as artificial intelligence and, in particular, machine learning. GPUs enable faster processing of complex algorithms and large datasets, accelerating advancements in these areas. Venture capital is increasingly targeting companies that are harnessing the power of GPUs to drive innovation in computing-intensive fields, recognizing the potential of these companies for substantial growth and breakthroughs.

I anticipate that venture capital funds focusing on businesses outside of these three categories will face challenges, particularly as many consumer and cultural innovations will now be created through decentralized funding methods.

NFTs as Financial Art

For me, the rise of non-fungible tokens (NFTs) represents one of the most intriguing developments in the ongoing mashup of culture and money, marking a pivotal moment in how we perceive and value art. NFTs, unique digital assets verified and stored on blockchain technology, exploded onto the scene in 2020 and 2021, capturing the imagination of artists, collectors, and investors alike. This new form of digital asset differs from traditional cryptocurrencies such as Bitcoin and Ethereum in that each NFT is distinct, with specific characteristics that prevent them from being interchangeable.

The NFT boom was fueled by the growing interest in cryptocurrencies and the recognition of blockchain technology's transformative potential to revolutionize various industries. What distinguished NFTs was their ability to attract a broader audience beyond typical crypto enthusiasts; artists and creators saw NFTs as a groundbreaking way to monetize digital art and content that was previously easy to replicate and challenging to claim exclusive title to. (This characteristic may prove of immense value in the age of AI tools such as ChatGPT and Dall_E, whose intelligence models are known to have been trained on many thousands of copyrighted visual and textual works through "scraping," resulting in a variety of lawsuits.) The March 2021 sale of the digital artwork "Everydays: The First 5000 Days" by Beeple for a staggering $69 million at Christie's auction house was a watershed moment for NFTs, showcasing their enormous economic potential and propelling them into the zeitgeist.

NFTs have since transcended the boundaries of digital art; their influence and prevalence have now infiltrated the worlds of music, gaming, sports, and entertainment. NFTs allow for the ownership, collection, and trading of everything from in-game items and virtual real estate in online video games to digital sports memorabilia and exclusive music files. This versatility has led to a diverse and dynamic NFT ecosystem, fostering communities and opening up fresh avenues for engagement between creators and their supporters.

In the final months of 2023, I found myself at the heart of the digital art revolution—an unexpected turn for someone who arrived relatively late to the scene. It was during this time that friends, sensing an opportunity in the market's lull, urged me to invest in a CryptoPunk. This unique collection of 10,000 digital avatars, once selling for as high as $23.7 million, seemed an extravagant gamble. Yet, there was one particular punk that bore a startling resemblance to me: wild hair, bold red lips, and (much to my embarrassment) a cigarette in hand. Against my better judgment and the values ingrained by my modest upbringing, I spent over $100,000 on this digital representation of myself—a decision I kept secret from my family (until now, I guess!), fearing their dismay over what could only seem to them like a frivolous indulgence.

My reservations ebbed away, though, when I stepped into the vibrant community at Art Basel that December. Surrounded by leaders, artists, and fellow punk owners within the cryptosphere, I found a sense of belonging and acceptance. It was here that I crossed paths with Masna, a renowned artist celebrated for immortalizing CryptoPunks in murals across global cities. His proposal to include my punk in his latest project in Miami struck me—an opportunity to embed my digital identity within the world of tangible art. I eagerly contributed to the endeavor, and soon, my punk adorned a building wall in the artist neighborhood of Wynwood, above Ben Zion's "Time to be Happy" gallery, a testament to the convergence of the digital and physical realms.

This mural, capturing the essence of my digital avatar, became for me a symbol of my journey, bridging my past, present, and future in both my personal life and my career. With each visit to Miami, standing before it, I'm reminded of the transformative power of creativity.

MONEY MYTH #3: Making money has to be boring.

One of the biggest misconceptions I was taught, early on in my career, is that making money has to be boring—that you have to choose between the practical and profitable path in life, and a career filled with creativity and joy. It wasn't until I moved to LA and entered the world of venture capital that I realized that making money is an art and, like any other art, it can be a source of happiness in and of itself.

Building brands, financing music venues, investing in start-ups, and making digital art: all of these endeavors start with a dream of creating something that was not there before. When I started working for Linkin Park, suddenly I was doing something more than just shuffling money into different anonymous piles—I was investing in new and inspiring products and services for the enjoyment of others. The most satisfying way, in my experience, to find your fortune is by branching out into not only what is new but also what is useful beyond wealth creation—into what will make money not only because people want it but because it brings a net benefit to society.

Throughout my journey, I have found two types of people: those who view money as some sort of evil, and those who embrace it as a byproduct of monetizing their talents and as a tool to do good in the world. The truth is, if you hate wealth, and treat it with disdain and skepticism, it will elude you. And if you use it for the wrong things, you are very likely to lose it. Your path to wealth should be about living out a dream because all innovation—both in the art and the technical worlds—starts with a dream. Most importantly, beyond dreaming up the impossible (which is high stakes and high risk), the truest path to wealth is to do something you really love. As Jim Carrey once said, "You can fail at what you don't want, so you might as well take a chance on doing what you love." If you have the opportunity, invest your time and money in what moves you. Whether you win or lose, you will have spent your time on something you believe in.

4

The Money Printer

In a world of magic wands, central banks have the best one: a money printer.

—Unknown

Before I embark on this chapter, I must say that this will be one of the most important topics we will cover in the book, but it will also be the most dense. Our financial system has been made increasingly and purposefully complex by our governments so that the population does not question its policies. Yet, it is important for all of us to understand how Western economics actually works. And even if you don't live in the US, it is important to note that American fiscal and monetary policies set the tone for the rest of the world—whether they like it or not—and often have painful ripple effects globally. Hence, understanding how the Federal Reserve and the US Treasury work together to manage the dollar is crucial for processing almost any bit of economic news, including global news. If you already know intimately how the money printer works, feel free to join me in despair, and in Chapter 5.

The Journey to My Parents' Basement

As the COVID-19 pandemic took the stage in the spring of 2020, it ushered in an era of collective upset. On January 5, 2020, the first case of coronavirus was discovered in Wuhan, China. By the end of February, several cases had appeared in the US, and by March, it had become clear that we were past the possibility of "containment." Fear and panic ensued, the economy slowed down, and the Fed was once again tasked with solving an economic crisis. The response? Print more money, of course. According to the IMF, governments worldwide unleashed an estimated $12 trillion in fiscal stimulus in 2020 to combat the economic fallout from the COVID-19 pandemic. The Federal Reserve's total balance sheet nearly doubled, from around $4 trillion at the start of 2020 to nearly $8 trillion by the end of the year, reflecting the scale of its asset purchases. This is about 10 times what the government spent on TARP, the program to mitigate the 2008 financial crisis.

As we were all forced into lockdowns, our worlds shrank to the confines of our homes, where the relentless barrage of grim news seemed inescapable. The markets, ever reflective of our collective psyche, were in disarray. On Monday, March 16, 2020—known as "Black Monday"—we saw an unfathomable market collapse. The Dow Jones fell by almost 3,000 points, losing nearly 13% of its value, which was its largest percentage drop since the 1987 "Black Monday" crash. For the third time in six trading sessions, "circuit breakers" were triggered on US stock exchanges, halting trading for 15 minutes after the S&P 500 fell 7% in an attempt to prevent a further free fall. Global markets were also deeply affected, with indices in Europe and Asia experiencing similar dramatic falls. By the closing bell on March 23, the S&P 500 had dropped by around 33%, to 2237.40, officially entering bear market territory (defined as at least a 20% decline from recent highs).

This upheaval on Wall Street was a mirror to the chaos unraveling across the globe. Global debt levels surged to a record high, reaching 356% of GDP in 2020 according to the Institute of International Finance (IIF), driven by the massive increase in borrowing by governments, corporations, and households. Oil prices, already beleaguered by a price war, went into a tailspin as demand evaporated overnight. Borders snapped shut, and cities became ghost towns, the pandemic's grasp promised a protracted economic slowdown—perhaps even a recession—as we grappled with our new reality.

Amid this chaos, I had begun to severely run out of money. The truth is, I had run out of money a long time ago. Although I had spent the last couple of years working, I cut every paycheck in half religiously to buy Bitcoin. Having witnessed an entire generation of Bitcoin millionaires created in the 2017–2018 cryptocurrency cycle, I realized that real money was made in the long trade. Millionaires were created, seemingly overnight, among people who had long-term conviction in Bitcoin and held it over a period of many years.

I had also begun to truly believe that Bitcoin was a better alternative to the financial system I had become intimately acquainted with during my time in investment banking and venture capital. I thought that the best thing I could do for myself and my future was to save at least 10 Bitcoins, and I had done exactly that, buying them at a price range of $3,000 to $8,000. On Black Monday, Bitcoin experienced a drawdown along with the rest of the market, reaching a low of $3,400. The 10 Bitcoins I held were everything I had to my name. Actually, that's not quite true—I also had about $50,000 in credit card debt.

I wasn't as irresponsible as that makes me sound. Although I indeed enjoyed a moderately high-end lifestyle, looking back on it, I didn't go overboard that much. I was fairly mindful of maximizing the value of my work-provided expense accounts and shopping for things on sale. I shared a house with a few friends in Venice Beach, significantly decreasing my housing costs. And yet, things always seemed to pile up, particularly the social pressures of living in LA. And the credit cards were too easy to obtain, making it difficult to say no.

But there was another reason I was hard-pressed for cash. In my early 20s, my biological father—yes, the one who sailed away on a ship after my parents' wedding night and came home to find himself no longer part of our family—had come back into my life, and he became very sick. Just a year earlier, in the fall of 2019, he had collapsed from a stroke, and I found myself on a flight to Saint Petersburg to possibly say goodbye for good.

When I got there, he was in a medically induced 30-day coma. His new family, a wife and their two daughters, were patiently doting on his every need. I felt like an outsider in every way: I didn't belong. I hadn't been raised in this family. The girls didn't like me much. And although my stepmother was more than appreciative of my arrival, she had her hands full.

It was just as well. I never did well with hospitals anyway. And so I did what I do best: I went to the office. As a former captain in the Soviet Navy, my father had built a successful manufacturing business, shipping products such as life jackets, flashlights, helmets, and first aid kits that outfitted most of the commercial and government ships sailing out of Saint Petersburg Bay. At the time of his stroke, he had about 50 employees, and with him being an in-the-trenches CEO, things started to fall apart in his absence. There were multiple legal disputes and accounting issues pending, as well as threats from former business partners to collapse the business.

I was only 31 at the time. My Russian was incredibly rusty. But the business was in crisis, so I got to work. I met with the staff lawyers daily. I had secretaries draft my emails to mask my linguistic shortcomings. I reorganized all the power-of-attorney documents to make sure capital decisions could flow through my stepmother when I was gone. I negotiated with shady characters, showing them that I was not going to be as nice as my father and would use my Western might and the gravitas of those three university degrees to squash any dispute. I reassured staff that the company had continuity. But most importantly, I put an envelope of cash in every safe in my father's office and his house. I told my family that I was doing well financially and that the cash was surplus, but that was simply not true. I was dead broke and was doing transfers to pull cash off credit card accounts. I figured I would make the money back. I was about to start my job with the Chainsmokers, and I was sure that after a year or two, things would stabilize.

After 30 days, in a turn of events that was nothing short of a miracle, my father woke up. It took him almost two years to fully recover from the episode, to learn to walk and talk and eat and drive again. But I knew his family had the time to see him through that journey, which gave me peace. Some years later, my father would call me to thank me for what I'd done for him and his family. He gave me what, as a girl growing into a woman in a man's world, I thought was probably the greatest compliment he could give me: "I love you," he said. "You are the son I never had."

A year after those trying days in Saint Petersburg, as COVID-19 descended on us, I departed my job earlier than expected, largely as a way of taking an emotional stance to live my life to the fullest and because at the time I did not fully appreciate my dire financial situation. And then the markets continued to collapse. As I sat at a friend's house in Venice Beach, taking stock of my accounts, I got a call from my mother. She had recently remarried and built a house with her new partner on two acres of land in Quebec, adjacent to a forest—a place too remote for me to ever consider visiting. But here we were, in the middle of a lockdown where the excitement of civilization had worn off, and my bank account was decidedly in the negative. And then my mother said, "Would you like to move into the basement?"

For what felt like the first time in my life, I allowed someone to help me, rather than carry the entire load myself. As I settled into my new underground headquarters in rural Quebec, after years of so much raucousness and noise, I had true quiet. There was a fridge full of food. There were no bills to pay. And, for better or for worse, there were absolutely no distractions.

I had decided that I would take this gift of time to focus on writing and building my personal brand as a financial thought leader. In the prior year, I had been asked to start contributing to Forbes.com as an expert in their cryptocurrency section. I figured this was a great time to lean into building out that column and my subsequent following on Twitter.

But then another opportunity emerged. As the markets continued to act erratically, my phone buzzed with questions from friends and acquaintances. *Is the stock market dead? Are we going to have a recovery? What does this mean for inflation? Are we heading into a recession? Is Bitcoin coming back?* Gradually, I realized that I could no longer deal with the one-on-one hand-holding on macroeconomic issues—and so the "MythOfMoney. com" newsletter was born. What started as a simple weekly Substack email blast to friends to summarize my thoughts on macroeconomic trends, tech developments, and, of course, cryptocurrency markets, became the greatest feather in my cap. The newsletter continued to grow organically to a wider readership, including not only TradFi (traditional finance) investors and VCs but folks from all walks of life who wanted to learn about the financial world in order to take control of their own finances.

The newsletter took on a life of its own, becoming ranked as one of the best financial newsletters by *TIME* magazine and NASDAQ and garnering a worldwide readership. But more importantly, it gave me an analytic outlet to explore all of the questions about financial issues that had been bubbling up in my mind and the minds of my readers. It is what led me to write this book today.

Key Schools of Economic Thought

Before we jump into the fiscal and monetary initiatives that took place during the COVID era, it is important to do a quick overview of the key schools of economic thought. If you've had some economics classes, this will sound familiar to you, but anyone who hasn't studied the field directly is likely to have only passing acquaintance at best with any of it.

Various schools of economic thought present distinct narratives on the mechanics of economies and, therefore, on the crafting of economic policies for maximum societal benefit. Each school, with its own set of principles and theories, offers a unique lens through which we can view the complex world of economics. And each contributes to a broader understanding of how economies can or should work, yet no single one captures the entire picture. As I navigate through these diverse economic philosophies in my own reading, I reflect that they are not just academic theories; they are living, breathing philosophies that shape the policies affecting our daily lives. They represent a kaleidoscope of ideas, each vying for prominence and relevance in a world where economic realities are constantly evolving.

Economic Theories Explained

Classical economics: Founded by Adam Smith and further developed by economists such as David Ricardo and John Stuart Mill, classical economics focuses on the idea that free markets lead to an efficient allocation of resources. It emphasizes the role of supply and demand in setting prices and wages and believes in minimal government intervention. The concept of the "invisible hand"—the idea that free markets incentivize individuals to act in their own best interest in a way that produces optimal results for society—belongs to this school.

Neoclassical economics: This school emerged in the late 19th and early 20th centuries as a response to classical economics. It focuses on how individuals make rational choices based on their limited resources, leading to the optimal allocation of resources. Neoclassical economists use mathematical models to analyze economic behavior. Classical economists believe the key factor in a product's price is the cost of production; neoclassical economists argue that the consumer's perception of a product's value is the most important factor in its price.

Keynesian economics: Developed by John Maynard Keynes, this school argues that private-sector decisions can lead to inefficient macroeconomic outcomes and that government intervention, through monetary and fiscal policy, is necessary to stabilize output over the business cycle. US monetary and fiscal policy is broadly considered Keynesian; President Obama's $787 billion stimulus package during the Great Recession, the American Recovery and Reinvestment Act, as well as all of the economic responses to COVID-19, are notable examples of this school of thought in action.

Monetarism: Led by Milton Friedman, monetarists emphasize the role of governments in controlling the amount of money in circulation. They argue that variations in the money supply have major influence on national output in the short run, and price levels over longer periods. When asked by a *60 Minutes* correspondent in 2020 if the Fed "simply flooded the system with money," Fed Chairman Jerome Powell responded: "Yes, we did. We print it digitally." That's unchecked monetarism. (More on this shocking interview later in the chapter.)

Austrian economics: Founded by Carl Menger and further developed by economists such as Friedrich Hayek and Ludwig von Mises, this school is known for its rejection of mathematical modeling and its emphasis on the importance of individual choice, spontaneous order, and the limits of government intervention. Menger explained that value is subjective—what is important to you might not be worth anything to me. The law of diminishing marginal utility (or "diminishing returns"), which states that all else being equal, the incremental utility received from the consumption of a good decreases with each additional unit consumed, has its roots in Austrian economics.

Marxist economics: Based on the works of Karl Marx, this school views the capitalist system as inherently exploitative, leading to class conflict. It emphasizes the role of labor in the creation of value and advocates for a classless society where the means of production are communally owned. As Marx famously prescribed: "From each according to his ability, to each according to his needs."

New institutional economics (NIE): This approach focuses on the role of institutions—laws, customs, norms, and practices—in shaping economic behavior and outcomes. It argues that economic behavior cannot be fully understood without considering these social and legal frameworks. NIE assumes individuals are rational and preference-maximizing yet lack complete information and

(continued)

have difficulties making and enforcing agreements. As a result, institutions form to deal with transaction costs. Transaction costs encompass all the hurdles and expenses involved in completing an economic transaction beyond the price of the good or service being exchanged. Transaction costs used to be invisible, but now you can often see evidence of them, on your Uber receipt, for instance.

Behavioral economics: Merging economics with psychology, behavioral economics examines how psychological, cognitive, emotional, cultural, and social factors affect economic decisions. This school challenges the assumption of rational decision-making in traditional economics. Why do you do the things you do? Behavioral economists, your mom, and your therapist all want to know.

The US economy is a dynamic, mixed system, weaving various economic principles into its fabric. At its heart lies market capitalism, wherein private ownership and profit motives drive production and distribution, reflecting classical and neoclassical ideologies. However, this practice is threaded with significant government intervention, in line with Keynesian economics, through monetary policies, fiscal strategies, and market regulations. Additionally, the US incorporates elements of a welfare state, with social security and health care programs providing some level of safety net for its citizens. Influences of monetarism, particularly in managing inflation, and the emerging recognition of behavioral economics in policymaking are also evident. This intricate blend creates a multifaceted and robust economic system, marrying market-driven forces with strategic government oversight.

A Creature Awakes: The Federal Reserve Steps In

In the wake of Black Monday, during the first few weeks of the COVID-19 panic, as the financial markets tumbled, Wall Street clung to the narrative that this crisis felt akin to the aftermath of 9/11 rather than a repeat of 2008. The 2008 crisis had been fueled by large institutions entangled in poorly structured and inadequately insured derivatives; this time, Wall Street was positioning itself as a victim of circumstance, an act of God rather than a consequence of its own machinations.

Both the financial sector and the government insisted that the system wasn't inherently at risk—that nothing fundamental had been amiss until the coronavirus emerged and drove everyone into quarantine. Yet, as more evidence surfaced, suggesting that we might be in the throes of another global financial crisis, public apprehension grew. Questions arose about whether the coronavirus was simply laying bare the fractures that already plagued our financial infrastructure. Was it possible that our economy suffered from deep-seated, potentially irreparable issues that had been veiled by years of a bullish stock market and unchecked consumption?

Financial professionals, business owners, and working-class American families all suddenly faced a gnawing uncertainty regarding our shared financial destiny. Many were driven to sell assets and hoard cash, leading to a liquidity squeeze in the markets. In an attempt to quell this burgeoning panic, the Federal Reserve introduced several new policies, which unfortunately sowed more confusion than confidence. With the task of deciphering financial news becoming increasingly exasperating, as they stockpiled toilet paper, hand sanitizer, and local currency, citizens the world over longed for some clarity. I tried to provide answers with my newborn newsletter. We started our discussions with the role and function of the Federal Reserve.

What Does the Federal Reserve Do?

The Federal Reserve (the Fed) is America's central banking system, first created in 1913 to deal with financial panics and crises. During the Great Depression, in the 1930s, its powers were significantly expanded. The Fed's main job is to monitor and control our nation's money supply, which is the total value of money available in our economy at any point in time.

Think of the economy as a rubber band that expands and contracts. When the band contracts, the Fed seeks a way to apply pressure to stretch it out again. To achieve its goals, the Fed uses tools from the Keynesian school of economics. Keynesian economists argue that aggregate demand is volatile and unstable (especially during a pandemic) and that recessions can be mitigated by monetary policy actions to stabilize the business cycle. If you are

(continued)

thinking that this sounds like "big government" and the opposite of a free market, that's because it is.

During turbulent times, the Federal Reserve has two main levers to pull: lowering the federal funds rate and issuing stimulus into the economy.

1. The Federal Funds Rate

The **federal funds rate,** or **overnight rate,** is the rate at which banks and credit unions lend funds to each other overnight. Why do banks lend money to each other? Because by and large, banks are required to maintain 10% percent of their total balance in reserve at the end of each day. This is done so that if someone wants to withdraw a balance the next morning, the bank has the funds available. The banks lend out and invest the other 90% of their funds in order to make a profit (more on this later).

When a bank is short on its capital reserves at the end of the day, it may ask a neighboring bank to lend it money at the overnight rate. The overnight rate has ranged from a 1981 peak of nearly 20%, in response to double-digit inflation, to lows nearing 0%, first seen after the 2008 financial crisis. After a brief period of increase, topping out at 2.42% in April 2019, the effective rate was again drastically lowered, to 0.05%, in April 2020. (By contrast, the effective rate in April 2024 is 5.33%, compared to 4.83% in April 2023.)

The federal funds rate serves as a basis for the cost of all other credit products, such as mortgages, auto loans, credit cards, business loans, student loans, and more. For example, say your mortgage lender has a business model where he makes a 3% spread on top of the overnight rate. If the overnight rate goes down, you should be able to get a cheaper mortgage.

Lowering the cost of borrowing across all products is the most obvious way of stimulating activity within the economy. When the cost of borrowing goes down, you are more likely to buy a house, start or expand a business, or even use a credit card for a shopping spree you can't afford. In a debt-driven society, low interest rates keep the wheels turning. But when the federal funds rate is already at or near 0% (as it was for much of the decade preceding the pandemic), how do you stimulate the economy further?

2. Quantitative Easing (QE)

During times of uncertainty—such as the dot-com bubble of 2000, the financial crisis of 2008, or the pandemic of 2020—businesses and workers start to panic. They are unsure of what the next three to six months will look like, so their instinct is to hoard as much cash as possible. The economy starts to slow down and head into a recession.

To increase economic activity and alleviate fear, the Fed needs to put more money into the system. If the Fed does not have enough money sitting in its vaults at the time, it may decide to rely on its emergency lending powers, given to it by the Federal Reserve Act, to create new money to put in the markets in "unusual or exigent circumstances." This process, known as **quantitative easing**, is implemented by the Fed buying Treasury and other government bonds directly from large financial institutions, thus raising the prices of those assets, lowering yields, and increasing the money supply. (More information about the specific tactics involved in quantitative easing follows in this chapter.) During 2020, the Federal Reserve's balance sheet, already at an all-time high at the start of the pandemic, expanded dramatically. Critics began to argue that the country had never truly recovered from the financial crisis of 2008 and that the economy was being propped up artificially by continued stimulus and low interest rates rather than real economic activity.

As the economic costs of the oncoming pandemic began to deepen, talk began to turn to the possibility of quantitative easing by the Fed. Quantitative easing initially came to public awareness during the financial crisis of 2008, a tumultuous period marked by failing financial institutions and economic instability. In response to the crisis, largely fueled by a fraudulent mortgage-lending system and the mispricing of bonds and derivatives by banks, the Fed acted as the lender (or, in some cases, the buyer) of last resort, initiating the purchase of $600 billion in mortgage-backed securities. By March 2009, its portfolio had expanded to include $1.75 trillion in bank debt, mortgage-backed securities, and Treasury notes. This initial phase of quantitative easing was followed by further rounds: QE2, in 2010, and QE3, in 2012. These efforts saw the Federal Reserve infusing trillions more dollars into the financial system, an attempt to stimulate an ailing economy that began to show signs of recovery by 2013, leading to the tapering of the program.

However, the saga of quantitative easing did not end there. On October 11, 2019, in anticipation of an economic slowdown and before any reports of a virus outbreak in China, the US government initiated another round of stimulus, injecting approximately $60 billion per month in Treasury bills into the economy. This move was seen as a red flag, suggesting that the nation might be on the brink of another liquidity crisis.

Stages of Quantitative Easing

Asset purchases: The central bank creates bank reserves and uses them to buy financial assets—typically government bonds, and sometimes corporate bonds—from banks.

Injecting liquidity: This process of asset buying increases the liquidity in the banking system, giving banks more cash reserves.

Lowering interest rates: By buying these assets, the central bank pushes up their prices, which in turn lowers their yield, because price and yield are inversely related. Lower yields on long-term securities aim to reduce the cost of borrowing across the economy, including for consumers and businesses.

Encouraging lending: With more reserves, and lower returns on investments in government and corporate bonds, banks are incentivized to increase lending to the private sector, which should spur investment and consumption.

Wealth effect: QE can boost stock prices, which increases wealth for consumers who own stocks directly or indirectly, potentially leading to increased consumer spending.

Currency devaluation: By increasing the money supply, QE can also put downward pressure on the value of the currency, boosting exports by making them cheaper on the international market.

QE is considered unconventional because it involves expanding the central bank's balance sheet to levels not normally considered appropriate. It's typically used when interest rates are already near zero and cannot be lowered further (a situation referred to as the "zero lower bound"). The ultimate goal of QE is to prevent deflation, encourage spending and investment, and jump-start an economy during periods of very low economic activity.

In response to the economic repercussions of the coronavirus pandemic, the Federal Reserve took several significant measures. Not only did it slash overnight interest rates to 0%, but it also unveiled a $700 billion stimulus package, with a provision allowing it to increase this spending to $1.5 trillion if necessary. However, the Fed's actions extended beyond these widely reported steps. It also employed a third, less commonly known tactic involving the overnight reserve requirement for banks. Traditionally, banks are mandated to retain 10% of their total deposits in their vaults at the end of each day. This reserve ratio is set based on statistical estimates of potential daily withdrawal demands. In times of financial strain, this requirement is often raised, to forestall a run on the banks—a scenario where large numbers of customers withdraw their deposits simultaneously due to fears over a bank's solvency. Bank runs have been witnessed recently in countries including Venezuela, Hong Kong, and Lebanon, often marked by long lines at ATMs. During these crises, it becomes patently apparent that the entire banking system is underpinned not by fancy math alone but by an emotion: trust. We trust banks to give us our money back when we want it, and they in turn rely on this trust to loan out all but 10% of our cash. Or at least, that's how it used to work.

In a somewhat understated but significant move announced on the Fed's website, effective from March 26, 2020, the Federal Reserve Board reduced reserve requirement ratios to zero percent, which we will discuss in detail in Chapter 9. This meant that depository institutions were no longer required to hold any cash reserves at all, a remarkable change that went relatively unnoticed by major media outlets but was critically relevant to the average American. With the elimination of reserve requirements, too many people attempting to withdraw their cash swiftly could lead to banks temporarily halting withdrawals or, in extreme cases, facing insolvency.

The Money Printer Goes *Brrrrr*

During the 2008 recession, the American government rolled out a slew of both fiscal and monetary measures and financial aids to keep public discontent from boiling over. We discuss the differences here.

Fiscal vs. Monetary Stimulus

Fiscal stimulus involves using government spending and tax policies to influence economic conditions. During a recession, a government might increase its spending to inject money into the economy directly through initiatives such as infrastructure projects, increasing public-sector employment, or providing subsidies to businesses. Simultaneously, the government might cut taxes to leave more money in the hands of consumers and businesses, encouraging them to spend and invest. Fiscal stimulus is a direct approach that requires legislation, making it subject to political processes and debates. It rests in the realm of politics, and can therefore be conducted primarily to appease voters. "AXE THE TAX" might make for a catchy slogan, but catchy slogans often are not informed by empirical data or economic theory.

Monetary stimulus is the domain of a country's central bank and involves managing the nation's money supply and interest rates. For instance, when a central bank cuts interest rates, borrowing becomes cheaper, encouraging individuals and businesses to take loans and spend money, thereby stimulating economic activity. The aforementioned quantitative easing is another form of monetary stimulus. Monetary policy decisions can be implemented more rapidly since, unlike fiscal stimulus, they do not require legislative approval.

During the COVID-19 pandemic, the US response once again featured significant monetary and fiscal measures to prevent a recession. As the Federal Reserve cut the interest rate to near zero and injected $2.3 trillion into the economy in the spring of 2020, Congress passed the CARES Act, which provided $2 trillion in direct monetary aid, including payments to individual Americans, expanded unemployment benefits, and funds for hospitals, small businesses, and state and local governments, as well as troubled essential industries such as airlines.

However, the execution of these measures faced challenges. Many Americans experienced delays in receiving aid, and the $1,200 payments proved insufficient to meet the needs of most. Meanwhile, large businesses and institutions, including Ruth's Chris Steakhouse, Shake Shack, and Harvard University, controversially received substantial loans through the Paycheck Protection Program (PPP), overshadowing the intended small-business beneficiaries of this aid. Reports of larger banks favoring wealthier clients in the loan process further highlighted the inequities in aid distribution. In response, Congress passed an additional $484 billion in aid, though its effectiveness remained uncertain. The pandemic exposed critical flaws not in the creation of money, but in its distribution, revealing deep, systemic issues.

The day after the Federal Reserve's significant monetary intervention in March 2020, Fed chairman Jerome Powell appeared on *60 Minutes* to elucidate the workings of the Fed to concerned Americans. His interview shed light on the central bank's perspective and actions during this critical period. While we sat glued to our televisions, wondering whether we were all going to be okay, Powell went on to give what would be remembered as one of the most dramatic and yet nonsensical interviews of a government official of all time. Personally, I couldn't help but feel that once again, we were being lied to, and that the "myth of money" was everywhere.

To kick things off, unsurprisingly, Powell predicted a substantial decline in economic activity in the second quarter. This seemed to make sense, as we would all be forced to stay home for an extended period of time. "Let's remember though that this is something that we're doing as a society, really, to protect ourselves from the virus," he observed. But then, Powell contended that the economy had been fundamentally sound before the pandemic. He pointed out that the current challenges weren't due to inherent problems, such as a housing bubble or issues in the financial system. "The economy was fine. The financial system was fine," he stated. Having lived through the 2008 financial crisis and several boom-and-bust cycles that followed, I had a hard time believing that things had been fundamentally sound before the coronavirus came along. But Powell's assertion was in line with what Wall Street and the government, wanted to believe, and wanted citizens to believe too.

Finally, in an admission that was jaw-dropping in its uncharacteristic clarity, Powell revealed that Americans had nothing to fear because, at the end of the day, the Fed had its magic money printer: "*We print it digitally*. So as a central bank, we have the ability to create money digitally. And we do that by buying Treasury Bills or bonds for other government-guaranteed securities. And that actually increases the money supply. We also print actual currency and we distribute that through the Federal Reserve banks," he said. The unspoken had been said; the cat was out of the bag. The money printer was working at full capacity.

Amid this turmoil, April 2020 arrived with an unexpected plot twist. The markets, defying the dire straits of the economy, began a magical recovery. This rally seemed at odds with the nation's crumbling GDP and pervasive economic malaise. Most investors and traders couldn't believe their eyes. A staggering 22 million unemployment filings had been recorded in just over one month, while economists predicted an 8.2% contraction in US GDP. Consumer confidence had plummeted to its lowest level in more than two and a half years. And yet, the S&P 500 rallied with seeming indifference, showcasing inexplicable surges in sectors such as live entertainment and home construction.

Detached from the tangible economy, Wall Street seemed to chart its course in the opposite direction from Main Street, through an alternate reality where traditional markers of prosperity held little weight. Wall Street and Main Street diverged. Unemployment swelled to levels unseen since the Great Depression, enterprises folded in droves, and the specter of financial despair loomed over working-class Americans. Despite this, buoyed by the Federal Reserve's unprecedented monetary policies and substantial fiscal stimuli, the stock market's rise persisted. A chasm emerged, severing the link between the financial sphere and the economic reality most of the country's residents inhabited.

The economy was at a standstill. Even before the virus's onslaught, America had been teetering on the brink of recession. But the CARES

Act had funneled a further $2 trillion into the economy, including a $500 billion lifeline for major corporations that, controversially, fueled share buybacks. It was also becoming increasingly evident that smaller, but still sizable, financial entities had managed to nimbly navigate the queues for PPP emergency loans, securing funds ostensibly meant for small businesses—funds that were now finding their way back into the markets. Some extreme examples included companies such as Uber, which saw its stock price soar by 74% in a 30-day span, despite the fact that most of its users were at home under quarantine.

Amid the economic turmoil, the oil market faced its own moment of reckoning on April 20, 2020, when the benchmark for US crude oil, the West Texas Intermediate (WTI), plummeted into negative pricing, a scenario beyond analysts' wildest predictions. This dip, to a staggering −$37.63 a barrel, was propelled by a precipitous decline in demand amid global lockdowns and a supply glut that left producers scrambling for storage solutions. Traders who had bought the dip were left holding expired contracts and being asked to come up with storage solutions for their oil, something no trader was equipped to do.

The K-Shaped Recovery

By May, the market was in an unstoppable, face-melting rally.

However, for the first time since World War II, the majority of the American workforce found themselves unemployed. Economic projections were dire, suggesting that up to $10 trillion in stimulus might be necessary to repair the damage inflicted by the pandemic. Considering that the US GDP in 2019 stood at $21.43 trillion, the potential stimulus required was nearly half the size of the entire American economy.

In the stock market, technology companies affirmed their dominance. While sectors such as restaurants and leisure travel grappled with near-total shutdowns, other industries such as entertainment, health and fitness, and retail swiftly adapted, pivoting their business models to online platforms such as Instagram, Zoom, and Shopify. The shift in consumer behavior toward online shopping resulted in a profitability surge for companies such as Amazon, with significant increases in consumer engagement and revenue. Meanwhile, tech giants such as Tesla, Twitter, and Alphabet continued their prevailing upward trajectory.

Conversely, the retail sector faced significant struggles. Prominent names such as Neiman Marcus, J. Crew, John Varvatos, and True Religion filed for Chapter 11 bankruptcy protection. The car rental industry, too, was in turmoil. Hertz, a century-old industry leader, found itself in negotiations with creditors, dangling on the brink of bankruptcy. The restaurant industry faced similar challenges: FoodFirst Global Restaurants, the parent company of Bravo Fresh Italian and Brio Italian Mediterranean, declared bankruptcy in April. Similarly, the fitness industry suffered major setbacks, with Gold's Gym filing for Chapter 11 bankruptcy protection, although its gyms worldwide remained operational as it sought restructuring.

The aviation sector also faced unprecedented challenges. Virgin Australia, one of the world's largest airlines and a part of Richard Branson's business empire, moved to seek bankruptcy protection in Australia. This move came despite Branson's offer to use his Caribbean island estate as collateral for funding and after the Australian government declined the airline's request for a loan of USD 903 million (1.4 billion Australian dollars).

As 2021 began, the aftermath of the pandemic's economic shock revealed a starkly divided trajectory, aptly characterized as a "K-shaped recovery." On the one hand, the upper echelon of the economy, including tech giants and well-capitalized corporations, not only weathered the storm but flourished, propelled by the surge in digital services and remote work adaptability. The stock market, buoyed by aggressive fiscal and monetary support, surged as well, reflecting this segment's rapid return to growth.

In sharp contrast, the lower segment of the K depicted a grim reality for industries crippled by the ongoing restrictions—travel, hospitality, and brick-and-mortar retail bore the brunt of lockdowns and changing consumer behavior. And the workers in these sectors, along with those in precarious employment, confronted escalating unemployment and financial precarity. This bifurcation underscored a troubling expansion in economic inequality: while wealth and opportunities grew for some, the pandemic exacerbated struggles for others, laying bare the disparities within the economic landscape of 2021.

During this period, an ever-more-noticeable wealth disparity emerged as numerous companies and affluent individuals significantly increased their wealth through the artificially buoyant stock and crypto-currency markets. In contrast, the middle and working classes largely did not benefit from these gains and were left behind. Simultaneously, the Federal Reserve's monetary policies led to a decrease in the real value of salaries. The rising prices of assets, goods, and services further exacerbated the financial strain on many, particularly those not invested in the booming financial markets. This situation underscored the uneven impact of these stimulus measures across different socioeconomic classes during the crisis.

As both pandemic- and economic-related panics continued to spread across the globe, inflation and unemployment skyrocketed. By the end of 2022, the US national debt had ballooned to a staggering $30 trillion (while GDP was only $25 trillion), a direct consequence of the extensive stimulus packages and relief measures deployed during the pandemic. These packages, which included trillions in direct stimulus payments, unemployment benefits, and business support, were crucial in stabilizing the economy but came at the cost of soaring government debt.

On the personal front, Americans faced growing financial challenges. Credit card debt, which had seen a slight decrease in early 2020, bounced back by 2022, with the average household credit card debt reaching around $6,200. Mortgage debt also surged, hitting an all-time high of over $10 trillion by the end of 2022, as homeowners took advantage of forbearance programs and low interest rates. Additionally, personal loans saw an uptick, with many Americans turning to them as a stopgap to address lost income and unforeseen expenses.

This increase in both national and personal debt levels illustrated the profound impact of the pandemic's economic disruptions and the resultant governmental response. While these measures provided essential relief and helped avert a more severe economic crisis, they also set the stage for long-term challenges associated with managing and eventually reducing this heightened debt. And yet, whatever pain we felt in the West was amplified by many orders of magnitude around the world. Bystanders began to wonder whether there would ever be a path back to normalcy and stability. As financial panic started to set in on families, domestically and abroad, many started wondering whether there was a better way.

Flight to Safety

The turmoil of that spring coincided with a long-awaited Bitcoin "halving" on May 11th, 2020, resetting the cryptocurrency market cycle. During unpredictable economic times, investors often pull their capital out of public and private markets and store it in less volatile assets, such as cash and gold—and, more recently, Bitcoin. Although Bitcoin had fallen more than 30% at the beginning of the pandemic with the rest of the market, as the Fed announced multiple stimulus measures, its price began to slowly recover.

The pandemic of 2020 is officially over, but today's perfect mix of chaos and mishandled monetary policy has continued to give credence to Bitcoin's ultimate test, a hedge against inflation and faulty monetary policies. In a future liquidity crunch, will it go down, like many other assets, or will it hold true to its promise and become an antidote to a shaky financial system? No one knows the answer for sure, and yet each of us will eventually be forced to place our bets.

MONEY MYTH #4: Regular people don't need to understand economic policy.

Many people believe that understanding economic policy is for PhDs and political junkies only, not for everyday people learning how to build wealth for themselves and their loved ones. Such policy is complicated, often opaque, and it's tempting to conclude that ultimately, it doesn't matter to us. We are encouraged to buy a home and to blindly put faith in the stock market in our retirement accounts, instead of asking the hard questions.

The truth is less comfortable but still knowable. Although it seems dictated from an ivory tower, economic policy has a tangible impact on our personal finances, influencing everything from interest rates and inflation to currency valuations and investment returns. A keen understanding of, and respect for, these levers allows us to better navigate economic landscapes and make more informed decisions.

Monetary policy in the US—a central fulcrum of the global economy—operates largely outside public scrutiny; it is not subject to legislative review or public debate. When it comes time to vote, we are given the option of two parties who will both use monetary and fiscal policy as they see fit to serve their own interests, not the interests of the average person trying to buy staples such as food, housing, and transportation. Policy decisions prioritize bailouts for large banks and institutions over safeguarding the purchasing power of a dollar, leading to inflation and eroding the value of our savings. Traditionally, individuals have been limited in their ability to shield themselves financially from government actions on this scale. Remember the old wisdom about storing money in a mattress? Due to the sometimes catastrophic impact of inflation, when you finally need it, that money might be worth a lot less than it was when you put it there. Yet the modern example of that practice—investing in whatever assets the conventional wisdom, as promoted by banks and politicians, claims will serve you best, without considering their motives—is all too common for those not paying attention.

These days, the rise of decentralized finance presents a compelling opportunity to work around the long arm of the state. Decentralized finance (popularly referred to as "DeFi") offers an economic landscape independent of centralized government, which resonates with a growing number of people wary of traditional finance's vulnerability to political imperatives. By learning and understanding how the Federal Reserve and the US Treasury impact the markets, you gain back a measure of control over the value of your assets and can hedge against the risks inherent in the current system (albeit by taking on a different set of risks). As global economic uncertainties rise, understanding alternative investment tools is crucial to preserving your wealth.

5

Once Upon a Time in El Salvador

Necessity is the mother of invention.
—Plato

In the summer of 2020, as the money printer continued to prop up the markets amid the chaos of the global pandemic, I continued writing at my parents' house in Canada. The COVID lockdown, combined with my financial status on the cliff's edge of personal bankruptcy, increasingly led me to ponder the intricacies of success, identity, and the ever-evolving nature of the financial world. It seemed that I was at my own personal crossroads. I had spent a decade immersed in the world of high finance, first as a lawyer, then as a derivatives trader, and finally as a venture capitalist for some of the biggest celebrities in Los Angeles. Yet, despite these impressive accomplishments, I had nothing tangible to show for my efforts. I still didn't have the financial freedom to buy a house or to work on the things I truly found exciting.

The elusive nature of true success led me to question the path I had been on. I had always managed to make enough money to cover my expenses, but never enough to truly build a solid foundation for the future. This conundrum seemed to be a common thread among those who had never dared to venture out on their own in business, no matter how shiny their job titles were. Determined to break free from this pattern and establish a successful career as an independent investor, I recognized the need to develop a strong personal brand, particularly as a woman in the financial sector. Creating a reputation as a thought leader, I reasoned, could open doors to speaking engagements and investment opportunities that might otherwise remain closed, especially now that I didn't have my former bosses lending me their credibility.

My first step toward building this new identity was to accept an unpaid contributorship with *Forbes*, where I would focus on money, markets, and, most importantly, crypto. The second step—crucial in today's digital age—involved sharing my work on every possible social media platform. I set up my Instagram, Twitter, and Substack, and began working to carve a niche for myself in the world of investing. In doing so, I hoped to create a tipping point of my own—one that would propel me toward a future of financial freedom. Much of my writing over the next few years would focus on Bitcoin and other cryptocurrencies.

The Birth of Bitcoin

In the hundreds of years of modern financial history, few moments can rival the quiet, unassuming birth of Bitcoin, the world's first mainstream digital currency.

The destruction of the 2008 financial crisis paved the way for the birth of a new asset—an exclusively digital one. In October 2008, an individual or group using the pseudonym "Satoshi Nakamoto" published the seminal white paper "Bitcoin: A Peer-to-Peer Electronic Cash System" to a mailing list on the cryptography platform Metzdowd, introducing Bitcoin to the world. This nine-page document provided a detailed blueprint for a cash system that was designed to be transparent, decentralized, and secure. The paper was both technical and philosophical, laying out the mechanics of how Bitcoin would work and the rationale behind its creation.

Often likened to digital gold, Bitcoin promised scarcity (with its preset cap of 21 million coins), divisibility, portability, and most crucially, decentralization. It gave people the hope of a financial system free from government control and manipulation, as well as the excesses and vulnerabilities of traditional banks. Amid the widespread and growing distrust of the financial system and banks brought about by the global financial crisis, many sought alternative ways to manage and invest their money.

And so, Bitcoin emerged as a groundbreaking currency for the masses outside of these institutions—a novel fusion of cryptography, economics, and computer science. It stood as a reaction to the shortcomings of the conventional banking system. It aimed to offer a decentralized, secure, and transparent alternative to centralized financial institutions. Satoshi's whitepaper laid the groundwork for a trustless payment network, allowing individuals to transact directly without intermediaries. By offering a decentralized and transparent alternative to the traditional banking system, Bitcoin emerged as a beacon of hope.

The technology behind Bitcoin, blockchain computing, promised a decentralized and transparent ledger system that would be immune to the whims and vulnerabilities of centralized financial institutions. Bitcoin was not just a new currency; it was a radical shift in how money could be understood and used. By design, it was immune to government control or inflation, offering a vision of a financial system where individuals had complete autonomy over their assets.

Key Features of Bitcoin

In its simplest form, Bitcoin can be thought of as digital gold—reminiscent of gold coins in a video game—that exists solely in the virtual realm, and has the following key features:

- **Decentralized and disintermediated:** Unlike centralized systems, which rely on a single entity (such as a bank or government) and multiple intermediaries, Bitcoin operates on a decentralized worldwide network of computers. This eliminates the need for intermediaries and reduces the risks associated with single points of failure or centralized control.
- **Transparency:** Bitcoin's underlying technology, blockchain computing, is a public, transparent, and tamper-proof digital

(continued)

ledger that records all transactions. It ensures the integrity and security of the system by employing cryptographic techniques and a consensus mechanism called proof of work. (It's a bit like keeping a record of what neighbors trade with each other inscribed on clay tablets in the olden days.)

- **Limited supply:** Bitcoin has a finite supply, capped at 21 million coins. This scarcity is designed to counteract inflation and mimic the monetary properties of precious metals such as gold. Part of Bitcoin's deflationary mechanism is known as the "halving" where the algorithmic difficulty to mine a new Bitcoin doubles every four years, further pushing the price upwards.

- **Privacy:** While not entirely anonymous, Bitcoin allows users to transact under pseudonyms (i.e. their account numbers), providing a level of privacy not available in traditional banking systems.

- **Divisibility:** Bitcoin is highly divisible, with its smallest unit, called a satoshi, being one hundred millionths of a Bitcoin (0.00000001 BTC). This makes it suitable for micropayments, such as buying a cup of coffee, in addition to larger transactions.

- **Portability:** Bitcoin can be easily transferred across borders and between individuals without the need for intermediaries, expensive transfer fees, or cumbersome processes, making it highly portable and accessible.

Bitcoin enthusiasts fundamentally advocate for "the disentanglement of money and state;" with Bitcoin, there's no need for paper currency, banks, or even governments. They argue that centralized structures such as governments and banks are prone to human fallibility and corruption.

Bitcoin is the money of tomorrow, today.

On January 3, 2009, the Bitcoin network came to life with the mining of the first block of the Bitcoin blockchain, known as the "genesis block." Referring to a front-page headline in that day's London *Times*, the embedded message in this first block was telling: "The Times 03/Jan/2009 Chancellor on brink of second bailout for banks." It was a clear nod to the financial chaos of the time and a pointed critique of the actions of central banks and governments. The gravity of this computing event would not be apparent for years to come, but as we now know, it would change the landscape of money and finance forever.

Public sentiment during this period was characterized by deep mistrust and skepticism. Many people felt betrayed by their banks, which they believed had engaged in reckless behavior and had faced little to no accountability for the damage they'd caused. Governments, too, were criticized for their perceived role in either enabling the crisis or not doing enough to prevent it. Against this backdrop, Bitcoin emerged as more than just a technological innovation; it was a political and financial statement. It symbolized a desire for change and a vision of a future where individuals, not institutions, held the power.

My own introduction to Bitcoin occurred almost a decade later, in 2017, when a neighbor in Venice Beach handed me a copy of *Bitcoin Magazine* during what was becoming the third cryptocurrency bull cycle. I dove headfirst down a 48-hour rabbit hole, voraciously consuming every piece of information I could find on the topic—an experience I later learned was quite common among newbies. By 2020, as the global economy continued to unravel, the subject of Bitcoin became the cornerstone of my writings. At the time, I had managed to accumulate ten coins, and despite my parents urging me to sell my holdings to pay off my mounting credit card debt, I felt convinced it was my most truly valuable asset and refused to sell. The average cost of my coins was around $5,000, accumulated during 2019 through cutting every paycheck in half and dollar-cost averaging into Bitcoin. Although the price of Bitcoin remained volatile, dollar-cost averaging—buying the same amount of Bitcoin on a regular basis regardless of the asset's price— allowed me to gradually accumulate a substantial holding while lessening the impact of that volatility.

In the midst of the ever-shifting terrain of cryptocurrency and blockchain in the early days of adoption, one figure stands out with a distinct blend of flamboyance and foresight: Brock Pierce. My journey into the heart of digital finance brought his name into my orbit more than once. Starting as a child actor, Pierce charted an unconventional path into the depths of digital entrepreneurship, pursuing ventures in online video and online gaming before finding his way into the world of cryptocurrency. He was a pivotal force behind the stablecoin Tether and the company Block One, leaving an indelible mark on the crypto-currency space. His role with the Bitcoin Foundation, though the foundation collapsed the following year, further cemented his status as a maverick in the crypto space. Pierce took an audacious leap in 2020, one that mirrored the boldness often seen in the crypto world, when he ran for president of the United States. It was a move that brought conversations around digital currency and technology into the political sphere, a domain often hesitant to embrace or even address such rapid change. His campaign, though not mainstream, was symbolic of the growing influence of cryptocurrency in wider societal discussions.

Brock was and is an incredibly controversial figure in the crypto-currency world, where opinions of him oscillate between "visionary" and "con artist." His business dealings and other ventures occasionally have left him embroiled in various allegations including defamation and securities fraud. Nonetheless, I always give credit where it's due—and Brock was the reason I started working in the cryptocurrency industry.

In late 2017 and early 2018, I informally joined Brock's crew of "deal runners." Our job was to vet potential initial coin offerings ("ICO's") coming through the door at one of his companies called DNA, which was akin to an ad hoc investment bank, and choose which ones to share with Brock's friendly network of investors. During this time, the "shop" operated out of a penthouse in Santa Monica overlooking the ocean. "The Penthouse," as we would come to know it, would bring together folks from all walks of life, including a Harvard lawyer, a failed consultant, a fintech entrepreneur, the former head of housing for the Fyre Festival, and many more.

The deals were just as eclectic: a blockchain supporting payments for porn stars, a tokenized airline, cryptocurrency Visa cards, and much more. If you thought the culture of investment banking was edgy, this scene presented something else. As teams would come in to pitch their ideas, the "judges" would roll marijuanna joints to make it through their "strenuous" days. It was as though a scene from *The Wolf of Wall Street* was unfolding in front of me, only without any rules or laws to be broken, as what we were judging at the time were not securities but totally unregulated assets. It was truly the wild, wild west of investing. I left that experience in 2018 completely disillusioned with the validity of future real-world crypto applications, aside from Bitcoin. I felt that most of it was one scam after another and would not bring anything of value to the world. But in my mind, I was convinced that Bitcoin was different.

During that time, someone handed me a collection of talks by Andreas Antonopoulos, compiled into a book titled *The Internet of Money*. Having obtained multiple degrees in computer science from University College London and honed expertise through years as an information-security researcher, Andreas had been making his rounds for years, lecturing to mostly empty university halls, trying to convince students that Bitcoin was the future.

Athens, Greece; November 2013

(Price of Bitcoin ranged this month from $200 to $1,100)

Bitcoin is digital money. It is money just like euros or dollars, only it's not owned by a government. You can send it from any point in the world to any other point in the world instantaneously, securely, and for minimal or no fees at all....

Here's why Bitcoin is important to me.

Approximately 1 billion people currently have access to banking, credit, and international finance capabilities—primarily the upper classes, the Western nations. Six and a half billion people on this planet have no connection to the world of money. They operate in cash-based societies with very little access to international resources. They don't need banks. Two billion of these people are already on the internet. With a simple application download, they can immediately become participants in an international economy, using an international currency that can be transmitted anywhere with no fees and no government controls. They can connect to a world of international finance that is completely peer-to-peer. Bitcoin is the money of the people. At its center are simple mathematical rules that everyone agrees on and no one controls. The possibility of connecting these 6 ½ billion people to the rest of the world is truly revolutiuonary....

Bitcoin is the internet of money. Currency is only the first application. If you grasp that, you can look beyond the price, you can look beyond the volatility, you can look beyond the fad. At its core, Bitcoin is a revolutionary technology that will change the world forever.

For me, I decided, that Bitcoin was the true north, the ultimate truth of money. Before I was 10 years old, I lived through the kind of financial collapse that most people only learn about in textbooks; before

I was 25, I lived through the near-collapse of 2008 that would similarly go down in the annals of history. I saw firsthand during my childhood in Eastern Europe how a faulty financial system can hurt an unprepared population, and I knew in my bones that the Western system wasn't perfect and could likewise succumb. I knew that we needed an alternative, and by the pandemic of 2020, I was certain that Bitcoin was the best shot we had.

Little did I know that my passion for the digital asset class would soon lead me to a small village in El Salvador, where an extraordinary tale of innovation, resilience, and the transformative power of Bitcoin was quietly unfolding.

A Love Story: Bitcoin's First Circular Economy

While working on my *Forbes* column, I became obsessed with the potential economic impact of Bitcoin on the developing world—in Africa, South America, and beyond. My interviews started to pick up steam as I was able to get one-on-ones with CZ, CEO of Binance; Charles Hoskinson, founder of Cardano; and none other than Sam Bankman-Fried, the later defamed and jailed founder of FTX. (Sam would become a close acquaintance who would later co-invest in a handful of my deals throughout the bull cycle. We'll touch more on this in Chapter 9.) My new column quickly gained traction, and it wasn't long before my phone began to ring incessantly with tips and information about happenings in the world of cryptocurrencies.

One day, I answered my phone and was greeted by a familiar voice. Lexie Cross was an old acquaintance I had met through mutual friends while spending a week on the coast of Nicaragua, in a small hipster motel called Maderas Village. Lexie embodied the quintessential cool girl: blonde, blue-eyed, and bronzed from her numerous sun-drenched escapades. A successful Instagram fashion entrepreneur, she mingled with New York City's fashion influencers and models. As a finance dork, I had never imagined hearing from her again after the trip. Yet, there she was, calling me from a village in El Salvador, some three years later.

Lexie had been drawn to the surfing culture of El Zonte, a beach destination popular among American tourists and known for its long, smooth waves. It was during her Christmas break there in 2019 that she met Roman "Chimbrera" Centeno, a local surfer with shaggy hair, and their shared love for surfing quickly developed into something more. When Lexie returned to El Zonte to visit Roman in March 2020, she faced a sudden decision: leave the country before the borders closed due to COVID-19, or move in with her new partner. Opting to stay in El Salvador, Lexie unwittingly found herself at the center of an economic experiment that would eventually capture the attention of the world.

El Zonte was a far cry from the bustling New York life that Lexie was accustomed to. The close-knit coastal town, with a year-round population of 3,000, offered a sanctuary for nomads and a glimpse into the struggles of a tourism-reliant economy. Most of the economy ran on crumpled American dollars that were stuffed into ripped jean shorts and exchanged at hostels and bars; local businesses tended not to meet the requirements that would enable them to accept credit cards. Banks and ATMs were nowhere to be found.

As a response to the COVID-19 pandemic, El Salvador implemented a militarized lockdown, with armed soldiers blocking highways and airports. El Zonte was particularly affected by these measures, as the lockdowns cut off the only roads leading in and out of the area. This had two major consequences: Firstly, the flow of American tourists and their much-needed spending came to an abrupt halt. Secondly, many families who relied on remittances from abroad for their survival were cut off from their usual access points; collecting these monies typically required an hour-long bus ride to the nearest Western Union. As a result, the pandemic's financial repercussions rippled jarringly throughout El Zonte, not too dissimilar from the challenges faced by countless other emerging-market communities.

The events that unfolded next in El Zonte were nothing short of extraordinary, a combination of luck, human ingenuity, and technology. Despite facing significant challenges, the inhabitants of El Zonte rose to the occasion and did something remarkable—to survive, they adopted Bitcoin as their primary currency. And so, Lexie, the quintessential cool girl from New York, bore witness to an incredible socioeconomic experiment, the world's first circular Bitcoin economy.

Following my introductory conversation with Lexie, she set me up with a phone interview with the founders of El Zonte's Bitcoin initiative, fittingly named "Bitcoin Beach." Three men participated in the call: Michael Peterson, an American in his 40s; Lexie's boyfriend, Roman;

and Jorge Valenzuela, a spirited local with the community's trust. The result was the first media account of El Salvador's incredible journey toward the daily use of Bitcoin, which went viral around the world. The article—aptly titled "This El Salvador Village Adopts Bitcoin As Money," and published in *Forbes* on July 14, 2020—would also put me on the map, as it would be cited by media outlets and academic papers worldwide.

The story that emerged from my interviews was this: Sometime in early 2019, an anonymous donor with a longstanding fondness for El Zonte had discovered a forgotten thumb drive loaded with Bitcoin. He had made the purchase when it was priced at around 5 to 10 cents a coin and had put it aside for several years. Upon realizing what his holdings were now worth, the donor spent several days attempting to unlock his wallet before finally succeeding. A believer in using blockchain technology to boost inclusion for the unbanked, he decided to seize this stroke of luck and allocate a multi-year, six-figure donation to El Zonte.

To his dismay, all of the regional philanthropic organizations the donor met with wanted to convert the donated Bitcoin into fiat currency. ("Fiat currency" is the term for government-issued money that is backed not by a physical asset, such as gold, but by the good-faith promise of the government that issues it. Most of the world's currency, including the US dollar, is fiat currency.) Instead, the donor opted to partner with Michael Peterson, a San Diego native who was already spending as many as nine months out of each year volunteering in El Zonte. Michael was given the opportunity to administer the Bitcoin on one condition: he would not cash it out. Beneficiaries would have to learn how to use Bitcoin itself, creating a Bitcoin economy. This initiative came to be known as Bitcoin Beach.

The proposal that Peterson developed established the beginnings of a circular Bitcoin economy that factored in remittances, tourism, public service, and small business. To bring Bitcoin into the local economy, initially, young people in the community were invited to work on public service projects that included trash removal, road repair, and fixing the local water system damaged by a recent storm, in exchange for payment in Bitcoin. Since the local school ended in ninth grade, the Bitcoin Beach program also provided educational grants in Bitcoin to students who decided to continue their education to high school and university, as well as funding to cover transportation and even snacks for their long commutes. The initiative also planned to make long-term investments in local infrastructure, and to do so it designed a system for paying suppliers, contractors, and builders in Bitcoin. Finally, parallel to El Zonte, Bitcoin was also injected into Punta Mango, another beach town three hours away. The idea was for Bitcoin adoption to grow in different communities and fill in the gaps between them over time.

The onset of the pandemic, which brought the financially devastating combination of unemployment and lack of access to overseas remittances to El Zonte, in some ways only served to accelerate the adoption of the Bitcoin Beach plan. To alleviate suffering, the initiative began making direct Bitcoin transfers every three weeks to about 600 needy families, covering about 50% of their basic household needs. Stores and businesses began to also accept Bitcoin, as they became desperate for income during the pandemic, finding themselves likewise cut off from access to any influx of dollars. By July 2020, when I wrote my story, Bitcoin was already accepted at several grocery stores, three restaurants, a barber shop, a nail salon, and two hardware stores. The local water utility was also accepting payment in Bitcoin, and the electric utility was working on doing the same. El Zonte had even gotten its first Bitcoin ATM, powered by Athena Bitcoin, despite still not having a regular cash ATM.

In addition to providing an injection of cash—any form of cash—to an economy that had been severed from its connections to the outside world, Bitcoin Beach had the potential to shake the foundations of one of the main pillars of the local economy: remittances. As of 2020, foreign remittances, sent primarily from the United States, were worth about $5 billion annually to El Salvador's economy, and the families of El Zonte were no exception in their reliance on these payments. During the pandemic, Western Union, the main source of these remittances, became impossible to get to, previously necessitating two-hour-long bus rides and returning with dangerously large amounts of paper money on hand. These transfers cost them 5% to 10% of the remittance in fees paid to the company for handling the transfer. To allow for a new channel for remittances, Bitcoin Beach began testing out a new product, the Strike app, which connected to the recipient's Bitcoin wallet and the sender's bank account, making transactions from the US to El Salvador fast and cost-effective. Families that embraced Bitcoin were able to keep more of their money and to receive it quickly and safely.

The creation of Bitcoin Beach was undoubtedly not without obstacles. In the early days of the project, Bitcoin itself was still working out some challenges, and many who doubted its long-term viability would point to high transaction fees and slow processing speeds on the network as critical failings for anything that aspired to be a daily-use currency. No one would buy a dozen eggs with a form of payment that might cost them two to seven dollars in additional fees to use, and no one would accept a form of payment for those eggs that might take hours to confirm a transaction. To solve this problem, Bitcoin Beach began using the Lightning Network, a second-layer payment protocol that operates on top of the Bitcoin network and enables instantaneous and affordable transactions. The group chose the Australia-based Wallet of Satoshi, a wallet that works for both on-chain and off-chain transactions, as its Bitcoin wallet for participants.

The Lightning Network: A Pivotal Innovation

The Lightning Network is a second-layer payment protocol for Bitcoin that enables instant, low-cost transactions. It does so by effectively grouping transaction activities between two parties, resulting in a single transaction bill for numerous transactions. For instance, a two-dollar transaction fee for a bill entered onto the blockchain could be divided among a hundred or more grouped transactions between the same customer and merchant.

Here's a straightforward explanation of how the Lightning Network operates:

1. **Payment channels:** The Lightning Network establishes off-chain, bidirectional **payment channels** between two parties. To open a channel, both parties create a multi-signature wallet, which necessitates signatures from both parties to validate transactions. The wallet's initial balance is determined by each party's Bitcoin contribution to the wallet.

2. **Transactions within the channel:** Once the channel is open, the two parties can transact as much as they want without recording every transaction on the Bitcoin blockchain. Instead, they exchange signed transaction updates that represent the channel's

current balance. Since both parties hold a copy, these updates can be kept off-chain.

3. **Closing the channel:** When the parties finish transacting, they can close the channel by submitting the latest balance sheet to the Bitcoin blockchain. This process entails creating a final transaction, agreed upon by both parties, which reflects the net result of all transactions that have occurred within the channel. The transaction is then broadcast to the Bitcoin network, and the blockchain is updated with the final channel balance. Only one transaction fee is charged for this update.

4. **Routing payments through multiple channels:** The Lightning Network permits users to send payments even without a direct channel to the recipient. Payments can be routed through multiple channels, finding the shortest and most cost-effective path to the destination. Each intermediate node in the path forwards the payment to the next node, maintaining the network's decentralized nature.

By conducting the majority of transactions off the main blockchain, the Lightning Network significantly improves the speed, scalability, and affordability of Bitcoin transactions. This has proved particularly beneficial for handling microtransactions and high-frequency transactions, which might otherwise burden the Bitcoin network. In doing so, it made Bitcoin viable for daily use in emerging markets and price-sensitive communities.

The other major challenge of implementing a Bitcoin economy in El Zonte was, of course, education. When the project began, many adults in the community expressed little or no interest in learning about Bitcoin, finding the details to be too technical. Young people, at least, were more receptive and quickly mastered the details. But the pandemic also proved to be a remarkable accelerant. Seeing that the younger generation was successfully and effortlessly making transactions in Bitcoin and that they were rapidly running out of other choices, heads of households and business owners became more open to Bitcoin's possibilities. To maintain social distancing, Bitcoin Beach initially set up a Facebook group where it would post instructional videos on the uses, advantages, and disadvantages of Bitcoin. As the world gained a greater understanding of how to stay safe from coronavirus, it became possible to set up outdoor education stations and, eventually, to conduct on-site trainings for business owners.

The unusual circumstances of a global pandemic made Bitcoin Beach a lifesaver for El Zonte. But even without the influence of the pandemic, by the time of my reporting—only a year into the project—it was already clear the initiative was having meaningful long-term impacts on the community. Jorge Valenzuela described it to me this way: "It's great to see youth excited and dreaming about their futures in El Salvador and seeing a path forward here, instead of thinking they need to go to the US. They are able to work, help support their families, and go to university.... Bitcoin has helped me understand what money really is and has given the resources to impact the lives around me." Roman agreed, in no uncertain terms: "Our kids start dreaming again. They have time to be kids, to swim and to play. Bitcoin gives them freedom."

I would have an opportunity to sit down with Lexie and Roman in person in the summer of 2023, when they came to visit me in my home in Malibu, California. As we sat beachside at the local Soho House, Lexie was struggling to get comfortable, as she was six months pregnant. Her and Roman's love story had continued to flourish, as did their home of El Zonte. When I wrote my article on El Zonte, the price of a Bitcoin was around $9,250; as we sat together and talked three years later, it hovered in the range of $30,000. Countless businesses and real estate developments had come to their little beach town, and they were excited to continue to build their future there. I asked whether Bitcoin was still the economic focal point, after COVID had subsided. They told me how commonplace it had become: how normal it was to walk into a coffee shop and scan your Bitcoin wallet, and how a new generation of Salvadorans were excited for their future.

The First Country to Make Bitcoin Legal Tender

El Salvador's Bitcoin journey didn't end in El Zonte. My article in *Forbes* was just the starting point of an incredible story that soon captured the world's attention. As news spread, media outlets flocked to cover the Bitcoin Beach phenomenon, and eventually, the project caught the attention of El Salvador's president, Nayib Bukele. Bukele, a popular but divisive figure, was a bit of an outsider himself; born to Palestinian immigrant parents, he had followed in his father's footsteps, managing businesses before venturing into politics. He started as mayor of a small town in El Salvador and eventually won the presidency in 2019 with promises to combat corruption, decrease gang violence, and boost the economy. But it was his casual demeanor and colorful social media presence that made him a favorite among many, especially the younger generations.

In June 2021, embracing his outsider spirit and riding the hype of the cryptocurrency bull cycle, President Bukele made history by declaring that El Salvador would adopt Bitcoin as legal tender, becoming the first country to do so. Bukele quickly became a social media celebrity, joining the ranks of prominent "Bitcoin bulls" like Michael Saylor, CEO of Microstrategy, and Mike Novogratz, CEO of Galaxy Digital. Bukele insisted that his Bitcoin policy aimed to foster financial inclusion, attract foreign investment, and facilitate remittances, which account for 22% of El Salvador's GDP. Despite global skepticism, El Salvador went ahead with its plan, and Bitcoin became legal tender on September 7, 2021, alongside the US dollar. The government even set up Bitcoin ATMs and offered $30 worth of Bitcoin to every citizen who downloaded a government-issued digital wallet called Chivo, often citing the Bitcoin Beach initiative as its blueprint.

The move was met with both praise and skepticism. Bitcoin supporters saw an opportunity to break free from traditional banking systems and attract innovative entrepreneurs to El Salvador. Skeptics raised concerns about the cryptocurrency's volatility and its potential for illicit activities and money laundering. Before the adoption of Bitcoin, the US dollar was the sole legal tender in El Salvador, having replaced the Salvadoran colón in 2001 in an attempt to put an end to a cycle of economic crises due to currency devaluations and hyperinflation. While the adoption of the dollar stabilized the economy to some extent, it also made the country more susceptible to US monetary policies. The move to Bitcoin represented an opportunity for El Salvador to achieve some form of monetary autonomy.

Despite continued global criticism, Bukele expanded his Bitcoin policy. In November 2021, El Salvador revealed plans for a Bitcoin mining facility powered by one of the nation's volcanoes, using geothermal energy to mine Bitcoin while minimizing the environmental impact of the process. The announcement went viral on social media, and the president was applauded for creating jobs. Further, to diversify its foreign currency reserves and reduce dependence on the US dollar, the treasury of El Salvador launched an active program to purchase Bitcoin. It's estimated that the Treasury holds over 5,690 BTC, valued at approximately $400 million in March 2024. Bukele has committed to buying one Bitcoin daily since November 2022. Many of these purchases were made at a substantial discount to the current Bitcoin price, which as of April 2024 is now over $68,000.

As Bukele expanded his Bitcoin dreams, the IMF and the World Bank expressed concerns that El Salvador could default on loans. Yet as of January 2023, El Salvador had successfully repaid one of two outstanding $800 million foreign bonds. Although the government still owes $367 million plus interest on an additional bond set to mature in January 2025, the successful repayment of the 2023 bond was a positive sign for the country's financial stability. Furthermore, earlier in 2023, El Salvador's congress approved a digital securities law, allowing the country to raise funds through the issuance of the world's first sovereign blockchain bond. The law permits the use of blockchain technology in the issuance, trading, and clearing of securities, increasing efficiency and transparency in the process. This move was perhaps another attempt to ride the digital securities trend and attract investment from tech-savvy investors. On April 1, 2023, Bukele officially signed and sent a bill to Congress—effectively removing all income, property, and capital gains taxes on technology innovations, including software programming, coding, app creation, AI development, and the manufacturing of computing and communications hardware.

El Salvador's bet on Bitcoin appears to be paying off so far economically. Granted, there are problems: back in Bitcoin Beach, locals are complaining about the price of property skyrocketing as foreigners continue to flock there, and there have been problems reported with Chivo, the government-designed digital wallet, causing some investors to balk and stalling adoption rates. As with any volatile asset, critiques of Bitcoin's holders will rise and fall with its price. Still, Bukele took a bold leap forward as the first sovereign leader of a nation to adopt Bitcoin as legal tender. (The Central African Republic followed suit in April 2022, though the country abandoned its plans a year later due to a number of factors, surely not the least of which was the fact that only about 10% of its population has access to the Internet.) The future success or failure of El Salvador's experiment will undoubtedly influence the way other countries approach cryptocurrency and its potential role in their economies, materially shifting the trajectory of global economic development.

As we've seen, the story of Bitcoin in El Salvador is more than just a tale of a single beach town. It is a narrative of resilience, innovation, and the power of embracing new ideas. From the grassroots movement in El Zonte to the highest levels of government, El Salvador's journey with Bitcoin has already left a lasting mark on the world of finance. Whether the experiment succeeds or fails in the long run, it has undoubtedly sparked conversations and shifted perceptions, paving the way for broader adoption of digital currencies and innovative economic models in the future.

The following is a Reddit post from @sleepapneainvestor that encapsulates Bitcoin perfectly:

I think I finally understand bitcoin.

It's a silent project that operates in the background. There's no face to it. The founders created it and walked away. It's like an elegant clock set into motion that continues to tick. There's no promise of some complex protocol to come 3, 5, or 10 years down the road. It does what it's supposed to now without self promotion from the founders. Since it doesn't need promotion to thrive, it doesn't fall victim to the vices of marketing from greedy, charismatic leaders, with overly complex projects. Sure, there's Saylor and Novogratz that sometimes fall into that role. But bitcoin doesn't need them to survive and won't need them when they die. The project works now. It does what it's supposed to and it'll continue to do what it's supposed to. It's the money of the future of our science fiction novels.

There's no Krypto Kris marketing shitty debit cards. There's no charismatic Do Kwon doing a Forbes, Steve Jobs photo shoot with a black t-shirt and a white background. There's no J Powell magically expanding the money supply with a … wand, creating a 9 trillion USD balance sheet out of thin air.

BTC takes out the corruption of humans, because the humans that created it stepped away. Sure, people will build corrupt systems around it, but BTC itself is a simple, pure, and elegant vehicle silently ticking away in the background until the ticking becomes so loud that no one can ignore it.

As Jorge Valenzuela astutely observed in El Zonte, the journey of discovering Bitcoin frequently prompts a reassessment of our perception of money's role in our lives. By acquainting ourselves with its distinctive attributes and constraints, we begin to discern how Bitcoin diverges from conventional banking and fiat currency systems. This newfound insight paves the way for embracing an alternative monetary framework.

The story of Bitcoin is as much about human ingenuity and the desire for freedom as it is about technology. It is a testament to the power of a dedicated community rallying around a shared vision, despite the skepticism and dismissal of the established financial order.

From the early days of mining in basements and garages to the dizzying heights of the 2017, 2021, and 2024 bull markets, the journey of Bitcoin has been nothing short of extraordinary. It is a story of innovation, resilience, and the relentless pursuit of a more equitable financial system. It is a story that, like the intricate strands of code that underpin this digital marvel, continues to unravel and evolve, challenging our preconceptions and reshaping the world in ways we are only just beginning to comprehend.

MONEY MYTH #5: Bitcoin is a scam.

You've heard it from the news, you've heard it from your boss, you've heard it from your grandma: Bitcoin is a scam. It's a popular talking point, one that's often being repeated by a person who either doesn't understand how Bitcoin works or is overinvested in the status quo. While Bitcoin, like any other asset, has its risks, labeling it a scam overlooks the fundamental principles underlying its creation and adoption. One of Bitcoin's core strengths lies in its decentralized nature. Unlike traditional currencies controlled by central banks, Bitcoin operates on a peer-to-peer network, eliminating the possibility of manipulation through arbitrary money printing or interest-rate adjustments. This very characteristic resonates with those who are wary of—or excluded from—the traditional financial system. Additionally, Bitcoin's finite supply, capped at 21 million coins, imbues it with a scarcity similar to that of precious metals, potentially leading to long-term value appreciation.

Critics often point to Bitcoin's volatility as evidence of its fraudulent nature. Volatility, a frequent criticism leveled at Bitcoin, is a double-edged sword. While it's true that Bitcoin's price can be volatile, this volatility is inherent in any emerging asset class, including stocks and commodities. Over time, Bitcoin has exhibited a consistent upward trend in price, outperforming traditional assets such as gold and stocks in terms of returns.

The idea that Bitcoin is a scam disregards its growing acceptance and adoption by reputable institutions and investors worldwide. Major companies, including Tesla and PayPal, now accept Bitcoin as a form of payment, signaling a shift in mainstream recognition and legitimacy. Additionally, renowned investors such as Paul Tudor Jones and institutions such as Goldman Sachs have invested in Bitcoin, further validating its credibility.

Dismissing Bitcoin as a scam oversimplifies a complex and revolutionary technology. While it's essential to exercise caution and conduct thorough research before investing in any asset, labeling Bitcoin as fraudulent ignores its transformative potential and the opportunities it presents.

6

Lebanon on Fire

Money isn't a material reality—it is a mental construct.
—Yuval Noah Harari

As the summer of 2020 unfolded, the echoes of monetary stimulus reverberated far beyond American shores. Various countries attempted to navigate their economic crises by essentially printing their way out of them. One particularly striking example was Lebanon, which by July 2020 was grappling with a staggering monthly inflation rate of 56%. This alarming figure was widely regarded as a point of no return, igniting calls for a radical overhaul of the country's entire monetary system.

The onset of the Lebanese currency crisis struck a personal chord. It presented an opportunity to illustrate an extreme case of the failures in traditional monetary systems. To many, the situation in Lebanon seemed like a distant anomaly, but for me, it resonated on a deeper level. I was transported back to my childhood, recalling vivid memories of my mother explaining the concept of hyperinflation to me at the tender age of seven. We had left my birth country in the aftermath of a bank run, an experience that imprinted in my young mind the frequently ignored fragility and volatility of financial systems.

Before we delve into the chaos that is unleashed when people stop believing in the integrity of money, let's begin with its origin story: the birth of money, and the original myths that surround it.

A House of Paper

First, let's try to answer one simple question: Why is the financial well-being of so many people around the world today at risk? Surely, after thousands of years of using money, human beings should be smart enough to develop a monetary unit of account that they could trust long-term, something they would feel safe passing down to their children. How is it possible, instead, that we live in a time when we can work for our entire lives, only to have our wages and savings eaten away by inflation?

In 2017, Netflix purchased the rights to a little-known Spanish series called *La Casa de Papel*, or *House of Paper*. The show follows an eclectic group of robbers who break into the Royal Mint of Spain and proceed to print themselves 1 billion euros, boasting that they did so "without stealing from anybody." Rereleased on the platform in English and renamed *Money Heist*, the show quickly captivated the hearts of millions—particularly those in the working class, because so many could relate to it. After all, if the government can simply print more money for itself whenever it wishes, why can't the rest of us?

Renowned historian and author Yuval Noah Harari once described money as a myth that we have all collectively chosen to believe in; coins and paper bills, he asserted, have value only in our common imagination. There's nothing physically valuable about their form, color, or shape—they have worth simply because we think they do. To most people, this thought will be a little unsettling. After all, money is how we buy the things we love, pay for our expenses, and, for some of us, even derive our sense of self-worth. Sure, the numbers on our bank statements are just representations of value, but cold, hard, cash—that's real money, right?

Today, we seldom think about how or why money was created. The story of money is a 25,000-year-long journey, one that began with the scribbling of simple IOUs as a method to help communities operate more efficiently: most historians agree that money began as a simple physical representation of who owed what to whom. Money is thought to be older than even writing; most early forms of writing that we know of now appear to be in the form of ledgers that record debts.

A Brief History of Money

Before we had money, societies engaged in bartering, the exchange of goods or services for other goods or services. The challenge of bartering is that it relies heavily upon the "double coincidence of wants"—each party must hold something that the other wants so that they can make a direct exchange without any monetary medium. When the double coincidence of wants is not met, people are forced to engage in multi-step bartering, wherein a chain of exchanges must be made among multiple parties to satisfy everyone involved in the trade. As communities grew in size and complexity, bartering became less viable, and people needed a simpler, more centralized medium of exchange to trade with each other. Thus, money was born. Some early forms of money included seashells, stones, feathers, and beads, as they were easy to carry and count.

Key Features of Money

No matter what form of money a community chooses to use, it needs to serve three functions:

1. **Unit of account:** a way to assign value to goods and services;
2. **Medium of exchange:** something to trade for goods or services;
3. **Store of value:** something to be saved for future purchases (or a rainy day).

At its core, money provides the functionality of a ledger of debts, or deferred payments to another party.

As economists and historians describe it, money developed in four distinct phases: commodity, gold, paper, and fiat.

Commodity Money

Money does not have to hold any intrinsic value, nor be sponsored by a government, so long as the community that uses it agrees that it is the primary unit of account. That said, money is most easily adopted if it has some intrinsic value. In ancient Babylon, the shekel, corresponding to a measure of barley, was used as both a unit of weight and a unit of currency.

Using barley solved the problem of trust: even if I don't need the barley myself, I have confidence that someone else in my village could use it for their next dinner. With incredible foresight, the Babylonians developed the earliest known system of economics, one that included debt, legal contracts, and even a system of private property ownership. Today, the term "shekel" is still used as the official currency of Israel.

Over time, commodities such as precious metals and jewelry-making materials (e.g., shells) began to be chosen as currency because they possessed qualities such as durability, divisibility, and scarcity—but humanity finds its way toward money, or symbolic representations of value for use in trade, in all sorts of situations. In prisons or prisoner-of-war camps, surprising items, such as cigarettes and canned mackerel filets, have been known to take on the role of currency.

Not all commodities meet all of the characteristics of ideal money, however, and where something better is available, commodities that do not satisfy these conditions will tend to fall out of favor as money. Barley and shells are easy to destroy, for example, and so are poor long-term stores of value. Gold bricks, on the other hand, are a great store of value, but not necessarily an easy medium of exchange, because they are difficult to transport or to break down into smaller units.

Six Characteristics of Ideal Money

The Austrian School of Economics describes six characteristics of the ideal version of money. It posits that money should be:

1. **Divisible**—money must be able to exist in small units to enable small purchases;
2. **Portable**—money must be easy to carry with us;
3. **Acceptable**—money must be accepted by most merchants;
4. **Scarce**—we must perceive the amount of money in circulation to be limited;
5. **Durable**—money must be difficult to destroy;
6. **Stable in value**—although it is normal for money to fluctuate in value, ideal money will tend to have a range within which it is acceptable for it to do so.

As trading between tribes became more common, the need for a more standardized form of money emerged to better facilitate economic exchange across wider areas.

Gold as Money

Gold became appealing as a more universal form of money, as it had intrinsic value in jewelry and ornaments and was used globally. Gold is scarce, durable, and inert. Gold is also stable in value. The price of gold in relation to local currency may change over time, but gold's purchasing power stays the same throughout centuries. Three grams of gold, the equivalent of $150 in 2019, could get you a three-course meal and drinks in New York. The same three grams of gold could get you a fancy meal with some wine in a tavern in Florence in the fifteenth century. Gold does have its imperfections, though. Gold is not easily divisible, as it has to be melted to create coins, and is also heavy, so not easily portable. Additionally, unlike the US dollar, these days, gold is not accepted just anywhere.

Paper Money

In an era when money needed to move faster and farther than ever before to accommodate international trade, merchants came up with the idea of depositing gold with their goldsmith and receiving a note in return stating, "I have your gold and I will exchange it for this piece of paper." And so, goldsmiths became the first bankers, issuing the first banknotes.

Thus began the rise of paper money, a distributed ledger of who held how much gold and where. Subsequently, governments started issuing their own banknotes, backed by precious metals, with Britain leading the effort in 1716. As more than 50 countries followed suit, it became apparent that the markets had chosen gold as the ultimate store of value. This decision was dubbed the gold standard: a new monetary system wherein paper money derived its value from gold held in a bank vault somewhere.

Fiat Money

During World War I, European governments needed additional funding for weapons and supplies, so they began printing "unbacked" money, effectively abandoning the gold standard they had used for almost two centuries. This was the first widespread version of fiat money: a currency that relies solely upon the strength of a nation's government. Modern fiat money is simply a system of IOUs; it has no intrinsic value and is rather a way of communicating or representing value.

The last 100 years of innovation in money has been a dance between fiat and gold-backed money, largely because of spending on wars. Wars tend to be expensive and are seldom fought with funds already present in a government treasury. If the actual (usually excessive) cost of war, or some other pricey government initiative, was collected from citizens through taxes, the people would protest. The cost is usually hidden from sight by governments printing new money to support excessive government spending.

In 1910 Europe, the printing of new, unbacked money resulted in the significant devaluation of European currencies, an effect known as inflation. Inflation is a sustained increase in prices and a resulting fall in the purchasing power of money.

WWII: A Financial Systems Overhaul

In 1913, after a series of financial panics, the United States established a central banking system known as the Federal Reserve or "the Fed." Throughout the last 100 years, each time the United States has endured an event leading to an economic downturn (such as the Great Depression, the oil shocks of the 1970s, the savings and loan crisis of the 1980s, September 11, the 2008 financial crisis, and now the pandemic of 2020) the Federal Reserve has stepped in to remediate the economy.

The genesis of the Federal Reserve goes back to 1910, when a group of influential bankers and policymakers met secretly on an island off the coast of Georgia to discuss a proposal for a central banking system. This resulted in a system of regional reserve banks overseen by the Federal Reserve Board, where bankers are included in the government's decision-making through a Federal Advisory Council made up of 12 representatives.

In his book, *The Creature from Jekyll Island*, G. Edward Griffin poses several critiques of the system and its creation, arguing it primarily serves the interests of the financial elite. According to Griffin, bankers created the Federal Reserve and disguised it as a government agency to give it legitimacy and authority while it engaged in practices that harmed the average citizen. Griffin makes the case that the Federal Reserve operates to bolster the wealth of entrenched elites, encourages war, and serves as an instrument of totalitarianism.

Central to Griffin's critique, and a key feature of the Federal Reserve Act of 1913, is the concept of "fractional reserve banking," which we discuss further in Chapter 9. At its inception, the Fed was required to hold the equivalent of 40% of the American money supply in gold. This was a partial gold standard system, intended to allow banks to expand the economy by freeing up capital for lending.

As the Great Depression of the 1930s created economic uncertainty, many Americans preferred to hold gold instead of dollars. On March 6, 1933, Franklin D. Roosevelt issued an executive order banning the "hoarding" of gold, under a penalty of up to 10 years' imprisonment. The main rationale for this severe punishment was that the resulting shortage of gold prevented the Fed from acquiring more of it to meet the 40% requirement needed to increase the money supply. By April 20 of that same year, the US dropped the gold standard altogether, aiming to increase the money supply and pull the country out of a prolonged economic downturn.

Six years later, in 1939, World War II broke out in Europe, while the US was still recovering from the Great Depression and had a record unemployment rate of 25%. For these and other reasons, the US remained officially neutral for as long as possible, until the Japanese attack on Pearl Harbor in December 1941, which acted as a catalyst for further involvement. In March 1941, the US passed the Lend-Lease Act to provide weapons and supplies to allied nations to support their war efforts. The support was positioned as a lease of equipment so that the US could maintain some pretense of neutrality abroad and, at home, bolster the illusion that Americans were not bearing the cost of this fight. The legislation gave the government authority to aid any nation deemed vital to US interests and to accept repayment "in kind or property, or any other direct or indirect benefit which the President deems satisfactory."

Furthermore, the agreement stated that supplies were to be used until returned or destroyed. Repayment, if agreed upon, could be made not in terms of money or returned goods but in the form of "joint action directed towards the creation of a liberalized international economic order in the postwar world," or by the recipient joining various world trade and diplomatic agencies. The repayment terms were purposefully left broad to provide for open-ended renegotiations. As expected, very little equipment was returned, and many nations were left struggling economically after the war, giving the US significant negotiating leverage.

The Triumph of the Dollar

The world was shaken in many ways during the Second World War. Although the United States lost 400,000 soldiers in the conflict, the economic boom generated by wartime manufacturing in the country meant that the United States reached the end of the war stronger than any other major power in the world order. Building on this American-centric momentum, in 1944, 45 allied nations came together in a small village in New Hampshire to seek to restore global financial stability. The event, known as the Bretton Woods Conference, resulted in a series of agreements regarding the new world economic order and international cooperation, with the goal of aiding eventual postwar economic recovery and reconstruction.

Two major institutions were created at Bretton Woods: the International Monetary Fund (IMF) and the World Bank, both based in Washington, DC. The IMF opened its doors in 1945 with 29 member nations with a distinct purpose of providing monetary loans to member countries during financial downturns and promoting economic stability; the early loans were made to Europe. As African countries began to join during the African independence movements of the 50s and 60s, lending expanded to that region as well. Today, the IMF has 189 member nations, and each one is required to contribute to the lending pool through preset quotas.

The World Bank was established as a lending institution to provide temporary loans to low-income countries that were unable to obtain loans commercially. In practice, the World Bank often provided loans in exchange for policy reforms in South America and the Middle East, using its position to spread democracy and free trade and combat communism (which is to say, to further American political hegemony abroad).

Countries that joined the IMF between 1945 and 1971 agreed that their currencies would be tied to the US dollar at a fixed exchange rate. As part of this agreement, the US dollar would, in turn, be backed by gold. To get the gold necessary to hold the dollar's backing, IMF member nations were required to pay 25% of their subscription by physically transferring gold to America, putting the member nations at the mercy of American economic policy.

The Bretton Woods Conference established the US dollar as the most widely used and trusted form of money in the world, making it the de facto "global reserve currency." In fact, it is the dollar's superior status that made the US the "leader of the free world," allowing it to exert influence over economic policies worldwide. The return of the US dollar to the gold standard at the close of World War II marked the greatest unification of global currencies in history and brought with it two decades of economic prosperity.

But the gold standard wouldn't last forever. On August 15, 1971, President Richard Nixon temporarily suspended the gold standard once again in order to print more money to stimulate the economy and fund war efforts, this time in Vietnam. By 1973, all major currencies began to float against each other, and in 1978 the IMF's articles were amended to bar members from fixing their currency exchange rates to gold. Nixon's abolition of the gold standard was a pivotal moment for the financial system, one that created a permanent crack in its foundation and marked the collapse of the Bretton Woods Agreement, as IMF members were now free to choose any form of exchange arrangement they wished.

Three types of currency systems emerged:

1. **Free-floating**—The price of a currency floats relative to others and is determined by global demand. Most currencies today are free-floating.
2. **Pegged**—The price of one currency is fixed to another at a specified rate. For example, the Chinese yuan was pegged to the US dollar from 1994 to 2005.
3. **Currency bloc**—Countries join their currencies together to form a monetary union, such as the Eurozone.

The American government's decision to let go of the gold standard signified a literal return to the "myth of money," leaving our most important measurement of material worth, the dollar, untethered to any asset of enduring value. The value ascribed to each dollar became wholly dependent on the collective faith we place in our government and its economic policies and decisions, marking a seemingly irreversible turn toward fiat currency. Today, the US dollar remains the world's dominant reserve currency, but the logic by which it historically became so no longer holds.

Crisis in Beirut: Hyperinflation Rocks the Boat

As 2020 unfolded, amid the turbulence of the pandemic, many countries discovered that their currencies were now considered too risky for international trade, highlighting the superior status of the US dollar and leading to significant imbalances in the currency markets. As demand for other currencies decreased, their inflation increased. Lebanon was a prime example of this phenomenon, but the waves of inflation reached Europe and emerging markets alike, affecting the middle and working classes the most.

In the summer of 2020, I received a call from my friend Sarah Himadeh, a Lebanese Canadian actress living in LA. Although Sarah had long been living the higher-end life, she was inspired that summer to go back to Lebanon and join the protests of the horrendous economic conditions now plaguing the country, fueled by decades of corruption. Cutting off her hair and swapping her Prada shoes for combat boots, she had become almost unrecognizable, and in the best way possible.

That August, tragedy struck: the port of Beirut, the shining capital of Lebanon known for its food, music, and culture, exploded due to a fire in a warehouse that held a vast store of ammonium nitrate. Sarah's brother was in one of the nearby buildings and was badly injured. The explosion resulted in the deaths of more than 200 people, injured thousands, and left an estimated 300,000 people homeless. In addition to the devastating human toll, the property damage caused by the event was estimated to be upwards of $15 billion USD.

In an article I penned for *Forbes* ("Lebanon's Currency Crisis Paves the Way to a New Future," July 9, 2020), I delved into the Lebanese financial crisis. At the time, the country was experiencing rolling black-outs, food shortages, and a monthly inflation rate of 56%.

Lebanon is a small Middle Eastern country, but it takes pride in its emigrant community; the Lebanese diaspora in nations including Canada, the US, and Britain is estimated to be about three times the size of the Lebanese population back home of approximately 5 million. Notable Lebanese figures include actress Salma Hayek, billionaire Carlos Slim, human rights lawyer Amal Clooney, writer and mathematical statistician Nassim Nicholas Taleb, and former Chairman of Fox Broadcasting Lucie Salhany.

As in many countries with significant diaspora populations, the Lebanese economy benefits enormously from remittances from abroad, to the tune of perhaps as much as 12.5% of GDP. Due to corruption and an unfriendly business environment, Lebanon lacks much in the way of domestic industry and imports a staggering 80% of its products, including most of the country's oil, meat, and grain. Its service-based economy is heavily dependent on tourism, which is largely paid for in US dollars.

In 1997, the Central Bank of Lebanon pegged the Lebanese lira to the US dollar, a move that further encouraged expatriate citizens to send money home, buy property, and even open local bank accounts. Over the subsequent two decades, the stability of the Lebanese economy depended on the lira's peg to the US dollar. However, the dollarization of Lebanon also contributed to its growing wealth divide, making it one of the most unequal economies in the world, with the top 1% of Lebanese earners bringing in 25% of the country's GDP. As tourism revenue began to diminish around 2011, owing to the civil war raging in neighboring Syria, the Lebanese government engaged in a series of moves designed to hide the growing currency crisis from citizens. To incentivize deposits, banks offered interest rates as high as 14%, which in turn created a necessity for more deposits to pay the higher interest rates—essentially resulting in an institutionally sponsored Ponzi scheme.

Finally, in 2019, the government began to require money transfer offices to pay out cash in lira rather than dollars, even those orders that were specifically denominated in dollars. The jig was up, and as citizens began to notice the scam, demand for dollars rose dramatically. A black market for dollars began to form, allowing purchases of dollars at prices notably higher than the official exchange rate. The pressure on the currency peg continued to grow, but worse was still to come. In August 2019, Fitch downgraded Lebanon's credit rating from B− to CCC; a few weeks later, a major Lebanese bank was forced to liquidate itself after being hit by US sanctions for allegedly helping to fund Hezbollah. The Lebanese government quietly began printing more lira.

On October 17, 2019, protests populated by thousands of angry citizens began. The immediate cause was a proposed tax on WhatsApp phone calls. Fundamentally, though, the protests were about decades of corruption and economic mismanagement, as well as Lebanon's political order, a complicated balance of power sharing, and sectarian quotas affecting the allocation of everything from public funds to entry-level jobs. These quotas, meant to form peace among the nation's many religious contingents—including Shia and Sunni Muslims, Druze, and various flavors of Christianity—instead continued to fuel a divisive atmosphere in Lebanon.

As we spoke on the phone the following summer, Sarah, whose family fled Lebanon in the 80s, amid the nation's brutal civil war, recounted to me her experience of the protests: "I was visiting my sick grandmother ... and the protests started the day before I was supposed to head back to LA. I knew that this was a transformative moment for my country and there was no way I was going to leave. There was no way I wasn't going to stand for my country... The Lebanese diaspora doesn't necessarily want to be scattered all over...We want to live in the Lebanon we all long for. In its mountains, and on its shores. In an incorruptible and secular Lebanon. That's where we want to live. And that's what we were fighting for."

Quarantine against the COVID-19 pandemic finally did what months of government intervention could not, sending the protesters back indoors. It also further exacerbated the dire economic conditions in Lebanon, as many Lebanese found themselves unemployed and without money to buy necessities. With a shortage of dollars available with which to import fuel, grain, and meat, most Lebanese began to experience power blackouts up to four days a week, and the specter of famine began to loom over the country. Pressure on the local currency began to rise even higher as citizens rushed to buy dollars on the black market, devaluing the lira by up to 85%. Banks began to limit, and then refuse, withdrawals of dollars, while merchants began to decline card payments for fear that banks would not honor them. Basic items became luxuries; the price of red meat soared from $9 for two pounds to $43 for the same amount. People began to line up in front of bakeries and butcher shops each day, hoping to buy goods before prices rose the following day.

At the time of writing this chapter, in spring 2024, a single US dollar is worth nearly 90,000 Lebanese lira. And all the time, the government was continuing to print more lira.

Hyperinflation: Triggers and Consequences

As I delved deeper into the phenomenon of hyperinflation, exploring Lebanon's ongoing crisis and reflecting on my childhood memories of a similar economic debacle, I wanted to understand how a country's currency gets to such a breaking point. Among numerous instances of hyperinflation in history, a few notable examples stand out: interwar Germany; Argentina, which has been grappling with inflationary pressures since at least the 1980s, and Zimbabwe, where the inflation crisis peaked in the late 2000s.

Germany, Post–World War I

In his book *When Money Dies*, journalist Adam Fergusson paints a haunting picture of post–World War I Germany engulfed in the throes of hyperinflation. The German government, desperate to finance the costs of the war, abandoned the gold standard in 1914 and turned to the printing press to fill the gap. This financial strategy, initially a wartime necessity, didn't cease with the end of the conflict. Instead, Germany continued to rely heavily on the printing of money, not just to sustain regular governmental functions but also to fuel its post-war recovery efforts.

As inflation spiraled out of control in Austria and Germany, the challenge of collecting taxes grew exponentially, especially for those levied in arrears. German businesses, grappling with the economic chaos, found refuge in dealing with foreign currencies. Unions, vigilant on behalf of their workers and aware of the situation, pushed for frequent wage adjustments. Remarkably, until the autumn of 1922, these adjustments managed to keep blue-collar wages somewhat aligned with the skyrocketing prices. However, the economic impact of the Treaty of Versailles was beginning to leave its mark. The treaty imposed heavy reparations on Germany, amounting to billions of dollars, in compensation for the damage caused by the war. To pay off its debt while keeping its own economy afloat, Germany resorted to printing more money, fueling inflation even further.

Ironically, despite the currency's rapidly diminishing purchasing power, the country saw little unemployment. The resultant urgency to convert cash into hard assets created a spending frenzy that kept the wheels of the economy turning, albeit in a weakened state. The frenzy of stock market speculation had become the norm, the only viable strategy for many to not just safeguard their savings but potentially to create a return. Amid this climate, a flurry of new bankers emerged, offering advice on how to escape the rapidly depreciating mark. This speculative wave wasn't limited to the financial elite; it permeated all social strata, sending stock prices soaring to dizzying, almost surreal heights.

The government saw that any attempt to stabilize the German mark would trigger a cascade of financial woes: bankruptcies, layoffs, reduced work hours, unemployment, strikes, hunger, civil unrest, and even the threat of revolution. Knowing employment numbers were fueled only by sell–offs and the paradoxical effects of the early stages of inflation, which was suspected to be short–lived, the German government found itself trapped between the dual threats of rampant unemployment and widespread insolvency.

Opportunistic profiteers exploited this dire situation. Valuable household items such as furniture, pianos, and carpets were snapped up en masse by the so-called "gold-currency people"—the occupying forces and foreigners from countries with stable currencies pegged to gold. As inflation trended ever upward, the price of goods soared so high as to be essentially meaningless: by November 1923, a loaf of bread, which had cost 250 marks in January, had risen to 200 billion marks. It cost more to print a note than the note was worth. The mark had fallen in value so much that it was used as wallpaper and burned in place of firewood.

Argentina, 1980– ?

My introduction to Argentina's inflationary woes came during an interview with Michael Saylor, CEO of MicroStrategy. Saylor, who has transformed his IT firm into a Bitcoin-centric enterprise, has been an intriguing figure in the financial world. As of May 2024, MicroStrategy owns 214,400 Bitcoins, purchased on average at $35,158.00 per Bitcoin for a total cost of $7.538 billion. As of May 2024, MicroStrategy had a market cap of $29.88 billion. Saylor's narratives about running MicroStrategy's subsidiary in Argentina were particularly insightful.

Argentina began to face significant hyperinflation in the late 1980s, rooted in economic mismanagement by the military dictatorship and fueled by fiscal deficits and unrestrained money printing. By 1989, the situation spiked out of control, with monthly inflation rates surpassing 200% and prices doubling in mere weeks. In July of that year, annual inflation peaked at an astounding 5,000%. Confidence in the Argentine peso plummeted, prompting a rush to more stable currencies. The economic turmoil led to widespread food riots and social unrest as people's purchasing power rapidly diminished. In response, Carlos Menem's government introduced the 1991 Convertibility Plan. This strategy pegged the Argentine peso to the US dollar at a 1:1 ratio, curbing inflation and bringing temporary economic stability.

The Convertibility Plan's rigid exchange rate system in Argentina, while initially stabilizing, eventually became a harbinger of new economic woes. The overvalued peso hampered exports, eroding the competitiveness of Argentina's economy. The government's inability to devalue the peso in response to shifting economic conditions culminated in a dire financial crisis by the end of 2001. The aftermath was chaotic: a default on a \$95 billion national debt, a drastic devaluation of the peso, and a renewed wave of inflation.

Amid growing rumors of the peso's detachment from the US dollar, Saylor's company, operating in Argentina, moved its funds to a dollar-denominated account at the local Bank of America. However, the unfolding crisis outpaced him: the peso was unpegged, and new regulations mandated the automatic conversion of USD accounts into the rapidly devaluing Argentine peso, a last-ditch net flung by the government to claw back fleeing capital.

As inflation accelerated, Saylor faced the urgent challenge of safeguarding the company's assets. However, stringent capital control regulations prohibited him from wiring the money out. At one point, Saylor even considered purchasing a yacht as a store of value to physically transport the funds to Miami. By 2018 and 2019, Argentina was gripped by another economic crisis. The peso's value plummeted, and inflation soared above 50%. In this maelstrom of financial instability, Saylor's efforts to salvage the funds ultimately proved futile.

Most recently, under the libertarian leadership of President Javier Milei, Argentina is taking a bold and somewhat drastic step toward economic stabilization with its latest "shock therapy" plan. This aggressive strategy, designed to tackle the nation's most severe economic crisis in recent history, is not without its pains and controversies. Spearheaded by Economic Minister Luis Caputo, the plan is a dramatic attempt to right a ship that's been battered by a fiscal deficit of 5.5% of GDP, soaring inflation projected to once again hit 200%, and a daunting debt exceeding \$100 billion. At the time of writing, Argentina is meeting with El Salvador and is considering adopting the Bitcoin standard.

Zimbabwe, 2008–2023

The inflation crisis in Zimbabwe, which peaked in the late 2000s, is one of the most extreme examples of hyperinflation in modern times. The crisis began after a series of aggressive land reform policies implemented by President Robert Mugabe in the early 2000s. These reforms displaced experienced commercial farmers (often white Zimbabweans whose families had acquired the land amid the brutality of the British colonial system) and disrupted the country's agricultural sector, the backbone of Zimbabwe's economy. The decline in agricultural productivity led to a significant drop in exports and foreign exchange earnings, further straining the economy.

The government began to print money to fund its expenditures, including veterans' pensions and public-sector wages, without the backing of an increase in production or reserves. This led to an excess supply of money, which, according to basic economic principles, devalued the currency and triggered inflation. The unchecked printing of money and the rapid loss of value in the Zimbabwean dollar caused a loss of confidence among the populace and investors, both domestically and internationally.

At the height of the hyperinflation, inflation rates escalated to astronomical levels, with prices doubling nearly every day. The government issued banknotes of increasingly higher denominations, at one point releasing a 100 trillion Zimbabwean dollar note, which quickly became worthless. Transactions became nearly impossible, as the currency lost value more rapidly than it could be exchanged, leading to a breakdown of the formal banking sector. Many businesses and individuals started to use alternative currencies, such as the US dollar or the South African rand, or bartered for goods and services to survive.

In response to the crisis, in 2009 the government of Zimbabwe effectively abandoned its currency and allowed the use of foreign currencies for transactions. A multicurrency system was adopted, and eventually, in 2015, the government officially demonetized the Zimbabwean dollar, confirming the multicurrency system as a formal measure. In spring 2024, Zimbabwe introduced a new currency backed by the nation's gold reserves, the sixth attempt to introduce a new currency in the nation since 2009.

★★

This historical context, alongside the crisis still unfolding in Lebanon, leads to the pressing question: Could the US face a similar level of inflation? Following the pandemic spending, by 2023 in the US, the signs of inflation were already visible across various sectors: food and lumber, real estate, and stock markets all witnessed substantial price increases.

Stephanie Kelton, in her book, *The Deficit Myth*, champions modern monetary theory (MMT), which presupposes that printing money is not always a bad thing. MMT proposes that many social issues—from education to health care—can be addressed by increasing the money supply, and it is justifiable to do so. Kelton's core argument is that the real constraint on money creation isn't an arbitrary ceiling dictating how much money can circulate in the economy. Rather, the constraint is inflation itself. This seems logical, yet it demands clarification: How can we avert soaring inflation when the treasury is printing over $3 trillion during a pandemic? Kelton revisits the Phillips curve, a classic economic principle suggesting an inverse relationship between unemployment and inflation:

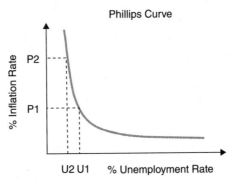

Source: www.economicshelp.org

In a pandemic, with much of the nation's productive capacity under-utilized (consider idle restaurant kitchens or scaled-back car manufacturing), there's insufficient income circulating in the system. Hence, monetary stimulus becomes essential to revitalize production. As stimulus funds circulate, employment rises, intensifying competition for labor, which in turn drives up wages and, subsequently, inflation. Given that US unemployment reached a staggering 14.7 percent in April 2020, the highest rate and the largest over-the-month increase in the history of data recorded by the Bureau of Labor Statistics, Kelton implies there is ample scope for money printing without immediately triggering inflation, so long as we have mechanisms and the political will to reign in inflation when needed.

Inflation must be viewed in conjunction with a country's GDP (gross domestic product). In the most basic terms, inflation is calculated by dividing the money supply by the number of units of production in the economy. For example, if Canada only produces one good, 100 bottles of maple syrup, and its entire monetary supply is $1,000 CAD, it would follow that each bottle of syrup is worth $10. If Canada prints an extra $1000, therefore doubling its money supply to $2,000 without a corresponding increase in production of maple syrup, the price of maple syrup will inflate to $20/bottle. If, however, Canada invested that extra $1000 into increased maple syrup production, the inflation rate would stay the same as the growth of the monetary base would correspond to the growth in production.

Most countries rely on a delicate balance between money supply and production. America, however, is the exception to this rule. The US dollar enjoys a superior status in the international economic order as approximately 80% of global debt is denominated in US dollars, as is the majority of global trade. The residual effects of the Bretton Woods Agreement continue to create a consistent demand for the dollar separate from the value of American production.

MONEY MYTH #6: All fiat currency is trustworthy.

The notion that a successful currency must be backed by a physical commodity such as gold is a myth rooted in historical precedent rather than economic principles. Conversely, the idea that a currency doesn't need to be backed by anything at all is also deeply flawed. The truth lies somewhere in between. A successful currency must be backed by *something*, but that something doesn't necessarily have to be an asset with inherent worth.

The myth that fiat currency (which is backed by the credibility of the government that issues it) is inherently trustworthy stems from a misunderstanding of financial systems. Not all governments have the same level of stability or financial health. The integrity of fiat money often depends on the government's ability to meet its financial obligations. Countries with higher debt levels or unstable political environments may face difficulties backing their financial commitments to foreign parties and their own citizens, potentially leading to default.

Even in stable economies, government-backed money is not immune to inflation risk. If the rate of inflation in an economy exceeds the rate of production, the real value of the currency can diminish over time, leading to a loss in purchasing power. Governments that face severe financial pressures might resort to printing more money, which can lead to inflation or hyperinflation. This devalues the currency, reducing the real value of money held by citizens and investors.

In an era of worldwide inflation, Bitcoin has gained significant traction and acceptance as a medium of exchange and store of value. Instead of being backed by a physical asset, Bitcoin is underpinned by its mathematical foundations and the principles of cryptography and decentralization. At the core of Bitcoin's value proposition is its fixed and limited supply, capped at 21 million coins. This scarcity, combined with the increasing demand for Bitcoin, creates a deflationary economic model that gives the asset inherent value. Unlike fiat currencies—which can be printed at will by central banks, leading to inflation and devaluation—Bitcoin's supply is predetermined and cannot be manipulated. As long as people continue to trust and use Bitcoin, it will maintain its value and utility, showcasing that a successful currency can thrive on the collective belief of its users rather than needing backing from a tangible asset or a government.

7

The Art of a Ponzi Scheme

A Ponzi scheme is a lie wrapped in high returns.

—Unknown

There are moments in life when, unexpectedly, you are put on a path that seems already laid out for you. Things happen to you that you did not eagerly seek out—or if you did, the seeking was buried so deep in your subconscious that when it unfolds, it feels as if a tidal wave has taken you and lifted you against your will. It is only after the thrill of riding the wave sinks in that you realize that maybe, just maybe, you wanted to be here all along.

In 1970, *Boston Globe* editor Bill Cardoso coined the term "gonzo journalism" to describe the fearless writer and journalist Hunter S. Thompson. Gonzo journalism describes the process of the writer becoming a protagonist in his own story, the way Thompson did during his famous exposé on the Hell's Angels. The writer becomes part of the story, portraying events through their own experience, which offers readers no less and no more than their version of the truth. More often than not, gonzo journalism is completely unplanned.

The following is a story I lived in 2020 and 2021, a story I became a part of. Like all stories told after the fact, it is shared from memory. Memories, of course, have a way of embellishing or distorting truths, facts, and events—sometimes for our personal benefit, sometimes for entertainment, and other times simply because we can't remember the details, so our minds fill in the blanks. All of the people in this story are real, but none are mentioned by their real names. Certain details have been changed to protect anonymity. Yet, the spirit of the story remains intact, and it is simply too crazy to make up.

Vegas of the Middle East

I arrived in Dubai in October 2020, amid a second pandemic-related lockdown and the beginning of the new crypto boom cycle. I had boarded a plane after packing my belongings into a storage unit in Venice Beach, leaving Los Angeles amid protests, lootings, and forest fires. I spent that first summer living in my parents' basement, building up my reputation as a writer, until I was invited to speak at a prestigious family office event in Dubai.

At the time, I was still working on my crypto column at *Forbes*. I was also investing and trading in both equities and crypto, trying to make enough of a living to pay my bills using my skills as a former VC and derivatives trader. Having worked at several firms throughout my career (both big and small), I had decided that firm culture—*any* firm culture— was not for me and chose instead to work on my own, focusing on my writing and investments. Just a few months earlier, I had quit my job working on the VC team for the Chainsmokers. It had seemed fancy from the outside but left me utterly unfulfilled, so I was looking for a new path, a new adventure, and, perhaps, a new life.

After 16 long hours, I landed in Dubai, a world away from everything I was used to. As we de-planed, the air was sticky and as thick as the traffic I could see on the roads as we landed. Immediately, I felt myself sweating under my blazer, craving the refreshing feeling of air conditioning.

It was my first time in the Middle East, but the streets were not as full of donkeys and merchant souks as I had naively imagined. Dubai, I would soon learn, has become known as the "Las Vegas of the Middle East," and in many ways, it is more Vegas than Vegas itself. The airport floors looked like white marble. The immigration kiosk, powered by futuristic tech, quickly scanned my face and eyeballs and let me through; no documents or human conversation were required. I was long gone from the chaos of LAX. I had arrived in the future.

I pulled out my iPhone and called an Uber. Within a few short minutes, a black Tesla X whisked me away, gliding past towering skyscrapers as far as the eye could see. They said Dubai was the new Singapore— clean, futuristic, and a tax haven for the ultrarich. And in the United Arab Emirates, a federation of seven unique emirates that gained its independence from British colonization in the 1970s, wealth was ubiquitous. Within a span of barely three decades, Dubai transformed itself into a glittering hub that attracted the world's ultrarich, including, recently, a growing number of cryptocurrency magnates.

Abu Dhabi, often recognized for its oil riches, stands out as the most prominent and established of the emirates. It is the seat of the ruling family, descendants of Sheikh Zayed, the visionary leader who unified the seven emirates and laid the foundations of their interconnectedness with a grand highway. (His legacy is omnipresent; his portrait graced every hotel in the nation.) Abu Dhabi exudes elegance and tradition. Its streets shimmer with cleanliness, and its restaurants possess a dignified air, closing their doors early. Women, though outwardly clad in traditional head garments and even at times burkas, often concealed designer labels underneath. They were chauffeured around in luxury cars such as Bugattis. As the financial and corporate epicenter of the nation, home to banks and business conglomerates, Abu Dhabi tends to regard Dubai (the more flamboyant sibling and the arrival point for most Westerners) with a certain lofty detachment.

Dubai carved out its own unique identity in the UAE under the visionary leadership of Sheik Mohamed Al Maktoum. His ambitious plan was to transform Dubai into an expatriate haven with luxury hotels and upscale dining experiences. To say that Dubai embraced excess would be an understatement: the city became a playground for the wealthy, where men flaunted their Richard Mille and Patek Philippe watches and cruised the streets in brightly colored Lamborghinis.

The lavish lifestyle of Dubai also attracts a certain crowd of women, from those seeking affluent partners to escort them through this opulent world to others more overtly involved in the nightlife scene. Clubs and hotels, I soon found, emanated extravagance and allure, with flashy attire and ostentatious displays of wealth being the norm. During Ramadan, the city's pulsating energy barely dims, a stark contrast to the more conservative practices of its neighbors. Despite its disapproval, Abu Dhabi maintains a begrudging tolerance for Dubai's extravagant persona, recognizing its role as a lucrative commercial hub that is good for business.

Ever since the market crash triggered by the pandemic in March 2020, different parts of the world began veering down a diverging path. We were witnessing the embodiment of the K-shaped economic recovery described by the media. On one hand, there were those who had capitalized on the chaos, amassing fortunes and thriving in the new economic landscape. On the other, there were many, many more who clung to their jobs and the conventional path of hard work and yet found themselves slipping further behind, an ever-growing number of people around the world who relied on unemployment compensation and food assistance to get by.

In this bifurcated world, I was keenly aware of having found myself landing on the prosperous arm of that divide. Checking into my suite at the Westin—something I could afford at the time only thanks to a friend's family employee discount—I stood on my balcony, watching the sun dip below the horizon of the Arabian Gulf, painting the sky with hues of orange and pink.

Then, my phone rang, shattering the tranquil moment and snapping me back to reality.

"Hi, Trav," I answered, jetlag and exhaustion in my tone.

"So? How is it?" Travis's voice was always warm and inviting, almost as if he was up to something.

At the sound of my friend's voice, I felt a pang of loneliness. Since our teenage years, Travis had been a notorious charmer with the ladies—his kindness, warmth, and the allure of a former pro hockey player were always on his side. To me, though, he was more than that—he was like an older brother, someone I had always looked up to. He'd made it big in the crypto world, first by investing early in Ethereum and then by building a string of successful enterprises in the industry.

I found myself confiding in him, "Honestly, I'm lonely. I barely know anyone. And this place just seems so … intense." I attempted to hide my growing despair. The world outside was unraveling, my finances were dwindling, and here I was, thousands of miles away from home. I missed the familiar, easy camaraderie of friends and the comforting presence of family. Amid the grandeur and relentless pace of Dubai, I felt adrift, grappling with a sense of isolation that often shadows those who tread the path less taken.

"Listen, I'm going to text Larry for you. He's one of my investors. I have to warn you, the guy is nuts. But you'll have a good time." His tone seemed mischievous.

"Thanks, Trav." I smiled. I was grateful for what felt like a lifeline.

"I'll see you soon. Oh—and be careful."

Be careful? Careful of what? But I didn't ask. I hung up the phone and got ready for bed.

Beep.

I looked down at my phone as a group text came through.

Tati is 10/10. Take care of her.

Travis had sent a text to me and an unrecognized number. And so my time with Larry Lau began.

I'm Rich, B*tch: Lessons from Larry's Crypto Suite

Some days of our lives blur into the undifferentiated past, but that scorching Tuesday in Dubai is etched permanently in my memory.

On Larry's instruction, I arrived at the Burj Al Arab, Dubai's landmark hotel and one of the tallest buildings in the world, standing majestically on its private island, shielded by security as tight as Fort Knox. My Uber crested the private bridge, approaching the massive structure shaped like a ship's spinnaker, a building that is a testament to a city obsessed with superlatives—"tallest," "biggest," and "most luxurious." At the building's base, a dazzling array of Bentleys, Rolls-Royces, and Ferraris in every conceivable color were lined up, befitting the entrance of the world's only seven-star hotel.

Navigating past the hotel's lobby, with its plush red velvet couches and a fountain that could seemingly flood the Arab Gulf itself, I made my way toward the gold-plated elevators. En route, I overheard a group of young women casually mentioning the $10,000 nightly price tag for their suite. The elevator swiftly whisked me to the 24th floor, opening to a colorfully carpeted hall leading to the opulent 5,000 square foot suite of Larry Lau.

Larry came into my life with a cautionary recommendation from Travis, who'd said to me, succinctly, "Larry is great. He loves his Lambos." That day, we went down to his poolside cabana, surrounded by a group of his closest friends. The gathering was like a scene from a movie, with wild stories, laughter, and bottles of 2008 Louis Roederer "Cristal" champagne flowing freely. As the (mostly) men around me intermittently checked their trading charts on their phones, Larry danced around the pool, repeatedly shouting, "I'm reeeeeeeech!" echoing a scene straight

out of *The Hangover*. The women in the circles were mostly plus-ones or
hired for the night, with few of us there for other career reasons.

Amid this extravagant display, I strove to maintain my composure,
though admittedly I was feeling a tad overwhelmed. The characters
around the pool seemed surreal, each one more colorful and larger-than-
life than the last. This was Dubai in all its excess and extravagance—a city
where reality and the cinematic often merged into one.

I met Louis, a trust-fund kid who continuously claimed to be a
French royal and who, according to whispers, had been financially dis-
owned by his family. He had resorted to running an investment-passport
scheme for wealthy money launderers coming to Dubai. He always
dressed as though he was ready to attend a polo match or a Formula
1 race, and had a new girl on his arm each day. Today he walked into
the cabana steaming from the ears after having placed a short against one
of Larry's trades the night before. Not a good call. His face was red, as
though he was ready to cry.

To Larry's left, lounged Jimmy, a congenial British chap known for
curating elite getaway experiences for the rich and discerning. Whether
it was securing tickets to an exclusive Grand Prix event, arranging a
helicopter ride to Everest's summit (why hike when you can fly?), or
planning a secluded week on a deserted island, Jimmy was the go-
to person. Not far from his side was Mandy, his indispensable junior
partner—a young, blonde, and spirited British woman who essentially
ran his enterprise, often playfully reminding Jimmy of her pivotal role.
Together, they managed all boat purchases and charters for their affluent
clientele, including Larry.

Larry, meanwhile, reveled in the role of the gracious host, regaling
his friends with tales and photos of his latest lavish acquisition—a sleek,
charcoal-colored 124-foot Rodriguez yacht named the *Zion*. It was the
first in a series of four lavish vessels he'd snapped up that month alone,
a splurge funded by his windfall in cryptocurrency. His enthusiasm was
infectious, and as he shared images of the *Zion*, the air around the pool
was charged with a mix of admiration and astonishment. "I'm a car guy,
and I like boats. This was my way of diversifying away from crypto."
Larry proceeded to explain to me the mechanics behind running a boat-
charter business; he noted that he "didn't believe in real estate." (A few
short years later, the Zion would be confiscated by the Emirati authorities on what was described to me as a "technicality.")

Larry Lau (a pseudonym for this narrative) is a name that resonates in the corridors of the cryptocurrency world. His life, seemingly enviable now, has not been without its trials and tribulations. Originating from humble beginnings in Hong Kong, Larry's journey took him to Vancouver, Canada, where he experienced the quintessential immigrant life: His parents, like mine, nudged him toward a secure and conventional career path. Early marriage and fatherhood soon followed, in line with the expectations set by his family. However, at the young age of 28, Larry encountered what seemed like an exceptionally premature midlife crisis. In a bold move, he liquidated all his possessions and set off for Silicon Valley, determined to reinvent himself. This decision marked the beginning of his transformation into the unique and eccentric figure he is known as today.

In 2013, Larry launched his first financial venture. However, the shadow of controversy was never far behind him. His firm later gained notoriety due to a series of early #MeToo allegations against one of his partners, igniting a spate of similar lawsuits across the US. Determined to distance himself from the scandal and seeking a fresh start, Larry moved to Abu Dhabi in 2016, splitting his time between his office there and the party scene in Dubai, a mere 45-minute drive away. There, amid the grandeur and tradition of this Middle Eastern gem, he found something unexpected—love. He would spend the next decade in an on-again-off-again relationship with a woman that drove not only him but his entire entourage crazy.

Larry knew that the Middle East invested a lot of money into attracting talent. "This is a place where you could come and plant your flag for growth. There is extraordinary sovereign wealth here, and limited quality investment opportunities. I wanted to be the guy who brings awareness to the blockchain space. The UAE has become my home," Larry told me later. Just a few weeks before we met, Larry had been granted a Golden Visa, which allows the most highly regarded scientists, doctors, and investors to maintain residency in the UAE for a 10-year period, and is considered one of the highest honors bestowed on visitors by the government.

By many accounts, Larry Lau had the Midas touch. Already, he had participated in some of the most lucrative investments in blockchain, from an early equity investment in Block One (now worth over 300 times its seed valuation) to a million-dollar investment in Blockchain Capital's tokenized fund, which is projected to yield 200 to 300 times its original capital due to its early investment in Kraken and Coinbase, two of the largest cryptocurrency exchanges in operation.

As I spent a few hours back in Larry's 5,000 square foot opulent suite observing Larry and his inner circle, several prominent investors came through arranging for wire transfers to co-invest in Larry's new scheme. Some even brought the occasional briefcase of cash. When you were in Larry's suite, if the room was quiet enough, you could hear the money counter clicking behind the office doors.

Larry's investment plan was deceptively straightforward. He had identified an obscure cryptocurrency, trading at about a penny per unit, with no remarkable technological edge—essentially, a faster but derivative version of Ethereum (the technical details of which I'll delve into later). It was during a leisurely day by the pool at the Burj Al Arab, a couple of years earlier, that Larry's path had crossed with that of a wealthy individual from Russia; for the sake of this story, we'll call him Mo. Living in Abu Dhabi under the auspices of a relative of the crown prince, Mo was rumored to be on the run after being implicated in a theft scandal in his home country.

Together, Larry and Mo orchestrated a strategy to inject hundreds of millions of dollars in capital from Russian and Emirati investors into this dormant cryptocurrency. Their pitch to the market was simple yet compelling: they branded this crypto "the new Ethereum," a tagline designed to create a buzz in the retail markets. As the currency gained traction among unsuspecting investors, Larry and Mo strategically offloaded their own holdings, reaping substantial profits in the process. This operation, unfolding in the opulent backdrop of the UAE, was a classic tale of market manipulation, blending the allure of emerging technology with the age-old lure of quick wealth. But it was not, technically, illegal.

Fraud is big business in the crypto world, though not as big as some pundits claim it is. Chainalysis estimates that around $24.2 billion in cryptocurrency was received by illicit wallet addresses in 2023, which is just 0.34% of the total on-chain transaction volume. While this number is significantly down from 2022, Chainalysis points out that while there has been a substantial decline in scamming and stolen funds, many crypto scammers have now adopted romance-scam tactics instead. In a romance scam, fraudsters target unsuspecting, unassuming, and often lonely individuals with whom they build relationships over time, as opposed to using widespread advertising. This tragic trend understandably leads to underreporting by victims, owing to embarrassment.

A Guide to Some Other (But Not All) Cryptocurrency Scams

As with any new and as-yet-largely-unregulated asset class, crypto-currencies have attracted their fair share of con artists looking to exploit unsavvy investors who hope to get rich quick on the back of a new technology. (For this reason, many serious crypto advocates and investors welcome further regulation, so long as it's intelligent and fair.) Many of the scams below are simply crypto-based takes on classic investment scams, but if you're relatively new to the world of investing, you should get to know them.

- **Rug pulls:** Scams where a cryptocurrency or NFT developer promotes a project to attract investors, only to close up shop and disappear, taking investors' assets with them.

- **Pump-and-dump coins:** These are cryptocurrencies created with the intention of "pumping up" their prices through coordinated buying and marketing schemes. Once the price is elevated, the creators sell their coins, causing the price to crash for the remaining legitimate investors, who are left holding the bag. Larry and Mo's scheme, described above, was a pump-and-dump coin.

- **ICO (initial coin offering) scams:** During an ICO, companies raise funds by selling their own tokens. However, with few reporting laws initially covering these pseudo-securities, there is nothing to protect investors from fraudulent issuances, which often don't bear fruit.

- **Ponzi scheme coins:** The classic, reinvented. The basics of a Ponzi scheme involve the promise of large, fast, returns, and the perpetrators can often deliver—but only in the beginning. That's because a Ponzi scheme relies on a manager taking money from investors and then paying off those investors with money taken from later incoming investors. Capital is simply transferred from investor to investor, without any actual wealth generation.

(continued)

> • **Copycat coins:** Derisively known as "shitcoins" in the crypto
> world, these are coins that are simply copies of existing technol-
> ogies and whose value is derived exclusively from hype. People
> invest in copycat coins due to FOMO—the fear of missing out
> on big, quick returns.

Larry developed a certain fondness for me, seeing an opportunity for
me to play a role in his scheme, (as I would later come to understand it)
by writing about it in *Forbes*. I was naively happy to oblige at the time,
although thankfully the article was never submitted for publication. At
the time, I thought he was one of the most enigmatic people I had ever
met. His invitations to extravagant dinners were frequent; one memorable evening at Nammos, he nonchalantly ordered a 50,000-dollar
T-bone steak for the table. It was f*cking delicious.

One day, Larry invited me to his base in Abu Dhabi. Our journey
from Dubai was an hour-long drive in a convoy of six cars filled with
groups of eager young 20-somethings. These youths, sons of Larry's
business partners and co-investors, were there to learn from him. Some
were novices in the crypto world, while others had already amassed fortunes. Regardless of their experience, they all looked up to Larry with
a mix of awe and reverence, treating him as a sage, a phoenix, risen with
wisdom and success.

Arriving at Larry's penthouse in the Four Seasons, I was greeted
by a spectacle—the living room, adorned with over 40 trading screens,
was a hub of ceaseless activity. Larry, despite his claims that he preferred to trade only his own funds, had earned such a reputation for his
investment acumen that he "occasionally" yielded to a request to manage outside capital. At the time, his various funds were overseeing about
$200 million.

My trip to Abu Dhabi culminated with a dinner with Larry at
Hakkasan, in the Emirates Palace. As we prepared to leave for the restaurant, Larry casually picked up a gold Rimowa briefcase containing
$4 million, a seemingly essential accessory for the evening. When I asked
about the necessity of carrying such an amount to dinner, he quipped,
"You never know who's going to show up." That evening presented an
opportunity for me to delve deeper into the enigma that was Larry Lau,
to peel back the layers of the man behind this extravagant, almost surreal
lifestyle.

The following is an excerpt from an interview I conducted with Larry that evening. Originally, the interview was written up with the intention of submission to my column in *Forbes*. In the end, the interview was never submitted or published, the reasons for which will become apparent later in this chapter.

January 18, 2021

TK: *We see almost a character-like figure on Instagram, with lavish parties and cars. What shaped your relationship with money?*
LL: *You know, growing up in a Chinese family, nothing I did was ever good enough. We had an import business for clocks and, through that, I learned the concept of hard work early on. The main message was always, "You have to provide for your family." But as an entrepreneur, if the market turns against you, things can get hard. So I got a lot of shit during those times from my parents.*

I got married and had kids at twenty-five. I had my midlife crisis by the age of twenty-eight. Money was how you got your worth in my culture. And I had to spend years unlearning those bad habits, like driving a car I couldn't afford. I thought if I could just afford a Lamborghini, I would be the happiest person in the world.

Being excessive is part of my personality. I fall in love to death. If I don't sleep, I don't sleep for days. Trust me, I have a full-time therapist to keep me in check.
TK: *What would you consider your big break?*
LL: *There was a ten-year gap when I was consulting and really struggling. My big break was when I was invited to go to the Summit Series. Some of my partners and first investors came from that event. After that, I truly realized the value of my relationships and how much more I could create... [Larry trails off]*

It feels like a lifetime ago. It's just been so long. I feel like I'm a hundred [years old].
TK: *How did you get in crypto?*
LL: *When I was twenty-eight, I went to San Francisco and sold everything. I had to let go of not only what I owned but who I was as a person. This incredible weight was lifted. I didn't own a car for almost ten years. I was driving my parent's old minivan.*

It took about six years of focus before I discovered Bitcoin. But what I learned from those six years is that people and relationships ... if you took away all my money right now, I would still be way richer because of my relationships. The social capital I have access to is the most valuable thing in the world. That's why I always take care of people first. I have been given this unique opportunity.

[Later, it would be revealed that Larry minted many millionaires in his close circle, even though even a larger subset of investors lost the majority of their funds.]

TK: Any missed opportunities?

LL: I missed the dot-com boom by about five years; I was born early. In my thirties, I missed the social media wave and my chance to go work at those companies. But when Bitcoin came, I was mature enough to understand that honesty and integrity was the most important thing when doing business. I was mature enough to run a hedge fund and run other people's money.

And that's actually been a big reason for my success. I do exactly what I say, often more.

TK: It's interesting to hear your responses. Because you are known as the wealthy crypto guy, but what I'm hearing now is a detachment from material things.

LL: Experiences are everything. We will never be here together this way again.

In terms of time, you cannot take it with you. How do you experience life? You experience it by sharing. I have my kids, I look after them. I have my staff and my friends, I look after them. Even when I spend, when we go on my yacht, my friends get to enjoy. You see the part where I spend. But you don't see the experiences we create together.

TK: That's beautiful. Larry, do you have any regrets?

[*Larry tears up.*]

LL: I wish I could spend more time with my kids. That's the time I will never get back. I'm over here, and they are in Canada. My kids will grow up to resent me. I had to do what's best for me, to do what's best for them. And hopefully one day they will understand that. I couldn't be the soccer dad—and I tried. If I'm not happy, I can't be a good father to them anyway. But it's been really hard.

By the end of the trip, I had become enamored with Larry. I wanted to learn what magical powers he possessed to have minted over a dozen millionaires among his close circle of friends. I wanted to understand why, in every room he walked into, he was treated as a king. I would tag along on several more trips to Abu Dhabi over the next few months and frequent multiple dinners and yacht parties.

Larry Lau would go on to be not just a mentor but also a guiding influence in my journey through the cryptocurrency landscape. My prior experience, during the 2017–2018 crypto cycle, had left me somewhat jaded, having seen the industry riddled with dubious schemes and opportunistic players. Yet, in Larry, I sensed a different vibe, an authenticity that piqued my curiosity and eagerness to learn. Over the ensuing months, our bond strengthened, marked by countless nights spent alongside him in Abu Dhabi, poring over trading screens and absorbing his insights into the nuances of crypto trading.

It was on Larry's bustling trading floor that I encountered a remarkable 24-year-old, affectionately dubbed "Smurf" due to his penchant for sitting cross-legged in a blue hoodie, immersed in all-night trading sessions. Smurf had an uncanny knack for predicting Bitcoin's price fluctuations, identifying tops and bottoms with an accuracy that seemed almost supernatural. Beyond his trading prowess, he was known for his generosity—using his earnings from the bull market to alleviate his family's financial burdens, including paying off his parents' mortgage and clearing their immigration debts. Little did I know then that this young man with a heart of gold would, three years later, become my partner in launching my first hedge fund.

The Genesis of Cryptocurrencies

Before we dive deeper into our narrative, it's essential to understand the nature of cryptocurrencies and their genesis in the broader context of the Internet's evolution.

In its early days, from the late 1980s stretching into the early 2000s, the Internet was a collective endeavor. It was an era defined by open protocols and a sense of communal governance. This period laid the groundwork for a digital environment that was both stable and predictable, fostering an ecosystem where individuals and businesses could confidently grow their online presence. It was a golden age for emerging digital for-profit corporations such as Yahoo, Google, Amazon, Facebook, LinkedIn, and YouTube, which flourished and reshaped the digital landscape. Their rise marked a significant transition, overshadowing centralized platforms such as AOL, which had once been at the forefront of the online world.

However, as we moved into the mid-2000s and beyond, the Internet witnessed a paradigm shift. Control began to consolidate as those for-profit corporations became industry-dominating giants, developing sophisticated software and services that far exceeded the capabilities of the open protocols of the earlier Internet era. The advent of smartphones further accelerated this shift, with a growing preference for proprietary applications over open-web services. This evolution led to a pronounced centralization in the digital realm, with most Internet users increasingly experiencing the web through the filtered lenses of these tech behemoths.

This shift toward centralization, while ushering in unprecedented technological advances and democratizing access to state-of-the-art resources, often at no cost to users, also brought its share of challenges. The concentrated control exerted by these tech behemoths began to overshadow the prospects of start-ups, independent creators, and diverse online communities. The unpredictability of platform policies posed a significant threat to the online presence and revenue generation of small initiatives, stifling innovation and diminishing the early Internet's diversity and dynamism.

This era of centralized control also gave rise to broader societal issues. We found ourselves embroiled in debates over misinformation and state-sponsored propaganda, grappling with concerns about censorship and privacy rights, and confronting the biases embedded within algorithms. Most recently, Elon Musk, who bought Twitter (now X) in 2022 for $44 billion, came under fire for censoring certain voices while failing to censor others for hate speech. Twitter, once the Internet's favorite public message board, now had to be viewed through Musk's lens on what was acceptable speech, as he censored certain types of speech as well as his critics. These challenges are not just passing phenomena; they are indicative of the deeper implications of the Internet's homogenization on our society.

A blockchain, a blueprint for a decentralized network, is a revolutionary technology in cryptography and computing that has transformed how we record and verify information. The basic function of a blockchain is to act as a distributed public ledger, akin to a giant spreadsheet that everyone can access and verify, but no one can tamper with. Information is grouped into "blocks" of data, with each block containing information and a unique cryptographic footprint called a "hash." Every block contains not only its own hash but also the hash of the previous block, creating a chain. If someone tries to improperly alter the data in a block, it changes the hash, rendering all subsequent blocks invalid. Bitcoin was the first major cryptocurrency to leverage the blockchain; Ethereum, which followed, goes beyond currency allowing for the creation of self-executing contracts and decentralized applications.

The Birth of Ethereum

Ethereum emerged as a solution to the growing concern of digital centralization. The brainchild of Vitalik Buterin, a prodigious programmer and cofounder of *Bitcoin Magazine,* Ethereum was originally envisioned as a significant advancement over Bitcoin's somewhat limited scripting language. In 2013, Buterin introduced the world to his idea through a white paper that described a blockchain platform capable of supporting financial transactions as well as a whole universe of decentralized applications.

The allure of Ethereum was twofold: it was a technological marvel, certainly, but it also heralded a philosophical revolution in the digital realm. Ethereum redefined the concepts of online trust, agreements, and collaboration. With the introduction of "smart contracts," Ethereum offered a framework where code became the law. These contracts could autonomously execute and enforce agreements in a way that was transparent, unchangeable, and without the need for traditional trust mechanisms such as intermediaries. This innovation was not just an alternative to conventional contracts; it was a complete reimagining of how agreements could be executed in a digital, trustless environment.

The official debut of Ethereum in 2015 marked more than just the launch of a new blockchain platform. It was the result of rigorous development, testing, and a steadfast commitment to a decentralized ethos. Ethereum was also the first ICO, facilitating the sale of cryptocurrencies to the public—a blueprint followed by thousands of projects over the next few years. In 2023, the combined trading volume of the top 10 cryptocurrency exchanges was around $34 trillion.

Ethereum represented a new chapter in blockchain evolution, offering a blank slate for redefining fields ranging from finance and law to gaming and art. It harnessed the power of community, attracting a dedicated and talented pool of developers who would continue to build and expand its ecosystem. Ethereum's launch was the beginning of a revolutionary movement toward constructing a decentralized digital world.

As the Internet stands at a pivotal point in its evolution, it is on the cusp of a significant transformation, likely to be spurred by the advent of crypto-economic networks. These so-called "Web3" networks blend the decentralized, community-centric spirit of the Internet's early days with the advanced functionalities of modern centralized services. Leveraging blockchain technology for consensus, and cryptocurrencies for incentivization, they promise a new era of collaborative growth and mutual benefit. In this emerging landscape, platforms such as Ethereum stand out for their versatility, catering to a broad spectrum of applications, beyond the more specialized roles of networks such as Bitcoin. (Another example of this phenomenon is the blue-chip project Filecoin, which has successfully tackled the problem of decentralized cloud storage.) These versatile networks transcend their technological foundations, embodying a collective pursuit of shared goals and network valorization.

Other Types of Cryptocurrencies

Since Ethereum's inception in 2015, the cryptocurrency landscape has burgeoned, giving rise to a multitude of networks and coins. Central to understanding this proliferation is the concept of "tokenomics." This term describes the economic frameworks and characteristics that endow a cryptocurrency token with value within its specific ecosystem. Tokenomics encompasses a range of factors, including the principles of supply and demand, the methods of token distribution and allocation, and the governing rules for token utilization.

To grasp the essence of crypto tokens and their value, a relatable analogy is the use of arcade tokens. Imagine stepping into an arcade where, to engage in the games, you first need to exchange real money for specialized arcade tokens. This exchange creates a self-contained economic system within the arcade: the more you participate, using tokens in games, the more tickets you earn, which can be redeemed for various prizes. This microeconomy, with its internal currency, mirrors how tokenomics works.

The concept of airline miles offers another parallel to this ecosystem. Every time I fly with Delta, I accumulate miles, which can be redeemed for future flights or other perks within Delta's network. Interestingly, these miles can also be purchased with cash, allowing for an infusion of external value into this closed-loop economy. This exemplifies how tokenomics functions in broader terms, creating and managing value within a specific network, much like the nuanced economies of cryptocurrencies in their respective digital realms.

Tokenomics 101: Examples of Token Functionalities

From smart contracts to digital storage to in-game currency for video games built on the blockchain, crypto tokens can serve a variety of purposes. Before choosing to invest in any crypto token, it's important to understand how it works and what value it represents to the future of digital technology (because in all too many cases, the answer could be "none"). Here are some of the key functions of crypto tokens.

- **Utility:** Tokens can serve as a means to access certain services or functionalities within a network. For instance, in a cloud-storage blockchain, tokens might be required to purchase storage space.
- **Incentive:** Tokens are used to reward network participants, like miners or validators, who help maintain the network by performing essential tasks such as verifying transactions or creating new blocks.
- **Governance:** In some networks, token holders can vote on decisions that affect the network, with the number of tokens correlating to voting power. This is part of what makes decentralized finance projects attractive, as it can give users a say in the project's direction.
- **Economics:** The supply of a token can be fixed or inflationary, affecting the token's scarcity and, potentially, its value. A fixed supply, like that of Bitcoin, means that there will only ever be a certain number of tokens in existence.
- **Exchange:** Tokens can be traded on cryptocurrency exchanges, which allows them to have a market value and be exchanged for other tokens or government-issued currencies.
- **Security tokens**: These tokens represent an ownership stake in the protocol, acquired by investors who wish to profit off the network's growth.

Three types of crypto innovations have received the most attention over the last three years:

1. **Layer 1 and layer 2 technologies:** Layer 1 and layer 2 technologies in the crypto space refer to different levels of blockchain infrastructure that are designed to solve various problems, such as scalability, speed, and interoperability. Layer 1 refers to the underlying main blockchain architecture. Examples of layer 1 solutions include Bitcoin's blockchain and Ethereum's blockchain. These are the foundations upon which various applications can be built and are often referred to as the "base layer." They have their own sets of rules for governance and consensus mechanisms (including "proof of work" or "proof of stake") and are responsible for the network's security and consensus. Layer 1 blockchains can be scaled and improved upon

directly through changes such as implementing protocol upgrades or "sharding" (dividing the database to spread the load).

Layer 2 technologies, on the other hand, are built on top of these layer 1 blockchains to enhance their scalability and efficiency. They don't require changes to the base layer itself, but offer an additional layer where transactions can be processed more rapidly or with different features. Examples of layer 2 solutions include the Lightning Network for Bitcoin and various rollups for Ethereum. By handling transactions off the main chain (off-chain) and settling only final states on-chain, these layer 2 solutions alleviate the congestion and high fees that can plague layer 1 blockchains during periods of high usage. Layer 2 can be thought of as an auxiliary framework that inherits security from layer 1 but operates at a higher speed and often at a lower cost.

The relationship between layer 1 and layer 2 is symbiotic; layer 1 provides the fundamental security model, while layer 2 delivers scalability and speed. This layered approach allows for a more flexible and efficient system that can adapt to a wider range of use cases and performance demands in the crypto ecosystem.

2. **DeFi:** DeFi, short for "decentralized finance," is a transformative technology within the crypto ecosystem that leverages blockchain and cryptographic protocols to create financial instruments without the need for traditional, centralized intermediaries such as banks, brokers, or exchanges. At its core, DeFi represents a shift from a centrally governed financial system to a transparent and open network of financial services that operates on public blockchains, predominantly Ethereum. By using smart contracts—self-executing contracts with the terms written directly into their code—DeFi platforms enable users to lend, borrow, trade, earn interest, and access a spectrum of financial products directly from their digital wallets, without the need for personal information sharing or third-party oversight.

This ecosystem has given rise to a multitude of applications that mimic traditional financial services, including decentralized exchanges (DEXs), lending protocols, stablecoins, and yield-farming platforms, while also innovating with new forms of economic coordination such as liquidity mining and automated market makers (AMMs). DeFi's permission-less nature means that anyone with an Internet connection can interact with these services, fostering financial inclusion and opening up the system to those who've historically been excluded from it. However, DeFi also comes with its own set of risks and challenges, such as smart-contract vulnerabilities and the absence of regulatory protection, which users must navigate with caution. In the Web3 space, at least $72 billion has been lost to hacks, scams, fraud, and other disasters since January 1, 2021.

3. **NFTs:** The third and most creative Web3 vertical, non-fungible tokens (NFTs), became a revolutionary aspect of blockchain technology, reshaping the concept of digital ownership and authenticity in the crypto world. Unlike cryptocurrencies, such as Bitcoin or Ethereum, which are fungible and can be exchanged on a one-to-one basis, NFTs are unique digital assets that represent ownership of a specific item or piece of content, such as art, music, videos, or collectibles, on the blockchain. Each NFT has a distinct, non-interchangeable identifier that certifies its authenticity and provenance, allowing it to be bought, sold, and traded with the assurance that each asset is one of a kind.

The innovation of NFTs lies in how they leverage the decentralized and tamper-proof nature of blockchain computing to secure digital collectibles in a way that was previously impossible. This has opened up new economic avenues for artists and creators, allowing them to monetize their work without intermediaries, and offering a new level of engagement with their audiences. NFTs have also begun to integrate with DeFi and virtual worlds ("metaverses"), where they can take on utilities beyond being mere collectibles—becoming access passes, in-game items, or digital real estate.

Washed Up in Monaco

Over the following six months, I found myself deeply immersed in Larry's world, oscillating between Dubai and Abu Dhabi. This period was an intensive masterclass in trading and the intricacies of hedge fund operations, knowledge that would become invaluable in the next chapter of my career. Yet, as I spent countless nights on the impromptu trading floor set up in Larry's penthouse at the Four Seasons, troubling details began to surface.

Among the regulars on the trading floor were several young men, mostly in their early to mid-20s, buzzing around Larry, absorbing every bit of wisdom he dispensed. These nights often extended into early-morning drinking sessions, where, after a few too many, conversations would slip into Russian, revealing secrets I was never meant to hear.

It was during these moments that the language of my childhood, long buried and seemingly useless, became an unexpected asset.

I learned that these young traders were sons of Larry's business partners and investors. The youngest was the son of Larry's co-conspirator in the "new Ethereum" scheme, Mo, who was now living under protection in Abu Dhabi. Another, more imposing and hefty, would drop in occasionally to oversee wallets containing immense wealth on behalf of his father, a figure deeply entrenched in Vladimir Putin's Kremlin.

Then, there was a name that kept cropping up, leading me to a late-night dive into Google, unveiling a web of tax evasion charges and control over a significant portion of Russia's oil wealth. The pieces began to fit together, painting a picture that was becoming alarmingly clear. Despite the years since I had left my birthplace, the rules of engagement in that part of the world remained familiar—and they carried inherent dangers.

One encounter, in particular, stood out. The Fixer, a towering Arabic man named Faisal, confronted me after a run-in with Louis, the French kid from Larry's entourage, who had actively pumped a meme-coin scheme and dumped it on all our friends. My outspokenness had ruffled feathers, leading to this unsettling meeting. Faisal's towering presence was intimidating as he sat me down, his voice calm but his message clear. The gentle but firm squeeze of my hand and his piercing gaze left no room for misunderstanding. "We're not going to have any problems, are we?" he asked, his words hanging heavily in the air.

This world I had stepped into was far from the clear-cut realms of finance and technology I was accustomed to. In the weeks that followed, my life became a tumultuous mix of anxiety and panic attacks. The world I had become entangled in, I now understood, was beyond anything I had ever imagined, filled with characters and situations that seemed lifted from a psychological thriller.

Amid this chaos, we were preparing for an important trip to the F1 Grand Prix in Monaco, a prestigious event and a significant occasion for Larry. Only a select group of 12 were invited, and I was among them. Navigating the labyrinth of COVID-19 travel restrictions, we boarded a private jet in Abu Dhabi, which stopped briefly in Cyprus under the guise of refueling in order to get around the restriction on flying directly from the UAE to Europe. Then the journey resumed, landing us in Genoa, Italy. Stepping off the plane, the mountain air hit me with a wave of clarity, reminding me of a world beyond the confines of the desert's opulence. I began to contemplate whether, perhaps, it was time for me to be planning my exit from Dubai, but I feared that I was in too deep to exit quietly.

From there, it was a helicopter ride to our final destination: a yacht moored at the Monte Carlo Grand Prix track. The days in Monaco blurred into a whirlwind of parties and heavy drinking—heavier than usual, even for us—fueled by the crypto markets' tumultuous correction that spring. Larry took things to the extreme, as he always did, ordering bags of cocaine straight to the boat. He also gave each of us thousands of euros in walking-around money—cash I would spend on my first luxury purchase, a classic Gucci purse, to commemorate the moment.

One night, in a hazy attempt to make a trade, my hardware wallet, a Ledger, catastrophically malfunctioned, melting in my hand. It felt like an ominous sign, mirroring the chaos around me. Noticing my distress, Larry led me to a quieter spot on the yacht. "You're not acting like yourself," he observed, concern etched on his face. At that moment, the dam broke: I confessed everything. I told him about my growing awareness of his scheme—the names, the origins of the money. Because I spoke Russian, I had been a fly on the wall and knew everything. His response was blunt: "You sound crazy." He urged me to return to my hotel and rest, and I took his advice.

The next morning, I steeled myself to join the others for breakfast on the yacht. But as I was approaching the dock, I was hit with a shock wave of disbelief: the yacht was sailing away without me, just out of reach. Confused, I tried to contact Larry and the crew, but my messages echoed into silence. The boat slid farther and farther out of the port, without a word to me from anyone on board.

So there I was, stranded in Monaco, left to navigate this foreign city alone. I watched the yacht leave into the distance, and my new life with it. Behind me, I could hear the clanking of fences being taken down; the roads of Monaco were finally returning to normal after four days of the Grand Prix. I sat at a coffee shop watching the sunset in the distance before walking back to my hotel. I could barely breathe. I realized that I had been right about everything. I'd been right about the schemes, right about the players, and right to fear the danger I could be in as a result. Larry's last words to me the night before echoed in my head: "You are my sister, and I will always protect you." I had been exiled, I now understood, because I knew too much. It was his last and final act of kindness.

It would be a full year before Larry responded to my attempts to reach out. When he did, his message was clipped and heavy with words unspoken: "I'm sorry." In those two words lay the end of an era, the closure of a chapter of life that had taken me through the highest highs and the lowest lows, a journey of learning, betrayal, and exposure to the harsh realities of a business operation shrouded in wealth and secrecy. I made a vow to never return.

Cashing In and Cashing Out

No matter who you were, being part of Larry's crew always meant being a big initial investor in his projects. At first, I was happy to be a part of something I thought was going to be huge, and more than happy to be along for the luxurious ride. I put in everything I could and watched as the numbers magically ticked upward.

Six months after being stranded on the dock in Monaco—intimidated, manipulated, gaslit, and abandoned—I decided I'd had enough. As a condition of participation in his investment projects, Larry forbade everyone in the crew from withdrawing their funds. But our relationship, I felt, was a bridge he had burned. Without a word, I pulled out my initial investment. And as soon as I did, it turned out Larry's fund was nothing but a house of cards: when one card was pulled, the entire structure, an elaborate Ponzi scheme capable of ensnaring even the most seasoned crypto investors, fell to ruins. The epic crash came soon after—and I was only one of two investors who cashed out on time.

MONEY MYTH #7: All cryptocurrencies are good investments.

The myth that all cryptocurrencies are good investments is a simplification that overlooks the nuances and extremes of the cryptocurrency market. While it's true that some cryptocurrencies have yielded exceptional returns for early investors, the landscape is diverse and includes thousands of digital currencies—each with different levels of risk, utility, and market acceptance.

Additionally, the regulatory environment surrounding cryptocurrencies remains uncertain and varies significantly by country. Existing in legal limbo affects the viability and stability of many cryptocurrencies, as potential regulatory challenges or changes in policy could adversely affect their value. One major challenge governments are currently grappling with is how to classify cryptocurrencies: are they commodities (like gold), securities (like stocks), or a new asset class altogether?

The pseudonymous nature of cryptocurrencies also makes them attractive to criminals, meaning that many jurisdictions are grappling with how compliance laws such as KYC ("know your client") and AML (anti-money laundering) laws should apply to them. The lack of consumer protection in the crypto space should add to your caution as an investor—if something goes wrong (say, you send Bitcoin to the wrong wallet, or invest in a scam company) there's no number on the back of a card to call, and no one to bail you out of that mess.

As of this writing, taxation likewise remains an uncertain variable surrounding crypto assets—is your crypto subject to capital gains or income taxes? The lack of international consensus on crypto taxation has created confusion and the emergence of potential loopholes. Don't get caught on the wrong side of the law—familiarize yourself with your country's legal regulations and abide by them. Or, if you'd rather not navigate this minefield yourself, remember that paying a good accountant means not having to pay a good lawyer.

It's also important to consider the technology behind each cryptocurrency you're considering investing in. Many cryptocurrencies lack the backing of solid use cases or technological support, making them risky and often speculative investments. Innovative fields such as blockchain computing are continually evolving, and newer, more advanced technologies or protocols could render older ones obsolete. This technological shift can directly affect your investment's longevity and profitability. Even if none of this gives you pause, don't forget the cryptocurrency market is notorious for its price volatility, which can result in significant losses just as quickly as it can yield substantial gains. Beware of the hype and the promise of guaranteed returns. Only invest what you can afford to lose. This is a new field, and not only do the old rules not apply, but we're not even really sure what rules *do* apply. Even celebrities with massive legal and investment teams have gone down on the wrong side of history, endorsing what turned out to be fraudulent financial "opportunities."

While certain cryptocurrencies may indeed present lucrative opportunities, and I'm not here to tell you not to invest in crypto (quite the opposite!), it is a myth to paint all digital currencies with the same broad brush, as "good investments." Prospective investors must conduct thorough research, assess their risk tolerance, and consult financial experts before diving into such a complex and rapidly changing field.

In summary: Do your own research. Approach with caution. Trust your gut, and don't believe anything that sounds too good to be true.

8

Leapfrogging to a Decentralized Africa

Africa is all the power you could never understand. It is all the beauty
you never get used to. It is all the mystery you can never resolve.
—Beryl Markham

The bull markets marched on throughout 2021 and into 2022, unabated
in both the traditional financial sphere and the developing world of
cryptocurrencies, or by any sense of logic or reason. By November 10,
2021, Bitcoin had scaled to unprecedented heights, peaking at a then
all-time high of $68,789. This surge in price wasn't an isolated phenom-
enon. It was part of a larger movement of adoption, powered by both
institutional interest and retail acceptance of digital currencies. The bull
market wave spread across continents, cascading from Dubai down to
the vibrant lands of Africa.

The swift adoption of cryptocurrency in Africa didn't catch me by
surprise. The continent is a cradle of youth, brimming with what is on
average the youngest population on the globe, a generation that carries
within it the potential to reshape social, economic, and political para-
digms. A significant majority of this population is under 25, a demographic trend that is projected to expand in the years to come. Given
its young population, African nations grapple with providing sufficient
educational and employment opportunities to this new generation, leading to a widespread problem of unemployment and underemployment.

Consequently, entrepreneurial in nature, African youth have shown an exceptional affinity toward digital and mobile technologies.

My first journey to the continent was in the warm summer of 2018 when I was asked to speak at a conference in Johannesburg, South Africa. This particular invite, a bit impromptu, came courtesy of Brandon Hiemstra, a longtime friend and a South African native. Brandon, now a Los Angeles resident, had recently launched House of Macadamias, a company connecting African farmers to the global market with an array of macadamia-based products. This latest business endeavor was gaining traction with endorsements from prominent podcasters and thought leaders, including Tim Ferriss and Joe Rogan.

The speaking engagement coincided with Brandon's visit to his home, and it was too intriguing an offer to pass up. Africa was uncharted territory for me, and I sensed that this journey would be unforgettable. I spent nearly 24 hours on the plane, half of it gliding over to Europe and the rest plunging down into the Southern Hemisphere. As we descended into Johannesburg, a surge of excitement washed over me, a magnetic pull, almost as if destiny had silently guided me there.

Brandon, ever the gracious host, picked me up in a Jeep Hummer. His striking appearance often made me playfully question his bachelor status, though he regarded me firmly as a friend, nothing more. He had arranged for my accommodation at a friend's house in Johannesburg—a wise choice considering the city's notorious reputation for safety problems. The house, nestled in a gated community, boasted a full suite of amenities and staff: a driver, cook, cleaner, and even a butler.

Our arrival, however, was greeted with an unexpected caution: "Please, stay in the car," the obviously agitated butler urgently advised us. The cause of the commotion? Jenny, the household's pet crocodile, had decided to take an unscheduled stroll outside her custom-built, terrarium-like enclosure at the heart of the house. This unexpected escape act was my first, somewhat startling, introduction to African pets, which differed slightly from the dogs and cats we had at home. It was an unconventional start to what would be an extraordinary trip.

The Fourth Industrial Revolution

The African continent became a source of fascination for many as the world entered a period of transformation commonly dubbed "the Fourth Industrial Revolution."

Reflecting on the past industrial revolutions, we see the following pattern: the first industrial revolution harnessed water and steam to revolutionize production, the second leveraged electric power to fuel mass production, and the third introduced electronics and information technology to automate production. Now, the fourth industrial revolution is marked by a fusion of the physical, digital, and biological realms.

At its heart is the digital transformation that touches every sector, from health care to finance, from education to agriculture. Advanced digital technologies such as artificial intelligence (AI), virtual reality (VR), machine learning, robotics, big data analytics, and cloud computing are driving unprecedented efficiencies, creating new business models, and delivering innovative services to meet the evolving needs of societies.

For Africa, a continent still bearing the scars of a colonial past, this revolution presents a unique and powerful opportunity. Historically, African nations have had to work with frameworks left by colonial powers—systems often alien to their intrinsic cultural and social fabrics. Decades into post-colonialism, many African countries still grapple with the legacies of conflict, corruption, and entrenched poverty. However, the infusion of new technologies offers a beacon of hope—a chance for Africa to sidestep the developmental pitfalls that ensnared the West, reshaping systems of production, financial services, and governance.

Africa is known for technological leapfrogging, where instead of following a linear progression of technological advancements, it bypasses certain stages and adopts more advanced technology directly. A prime example of this is the continent's widespread adoption of mobile phones, skipping landline infrastructure altogether. This leap has not only revolutionized communication across the continent but has also paved the way for mobile-based solutions in sectors such as banking, education, and health care.

Mobile banking, for instance, has brought financial services to millions of unbanked Africans, transforming economic participation without the need for traditional banking infrastructure. Africa leads the world in mobile money adoption, with Kenya's M-Pesa being a standout example. Mobile money services have reshaped the financial landscape, allowing millions of people without access to traditional banking to perform transactions and manage their money via their smartphones. As anyone who has ever tried to bank via an actual phone call can attest, this step could be missed. This ability to skip over outdated technologies and move directly to more efficient and scalable solutions showcases Africa's key advantage over the ingrained technological systems of the West.

While still in its infancy, the roots of decentralized technology have already taken hold in the mobile-first African population. These technologies are beginning to address some of the continent's most pressing challenges, offering new solutions to age-old problems and painting a picture of a future where technology is not just an imported solution but a homegrown beacon of progress and change.

The continent's potential for widespread adoption of digital currencies hasn't gone unnoticed by the titans of the crypto world. Binance, which operates the world's largest crypto exchange by trading volume and the world's leading blockchain ecosystem, has put down roots with its Binance Africa operation. In 2020, Binance educated over 70,000 Africans about crypto fundamentals. In 2021, they held a blockchain app creation masterclass attended by over 1000 developers. FTX, the now-defunct industry heavyweight, marked its entry into Africa with a significant investment in 2023. Joining the roster is Coinbase, which is making its own strategic advances in African markets. Meanwhile, homegrown African blockchain companies raised $91 million in the first quarter of 2022, a 1,668% year-on-year increase in cash inflow compared to 2021. Fintech start-ups (seeking to innovate on Africa's malfunctioning banking system) attract approximately 60% of all crypto VC funding in Africa, replacing traditional financial infrastructure for remittances, lending, and peer-to-peer payments.

In 2021, Nigeria, in a pioneering move, became the first government outside the Caribbean to launch a Central Bank Digital Currency (CBDC), the eNaira, signaling a growing governmental interest in the crypto realm. Because of the fear that eNaira would be used by criminals, especially money launderers looking to evade taxes, the government imposed regulations requiring different levels of personal authentication in order to access different user tiers; each tier was associated with different transaction limits and freedoms. Unfortunately, these government controls effectively massively centralized the digital currency, bringing as much power as possible to the government, not the people.

Africa has become a focal point for global powers, each vying for influence, partnerships, and a stake in its future. It holds about 30% of the world's mineral reserves, 12% of its oil, and 8% of its natural gas. It also has vast quantities of diamonds, gold, uranium, cobalt, and platinum. The Democratic Republic of Congo alone is estimated to have $24 trillion worth of untapped mineral reserves. The United States, Russia, and

China, in particular, have each carved out their own spheres of influence on the continent, driven by strategic, economic, and geopolitical interests. All three are making significant deployments in both physical and digital infrastructure across the diverse landscape.

American involvement in Africa has traditionally been interwoven with the tools of aid, diplomacy, and development. The US has positioned itself as a partner in Africa's development, focusing on humanitarian aid, health initiatives such as the President's Emergency Plan for AIDS Relief (PEPFAR), and investment in democratic institutions. However, this relationship has also been tinged with strategic military interests, particularly in counterterrorism efforts in regions such as the Horn of Africa and the Somali Peninsula. In recent years, the US has sought to counterbalance rising Chinese and Russian influence by bolstering economic ties to African nations, exemplified by initiatives such as the Prosper Africa strategy, aimed at increasing two-way trade and investment.

Russia's approach to Africa is rooted in its historical ties from the Soviet era, with a renewed focus on the continent under Putin's leadership. Russia's presence in Africa is characterized by arms sales, military training, and security cooperation, alongside investments in the mining and energy sectors. Unlike the US, Russia's involvement often comes with fewer conditions related to governance or human rights, making it an appealing partner for some African nations. Russia has also been leveraging "soft power" through cultural exchanges, education, and media, aiming to bolster its image and influence.

China's engagement with Africa is perhaps the most visible and economically substantial. Under the umbrella of the Belt and Road Initiative, China has invested heavily in infrastructure projects across the continent, including roads, railways, ports, and telecommunications networks. These projects are often linked to resource extraction, providing China with vital access to African minerals and oil. Chinese involvement, however, has drawn criticism for creating debt dependency and not sufficiently prioritizing local labor and sustainable practices.

In this tripartite dynamic, African nations are not merely passive recipients but active participants, navigating these international relationships in their own pursuit of economic growth, stability, and sovereignty. The continent's engagement with these global powers reflects a delicate balancing act, one that seeks to leverage foreign interest for its own developmental, political, and economic goals.

The Camp David of South Africa:
A Presidential Visit

During my first visit to the continent, I met Tumelo Ramaphosa, commonly known as the first son of South Africa. His father, President Cyril Ramaphosa, ascended to power in a pivotal moment for the nation, as the country's fifth president, heralding a promise of reform and renewal. Ramaphosa's presidency, following the troubled presidency of Jacob Zuma, was significant for its focus on tackling corruption and reviving the economy. His legacy, still in the making, was one of steering South Africa toward stability. It was also marked by the mass emigration of the wealth of educated white South Africans, partly due to a feeling of being unwelcome by the new regime and partly due to recent issues with currency instability.

In recent years, South Africa's currency, the rand, has seen significant fluctuations. For instance, during the early stages of the COVID-19 pandemic in April 2020, the rand dropped dramatically to a record low, trading at over 19 ZAR to the US dollar due to global economic uncertainty and a halt in economic activities. This was a steep fall from more stable times such as early 2019 when the rand was about 14 ZAR to the USD. Political issues, including leadership changes and corruption scandals, have made investors cautious, adding to the rand's instability. By 2021, the rand had regained some ground, appreciating back to 2018 levels, but it continued to face global economic uncertainties and domestic problems such as power shortages and high government debt. This volatility has significant implications for South Africa's economy, affecting inflation and import costs, making it challenging for policymakers and businesses to plan and operate effectively.

During my visit, I had the opportunity to watch the digital evolution unfold firsthand.

As the youngest son of the president of South Africa, Tumelo Ramaphosa was no stranger to turmoil. Throughout the governmental transitions, his one constant was his family's farm. His passion for wildlife was inherited from his grandfather, reflected in the family livestock business that has been passed down from one generation to another; Tumelo recalls helping his mother deliver baby lion cubs at the age of three. Even though by the time I met him, he now worked in the crypto space full-time, he continued to spend significant time on his family farm, citing a strong connection to the craft of his forefathers. After discovering Bitcoin in 2010, Tumelo started to ideate a digital version of his family farm within the cryptographic space. The original idea was to create a currency to sell animals, which then quickly grew into a movement to protect and conserve rare wildlife through impact-focused capital.

After the conference, Tumelo orchestrated an exclusive retreat for a select group of speakers to his family's safari compound, a serene sanctuary three hours from Johannesburg. Often dubbed "the South African Camp David," this secluded haven was a customary retreat for esteemed political and business leaders. Our journey there was unassuming: a caravan of worn-out Sprinters weaving through the landscape, a strategic choice for safety over ostentation. Upon arrival, though, the stark contrast of desert plains and luxurious amenities was striking.

As we disembarked, I committed a faux pas that would become an amusing anecdote for years to come. Weary from travel, I inadvertently handed my luggage to a woman near the bus in a safari uniform, mistaking her for a member of the household staff. She was, in fact, the First Lady of South Africa. I was mortified as my travel companion looked at me in dismay, pointing out my error. The First Lady, luckily, was gracious and warm, taking my panicked apology in stride, and she and I would spend the ensuing days in amiable conversation, sharing stories over tea.

The days unfolded with leisurely excursions amid African wildlife—giraffes and buffaloes roamed the vicinity, and I even experienced the unique joy of riding elephants. A particularly endearing memory was watching a young boy play soccer with an elephant, the animal skillfully using its trunk to kick the ball. Evenings were reserved for camaraderie by the campfire, under the sky strewn with stars, our conversations meandering from the future's possibilities to the rhythmic backdrop of African music.

One such evening, as laughter and music melded into the night, impromptu dance sessions began. It was during these lighthearted moments, amid the dance and revelry, that I was affectionately christened with my African nickname: Tay Tay. The nickname would stick on subsequent visits during moments of sheer joy and laughter. This first trip to Africa, woven with unforgettable experiences and new friendships, was more than a journey. It was a moment where my eyes were truly opened to a greater future of everything we have been creating in our industry.

On this trip to South Africa, my path crossed with that of Charles Hoskinson, a luminary in the world of cryptocurrency, renowned as one of the "Ethereum Eight"—the group of eight engineers who were instrumental in the creation of Ethereum. This venture propelled Ethereum to the forefront of the crypto world, marking it as one of the most successful cryptocurrencies globally. But Charles's vision extended beyond Ethereum. In 2015, he embarked on a new endeavor, founding Cardano, a cryptocurrency with an ambitious mission to redefine and unlock the potential within the African landscape. The Cardano blockchain empowers users to verify their identity, credentials, and legal ownership of land or other natural resource rights. It also allows them to free capital for getting loans, a process people in Western countries often take for granted. In societies where central government agencies might be difficult to reach, underfunded, or corrupt, storing property deeds on the blockchain—accessible via mobile phones—is transformative. This technology ensures that all parties can retrieve and trust the authenticity of these documents, thereby enhancing transparency and security.

Charles' commitment to leveraging Cardano in addressing Africa's challenges highlights a crucial aspect of technological progress—the ability to tailor innovations to meet the unique needs of diverse regions, particularly those as dynamic and varied as the many nations of the African continent. Cardano would later base itself in Ethiopia, creating new infrastructure for utility payments across the country.

I departed Johannesburg inspired by the possibilities for Africa's future, yearning to come back and explore the continent further.

A Detour to Necker Island

It would take another four years before I would return to Africa. Many journeys were taken in between, and one would lead to a chance meeting with Kate Kallot, a new friend and founder, whose venture in Kenya would become one of my proudest investments to date.

At the height of the bull market in December 2021, I took a trip to Necker Island, Sir Richard Branson's private island off the British Virgin Islands in the Caribbean. The trip came about as a last-minute invite by some friends who were joining a contingent of 50 folks looking to do an artificial intelligence–themed trip to the island. The group was a vibrant mix of founders, investors, and artists, boasting an impressive lineup of attendees, featuring notable figures such as presidential candidate Andrew Yang and Grammy Award–nominated musician Mike Posner.

Amid this extraordinary setting, I marveled at how far I had come from my immigrant beginnings and my early struggles to find my place in the world. A mixture of hard work and opportunity had landed me in environments that previously I could only dream of, sitting on an island with one of the most accomplished entrepreneurs in the world. Sequestered on the island for four days, we played with lemurs and delved into the world of kite surfing with none other than Sir Richard himself. Our days were filled with rich discussions on the future of AI, interspersed with leisurely rounds of surfing, tennis, chess, and my newfound passion, backgammon.

One memorable evening, I arrived fashionably late to dinner, my hair still damp from the shower, to find the gathering in full swing. Amid the laughter and engaging conversations, a single empty chair remained, located conspicuously beside Sir Richard Branson. It seemed as though everyone had deemed that seat reserved for someone more significant than themselves. Without seeing an alternative open chair, I approached cautiously, inquiring if the seat was claimed. Richard was surprised yet welcoming, jokingly exclaiming, "Oooo! A girl!" as he offered me the only open seat in a sea of "tech bros." During our dinner, Richard was warm, sharing his philosophies on family and business success, and background on the evolution of Virgin from a record label to a conglomerate spanning various industries. He also emphasized the importance of family.

Inspired by Richard's daily 7:00 a.m. tennis ritual, I resolved to join him, a commitment that saw me down at the courts each morning, coffee in hand. My initial attempt to participate on the courts was met with gentle advice to improve my skills—a challenge I eagerly accepted, though my efforts on the tennis court never quite matched up to the competition. It was at the chess and backgammon boards, one sunset-lit afternoon, that I found my moment.

Challenging Richard to a game, I surprised us both with my victories, my mathematical skills shining through across 17 games before he could claim a single win. This unexpected turn of events earned me the playful nickname "Baby-faced Killer" from Richard, a testament to the respect forged not just through sportsmanship but through intellectual prowess on the board. Like life, backgammon is a game of skill as well as a game of luck, where one roll could wipe out the most experienced of opponents. But preparation is key; a well-positioned opponent can defend against most lucky rolls turning against him. Richard would often say that respect is earned "on the board or on the court."

At our last breakfast together, Richard slid across the table a piece of paper bearing an incognito email address—a discreet channel of direct communication. With a smile, he simply said, "Reach out if you ever need anything." In that moment, a unique bond was cemented, marking the beginning of a cherished friendship.

The culmination of our island escapade was a dazzling disco-themed soiree, where sequins sparkled as brightly as the personalities gathered around the dinner table. I was nestled to the right of Andrew Yang, engaging in a heartfelt conversation about his recent presidential campaign and his aspirations for a future America rooted in justice and equity. Directly across from me sat Mike Posner, the evening's musical guest, whose enchanting voice was set to captivate us later. Yet, it was a different moment that etched itself into my memory.

Amid discussions on the trip's serendipitous nature and our diverse paths that led us to this shared moment in time, Mike Posner interjected with a whimsical quirkiness that caught everyone off guard. With a play-ful glint in his eye, he tossed out the question: "Hey guys, what's AI?" The table erupted in laughter, not just at the jest, but at the realization that so many of us were woefully ill-equipped to answer that very ques-tion while at an "AI-themed" gathering.

So, What Is Artificial Intelligence?

The evolution of artificial intelligence (AI) stands as one of the most transformative journeys of human ingenuity, starting with the mid-20th-century concept of "machine intelligence." The 1956 Dartmouth Conference is often cited as the birthplace of AI, where pioneers including John McCarthy and Marvin Minsky laid the groundwork for a discipline that aimed to replicate human cognitive processes through machines.

AI's initial decades focused on rule-based systems, where computers were programmed to perform tasks by following coded instructions. This era saw the development of languages such as LISP, designed specifically for AI programming, and the emergence of expert systems in the 1970s and 80s, which could mimic the decision-making abilities of human experts in specific domains. Despite these advances, early AI struggled with limitations in computational power and an inability to process the nuances of human language and learning, leading to what is known as the "AI winter"—a period marked by skepticism and reduced funding.

The resurgence of AI, in the late 1990s and early 2000s, was fueled by leaps in computational capabilities and the advent of the Internet, which provided vast datasets for training algorithms. The field of machine learning, where computers learn and adapt from data without being explicitly programmed for each task, began to flourish. This shift from hard-coded logic to data-driven learning marked a pivotal evolution in AI, enabling breakthroughs in natural language processing, image recognition, and predictive analytics.

The significance of AI in the contemporary era cannot be overstated. Its impact is profound and pervasive, revolutionizing industries from health care, where AI-driven diagnostic tools can identify diseases with astonishing accuracy, to finance, with algorithms now capable of executing trades and managing portfolios. In the realm of everyday life, AI powers the virtual assistants in our smartphones, curates the content on our social media feeds, and drives the recommendation engines that suggest what we should watch next on streaming platforms.

Yet, the ascendancy of AI also poses ethical and societal challenges, including concerns about privacy, the displacement of jobs, and the potential for bias in decision-making algorithms. The ongoing dialogue around these issues underscores the need for a thoughtful approach to the development and deployment of AI technologies.

As AI continues to evolve, its trajectory points toward even more sophisticated forms of intelligence, such as artificial general intelligence (AGI)—a (currently) hypothetical AI that exhibits humanlike understanding and reasoning across a wide range of domains. While the realization of AGI remains a subject of debate and speculation, the rapid journey of AI from its inception to its current state highlights humanity's relentless pursuit of creating machines that can think, learn, and, perhaps one day, understand the complexity of the human experience itself.

Artificial intelligence became a hot topic for VCs everywhere with the launch of OpenAI. OpenAI, founded in December 2015 by Y Combinator partner Sam Altman, emerged as a pivotal player in the AI landscape. Initially established with the goal of promoting and developing friendly AI for the benefit of humanity, OpenAI transitioned from a nonprofit to a capped-profit entity, attracting significant investment, and notably a billion-dollar commitment from Microsoft. OpenAI's ChatGPT has gained widespread acclaim for its ability to generate humanlike text, offering applications ranging from writing assistance to customer service automation. Beyond language models, OpenAI has also made strides in robotics and computer vision, contributing to the broader AI research community through the open sharing of research papers and software. At its peak, the foundation was valued at over $100 billion before facing several organizational challenges. Most recently, the company found itself embroiled in a scandal over allegedly using Scarlett Johansson's voice without her permission, a voice notable for its appearance in the 2013 movie *Her* where a man falls in love with an AI persona.

★★

My journey to Necker Island resulted in a new friendship with tech executive Kate Kallot. Kate grew up in Paris with her family originally from the Central African Republic. She had gone on to make her mark in the AI world as an executive at NVIDIA, in New York. After a long walk and heartfelt talk on the beach one day, Kate shared with me her aspirations of going back to Africa and launching her own AI project to solve the problem of climate and agriculture data scarcity in Africa. To explain it simply, Kate's idea—which would later turn into her start-up Amini, funded by top-tier investors such as Melinda Gates—sought to gather satellite data in Africa, process it using AI algorithms, and sell it to insurance companies and property developers.

Years later, Kate would call me, ready to take the leap to become her own boss. Without hesitation, I would write the very first check into the company, for $10,000, enabling her to sign an office lease in Nairobi, Kenya. At the end of our call, Kate would extend a sweet invite: "Come back with me to Africa."

Into the Lion's Den: Blockchain Applications Kenya and Nigeria

My journey back to Africa started with a short detour to Nigeria, to meet with a portfolio company that was building neo-banking infrastructure for the region. Embarking from Doha on a flight bound for Lagos, I had mentally prepared myself for heightened security measures, but the reality that awaited me was beyond anticipation. Stepping off the plane, I was immediately met by three men, a protective detail arranged by the company, who efficiently whisked me away, making the usually daunting immigration process a breeze through discreet exchanges with officials. Amid the bustling crowds of African and Middle Eastern travelers, my presence was an anomaly, a sensation amplified by the stares that followed me, the only white woman walking through the airport.

Our departure from the airport was swift, accompanied by a police escort, signaling the lengths to which security measures had been extended. The journey to my accommodation was an eye-opener; Lagos unfurled before me in layers of complexity and contrast. The stark poverty and the hustle of daily life were on full display as we navigated through the congested city streets. Women walked barefoot, with baskets of goods balanced atop their heads. Riverbeds were filled with haphazardly made shacks. I couldn't help but wonder what my life would have been like if I had been born into this type of environment. How successful would I be if I hadn't moved to the West and had my set of opportunities presented to me?

Our ride from the airport ended at the Sheraton, reputedly one of Lagos's finest hotels, the standard of which was well beneath the accommodations I had been used to in luxurious Dubai. It was a frank reminder of what money makes possible. A janky gate framed by armed guards opened for our arrival and then firmly closed behind me, welcoming me to a tumultuous new world.

I spent the next four days in meetings, at the same time aiming to see as much of Lagos as my schedule would allow. Amid the apparent chaos, there was an undeniable vibrancy, a testament to the resilience and spirit of the Nigerian people. Like much of the rest of Africa, Nigeria's demographic is notably young, a factor that defines much of its cultural and economic landscape. The nation's leapfrog into the digital age mirrors its inhabitants' adaptability and ambition.

Nigeria is not only the most populous country in Africa but also a pivotal economic powerhouse on the continent. Tracing its history back to ancient civilizations, Nigeria has been shaped by centuries of trade, colonialism, and the quest for independence, culminating in its emergence in 1960 as a sovereign nation composed of diverse cultures, languages, and landscapes. Its rich cultural heritage, from the historic kingdoms of Benin and Ife to the powerful Sokoto Caliphate, laid the foundation for a country marked by a profound depth of diversity and tradition.

In the decades following independence, Nigeria experienced a series of political upheavals, including a civil war and periods of military rule, which have shaped its modern political landscape. The return to democratic governance in 1999 heralded a new era of economic and social reform, with the country leveraging its abundant natural resources, particularly oil, to fuel economic growth. Nigeria's oil reserves, among the largest in the world, have been a significant driver of economic expansion, though the country is working to diversify its economy to reduce reliance on the oil sector.

Today, Nigeria stands as a giant in Africa both in terms of its demographic and economic stature. With a population exceeding 200 million, it is poised to become the third most populous country in the world by 2050, according to United Nations projections. This demographic boom presents both challenges and opportunities; the young population drives innovation and a vibrant digital economy, particularly in fintech and entertainment sectors such as Nollywood—Africa's answer to Hollywood—which produces thousands of films annually.

Nigeria's journey is one of resilience and transformation. However, Nigeria also grapples with issues such as unemployment, infrastructure deficits, and regional disparities in wealth and education. Sitting at $440 billion, the country's GDP, the largest in Africa, reflects its economic potential, but the benefits of its growth have not been evenly distributed, prompting initiatives aimed at fostering sustainable development and reducing poverty.

Following my whirlwind introduction to one of Africa's great powerhouses, I was off on a five-hour flight to Nairobi to meet up with Kate. Kate and I would spend the next two weeks exploring Kenya, going to dinner with friends, trying new foods, and partying in the clubs of Nairobi. We would explore the coastal town of Lamu, staying at Peponi Hotel, the same little beach hotel that hosted President Obama and actress Gwyneth Paltrow. We would visit the fish shacks in Vipingo, eating all the fresh seafood we could manage, before our final journey to the safaris of the Maasai Mara.

Unlike in Nigeria, where tensions among different groups were more evident, Kenya felt like a haven, a place where diverse cultures blended seamlessly. Here, women of every background moved with an air of freedom, unbound and solo, carving paths through the vibrant streets. My days were filled with Uber rides to visit friends, whose lavish homes, nestled against the backdrop of sprawling jungles, boasted pools and guest quarters for less than $5,000 a month—a fact they'd share with a chuckle. Many of them worked remotely, earning Western salaries and living the lifestyle of the top 1% in the country. The difference from Nigeria, I realized, lay in Kenya's subtle embrace of the West, a thread woven into the very fabric of its society, making it more familiar. To me, Kenya had a sense of order around it that many other African countries still lacked.

Kenya's colonial history strongly shaped the nation's identity, culture, and sociopolitical landscape. The scramble by the Western powers for a presence in Africa in the late 19th century saw the British Empire establish its dominion over the territory, formally declaring it the British East Africa Protectorate in 1895 and, later, the Colony and Protectorate of Kenya in 1920. This period marked the beginning of a complex and often tumultuous relationship between indigenous communities and colonial powers, fundamentally altering the region's trajectory. British colonization was driven by strategic interests and the allure of Kenya's fertile highlands, which were soon appropriated for European settlement and agriculture, notably tea and coffee plantations. The introduction of the cash economy, European legal systems, and Christian missions were aimed at transforming Kenyan society to serve colonial needs. The construction of the Uganda Railway, famously employing laborers from British India, epitomized the colonizer's imperial ambition, despite the human and financial costs involved.

The imposition of colonial rule was met with resistance from the outset. Notably, the Mau Mau uprising in the 1950s, primarily among the Kikuyu people, stands as a testament to Kenya's struggle for independence. The rebellion was characterized by guerrilla warfare against British forces and settlers, prompting a brutal counterinsurgency campaign by the colonial government. The Mau Mau revolt, while ultimately viciously suppressed, ignited nationalist fervor across the colony, setting the stage for the independence movement.

Kenya's journey to independence was spearheaded by figures such as Jomo Kenyatta, who became the nation's first prime minister, in 1963, and later its first president when Kenya became a republic the following year. The transition from colonial rule to independence was marked by efforts to redress the inequalities and divisions sown under British rule, including land redistribution and the establishment of a national identity. The legacy of colonialism in Kenya is nonetheless enduring, reflected in the country's political institutions, land ownership patterns, and economic structures. The colonial era's impact on ethnic relations, particularly the privileging of certain groups and the marginalization of others, continues to influence Kenyan society. Despite these challenges, Kenya has made significant strides in forging a cohesive national identity, becoming a regional leader in East Africa in terms of political, economic, and cultural influence. These factors make Kenya one of the most fertile and low-risk environments to explore new business and technology models among the 49 countries in Sub-Saharan Africa.

One of the most unique aspects of Kenya's evolution in the digital sphere is the introduction of M-Pesa, which became a part of everyday life for most residents. M-Pesa, which originated in 2007, was launched by Safaricom and Vodacom, the largest mobile network operators in Kenya and Tanzania, respectively, eventually expanding to other African and even Asian nations. The name M-Pesa comes from the Swahili word "pesa," meaning money, and "M" for mobile. The service allows users to deposit, withdraw, and transfer money to pay for goods and services easily with a mobile device, making it particularly transformative in regions where access to traditional banking services is limited. Instead of relying on brick-and-mortar banks, M-Pesa users can use their mobile phones to manage their finances with simplicity and efficiency. This has dramatically changed how money is saved, spent, and managed, promoting financial inclusion at a grassroots level.

Studies have shown that M-Pesa has helped reduce poverty in Kenya, particularly among women, and has fostered a culture of saving. It also plays a critical role in providing remittance transfers, thus linking migrants with families in rural areas. The platform's success has made it a global example of the power of mobile banking in emerging markets, proving that technology can drive financial inclusion and transform economies. During my time in Kenya, M-Pesa became a part of our daily method of getting anything done. The technology has become so ubiquitous that even as tourists, we had no choice but to upload it on our phones.

Our Kenyan adventure culminated in a breathtaking eight-seater charter flight over the expansive Maasai Mara, a landscape where the term "vast" finds its truest expression. The term "Mara" is translated from Maa, the language of the Masai people, as "spotted" and refers to the appearance from afar of the landscape, which is dotted with trees, shrubs, savanna, and cloud shadows that look like spots. From the plane, an otherworldly palette of earthy oranges and burnt yellows unfurled, punctuated by meandering streams and darting wildlife—a sight so majestic it seemed endless. A fellow passenger mused on the continuity of this vastness into Tanzania, where the Maasai Mara's grasslands seamlessly transition into the Serengeti, unmarked by visible borders. Here, the Great Migration, with wildebeest, zebras, and gazelles—a spectacular annual journey of wildlife—unfolds annually without regard for human-imposed boundaries, a poignant reminder of a time when the earth was unpartitioned and movement was dictated not by passports but by the rhythms of nature.

Our bush camp, Ishara, was an oasis of comfort where indulgence met wilderness, with opulent linens, golden baths, and an ambiance that rivaled the finest hotels, yet with a wild chorus of hippos as our nightly serenade. Cautionary tales of hippos and lone lions wandering through underscored the untamed essence of our surroundings, necessitating Maasai escorts within the camp—a thrilling blend of luxury and the untamed. And the welcome dance by the Maasai, vibrant with color and tradition, was a vivid testament to the preservation of their heritage. This infectious pride was palpable in their music, indigenous attire, and joyous smiles.

As we embarked on guided excursions, capturing the wild beauty of the Mara through the lenses of professional Kodak cameras, each moment felt like an intimate glimpse into the heart of the wilderness. Yet, it was an impromptu evening venture that would forever imprint on my memory. Our usual dinner was interrupted by a guide hurrying us from our table—"It's time to go!" We drove out into the pitch-black expanse, barely seeing the bushes ahead with the jeep headlights. As we arrived at what seemed to be our destination, we toned down the noise and the lights. And there, we encountered the raw, unfiltered dance of the ecosystem: a lion family partaking in the bounty of their hunt. The prey? An antelope, picked apart, limb by limb. This spectacle of life, stark and primal, offered a meditation on existence itself. *Crack!* We watched a baby lion pull off a leg, blood splattering everywhere. We watched in awe as the cub chewed on the raw meat.

In the hushed reverence of that moment, I pondered the complexities of human society—our inventions, our conflicts, our endless quests for more. Here, life's fundamentals were laid bare: survival, community, and the cycle of life and death played out under the canopy of stars.

Yuval Harari, in his bestseller *Sapiens: A Brief History of Humankind*, explained it best:

On a hike in East Africa 2 million years ago, you might well have encountered a familiar cast of human characters: anxious mothers cuddling their babies and clutches of carefree children playing in the mud; temperamental youths chafing against the dictates of society and weary elders who just wanted to be left in peace; chest-thumping machos trying to impress the local beauty and wise old matriarchs who had already seen it all. These archaic humans loved, played, formed close friendships and competed for status and power—but so did chimpanzees, baboons and elephants. There was nothing special about humans. Nobody, least of all humans themselves, had any inkling that their descendants would one day walk on the moon, split the atom, fathom the genetic code and write history books. The most important thing to know about prehistoric humans is that they were insignificant animals with no more impact on their environment than gorillas, fireflies or jellyfish.

This reflection led me to question how far humans have moved away from their original existence in the animal kingdom, and whether that progress has been entirely fruitful. In our pursuit of progress, have we strayed too far from the elemental truths that bind us to this earth? Could the essence of life be found not in the constructs we've built but in the primal connections we share with the world and each other? Kenya, with its untamed beauty and timeless rhythms, offered no answers, only space for the questions.

MONEY MYTH #8: Blockchain technologies do not have real-world impact.

For many Western investors, blockchain-based technologies such as cryptocurrencies are just a speculative investment. For those in emerging economies, it can be a lifeline.

The myth that cryptocurrencies don't have a real impact, especially in emerging markets and regions such as Africa, overlooks the transformative role that digital currencies can play in these economies. In many parts of the developing world, access to traditional banking services is limited, leaving a significant portion of the population unbanked. Cryptocurrencies offer a viable solution by providing access to financial services through mobile technology, which is widely accessible even in remote areas. This technological revolution in finance has enabled individuals and businesses to engage in transactions, build savings, and use credit—tools that were previously out of reach—thereby fostering economic inclusion and empowerment. Blockchain-based smart contracts and official documents bring these instruments into the literal hands of citizens who may not otherwise have access to them.

In Africa, for example, cryptocurrencies are not just theoretical tools; they are actively reshaping financial interactions. They facilitate remittances from the diaspora without the hefty fees associated with traditional banking systems, allowing more money to flow directly into local economies. Blockchain technology offers transparency and security in financial transactions, which can be particularly valuable in regions plagued by corruption and fraud. This aspect of cryptocurrencies can help establish trust in economic systems and can encourage investment and economic growth. In countries that experience high inflation, cryptocurrencies provide a more stable store of value compared to the local currency, thus offering a hedge against economic instability. The real impact of cryptocurrencies and the blockchain technology that backs them is profound, challenging the myth that they are without tangible benefits, and underscoring their potential to drive significant socioeconomic development.

9

Breaking Point

Gravity is a harsh mistress. The higher you climb, the harder you fall.
—Anonymous

In the second half of 2022 and the beginning of 2023, I lost about 50% of my net worth. The bear market of that period was an array of disasters across both the cryptocurrency and the traditional financial worlds, wiping out $2 trillion in value in what was dubbed the "crypto winter of 2022." The S&P 500 lost 19.4% in those twelve months, having, in 2023, the worst six-month start to a year since 1970.

I often say that "crypto is a caricature of real life." In my view, the crypto world merely amplifies issues already present in our financial institutions, due to government inefficiencies and human psychology, across all asset classes. The traditional stock market, just like the crypto market, is well known for its irresponsible use of leverage and media buzz to exaggerate prices. Those of us who worked in finance in the era of the 2008 financial crisis are no strangers to how convoluted derivatives products can be, and to how the lack of regulatory guardrails in place can bring down an entire financial system.

The crypto world follows the same patterns of manipulation, creating the same drama but multiplied tenfold. Twenty-x leverage on a trade? No problem. Copious amounts of multilayered debt collateralized by vaporware? Why not. Eight-figure pre-seed cap tables for companies with no working product? Sounds good! No need for a board, or any investor oversight, either. The Bitcoin network first gained popularity (and notoriety) by facilitating an online marketplace for drugs (Silk Road comes to mind) where college kids could buy grams of weed for 3 BTC, but now moves vast fortunes. Billionaires were created within a matter of years, and in a few more they could lose it all, without ever opening a bank account. In retrospect, the calamities experienced over the crypto winter of 2022 were perhaps not all that surprising.

The crypto winter was felt across the industry, but the impact on Bitcoin was remarkable, with a drop of 64 percent in 2022. I was starting to feel the chill of the deep bear market. After finally having begun to feel financially secure, the result of success built on a lot of work and hard-won lessons, I began to feel once again that no matter what I did, or how hard I fought, I would always be one step behind. I was chasing an intangible target that was moving so quickly and unpredictably that I could never hope to catch it.

When Your Mind and Body Fail: Retreat to Bali

Amid the turmoil engulfing the crypto markets, in April 2022, I realized the toll the last couple of years had taken on my health. During two years of a nomadic lifestyle filled with endless industry gatherings and luxurious escapades, living out of my suitcase, my well-being had taken a backseat. I had a collection of adventures to recount to family and friends—from Dubai and Abu Dhabi to Nairobi, Lagos, Monaco, and so many other places in between, I felt I had lived an entire lifetime during COVID-19. But now, I felt sick and lethargic, all the time. I had just come off another three-week bender and was making a dizzying amount of mistakes in my personal and professional life. It seemed that every trade I made went against me. Falling further into despair, I started drinking heavily. One time, I distinctly remember making a leveraged trade on my phone while out at a mansion party. I pressed the wrong button, and—poof!—a quarter of a million dollars just disappeared.

As Bitcoin hit an all-time cycle low of just under $16,000, our industry was filled with despair. Traders started returning their Lambos to the dealerships, and prices on secondary sales in the watch market began to plummet. The desperation with which the entire industry was wishing the bull market back to life was palpable. It seemed that a mental health crisis was spreading all around me. The cognitive dissonance of having no one to blame but yourself for not having pulled your chips off the Ponzi table on time resulted in the collective lashing out at everyone around them.

I knew in my bones it was time to walk away. I decided I needed a real break, and so, for the first time in two years, I exited my trades, closed my laptop, and impulsively booked a flight to Bali.

The night before my flight, I went out with a group of friends for my last night in Dubai, another sunrise-capped escapade. The morning was, unsurprisingly, a harsh awakening: I awoke after a mere two-hour sleep, plagued by tequila-inspired nausea and stomach pains. Eventually, I finally fell back asleep, and as a result, I missed my flight. This was perhaps the first step in my journey of realizing that there were no accidents and that everything in life happens for a reason.

There were only three direct flights a week from Dubai to Bali, so I parked myself in yet another hotel suite and waited another two days. On a Thursday morning, I boarded an Emirates flight to Denpasar, Indonesia. As I hazily got on the plane, I encountered an old friend. Confused, we both had to do a double take, as we were wearing our COVID masks. When our eyes met, we recognized each other's familiar curly hair.

"Marc?"

Marc had been my roommate back in 2017 in a house in Venice Beach. Coming from a traditional investment banking background, he had ventured off into the world of music and festivals before eventually finding himself in the tumultuous world of crypto. Marc became somewhat of a mini-celebrity after appearing in the Netflix documentary *Fyre,* about the infamous Fyre Festival, for which he had been the unfortunate head of housing, trying to warn Billy McFarland and his team of the impending doom.

For those of us living under a rock, the Fyre Festival had been marketed as the ultimate luxury music festival experience, set on the picturesque Bahamian island of Great Exuma, but instead had spiraled into a notorious debacle that temporarily captivated the world. Promoted with glossy social media campaigns featuring top models and influencers, including Kendall Jenner and Ja Rule, the festival promised opulent accommodations, gourmet meals, and performances by top-tier artists. However, upon arrival attendees were met with disaster: unfinished, makeshift refugee-style tents instead of luxury villas, cheese sandwiches instead of gourmet cuisine, overflowing Porta-Potties, and a complete lack of organization that led to the event's abrupt cancellation. With attendees who had paid $1,500 per ticket (and even more for a VIP package) stranded and furious, the fallout was swift and severe. Lawsuits piled up, and the festival's mastermind, Billy McFarland, was eventually sentenced to prison for fraud. (Ironically, Billy's playbook was somewhat similar to that of the many failed crypto founders and fund managers who would flame out in the years to come.) The Fyre Festival became a cautionary tale about the dangers of overhype and the stark realities that can lie behind a well-curated digital facade.

After the debacle in 2017, Marc had, understandably, wanted to disappear. "I told them we had to cancel ... I really did," he would often mutter under his breath, still shaking from PTSD, while cooking his breakfast. Marc eventually found his footing, discovering a passion for crypto investing and rising to lead a top-tier crypto fund out of Puerto Rico.

Our chance meeting on the flight to Bali was fortuitous; Marc was en route to a spiritual retreat led by a renowned Vedic guru, aptly named Guruji. The event was to be a gathering of the tech elite, including the sage-like Naval Ravikant and dear friends Jack Herrick and Niraj Mehta, among other Silicon Valley titans. And since I was already on my way there, with no plans for myself except to stop doing everything I'd been doing, I decided to join them.

Bali offered me the rare opportunity to disconnect completely. As a group, we would practice Shakti meditation to the "goddess of truth" in the Vedic tradition, calling in our true path for this lifetime. "Truth, consciousness, bliss—the divine right of every human," Guruji would often chant during his sermons. I embraced the tranquility, meditating on a cliff in Uluwatu, watching surfers dance with the waves below, and embarked on a profound spiritual journey.

Amid the global financial chaos, I began to perceive money as a flow of energy, a means of sharing our resources with those we cherish, rather than just a means to an end. Money, I understand now, is inherently tied to our emotions and the way we see ourselves in this world. Do I have more than my neighbor? Am I more successful than a former classmate? Do I finally have enough to take some time off? Understanding the psychological underpinnings of financial decision-making is crucial, as our emotions and behaviors deeply influence how we handle money. Envy, greed, and optimism, for example, are potent forces that can drive people to make risky financial choices, accumulate unsustainable debts, or squander their resources. To grasp the full impact of these emotions, one must consider not just the economic but the emotional investment we have in our financial decisions.

Money, far more than being just a medium for transactions or a reserve of value, plays a pivotal role in shaping our mental and emotional landscapes. It influences our thoughts, feelings, and actions in profound ways. And so by fixing our emotional and mental health, we can fix our unhealthy relationship with money. We can begin to let go of the attachment we have to financial success or to the numbers in our bank accounts. Rather, we can begin to view money as a tool to better our lives and the lives of those around us—as an exponential power that is meant to be shared with others, an energy that is meant to be passed on rather than hoarded.

This period of retreat also led me to my first holistic health consultation. Twenty pounds over my normal weight and plagued by depression, anxiety, and panic attacks, I received a stark diagnosis from the Bali BSI Clinic. My liver toxicity was alarmingly high, a clear indicator of the intensity of my lifestyle, driven by the relentless crypto market. I embarked on a six-month liver detox, quitting alcohol, processed foods, and red meat.

My time in Bali marked a pivotal shift in my worldview. Upon returning to the US in June of 2022, after almost two cumulative years abroad, the contrast of Venice Beach, marred by chaos and homelessness in the pandemic's aftermath, made me yearn for serenity. I found solace in Malibu, where I settled into a beachfront apartment, surrounded myself with spiritual readings, adopted a daily meditation practice, and took a nearly yearlong hiatus from my phone and the tumultuous world it connected me to. That summer, I also said goodbye to a friend, whose passing made me question everything I have worked so hard for.

Market Collapse: A (Block)chain Reaction

As it became clear that good times were not coming back to the cryptocurrency markets anytime soon, outside my Malibu sanctuary, a number of alarming developments began to shake not only crypto investors' portfolios but our entire faith in the asset class. Cryptocurrencies were increasingly the subject of prominent media coverage following the COVID-era bull market cycle, and the consequences of their collapse were felt not just by industry pros but by numerous inexperienced retail investors who had sprinkled their savings far and wide across crypto projects of highly varied quality, stability and, frankly, legality.

The First Domino Falls: TerraLUNA

In May 2022, in a dramatic unraveling that shook the foundation of the crypto world, Terra (known as LUNA) and its stablecoin counterpart, TerraUSD (known as UST), experienced a catastrophic collapse, erasing billions of dollars from the markets in a matter of days. This event not only highlighted the volatile and speculative nature of digital currencies but also raised serious questions about the viability of algorithmic stablecoins, which seek to maintain their peg to traditional currencies through mathematical formulas rather than through reserves of fiat currencies or other assets.

The price of LUNA plummeted from over $100 to mere pennies in a matter of days. With almost $40 billion erased from the markets (between UST and LUNA), a number of brand-name funds and financial firms were severely affected.

The Second Domino: 3 Arrows Capital

Three Arrows Capital (3AC), co-founded by Kyle Davies and Su Zhu, was the next domino to fall in the crypto bear market that summer. Established in 2012, 3AC was once among the most respected and influential hedge funds in the crypto space, managing upward of $18 billion in assets and known for its aggressive investment strategies.

3AC's troubles began to surface publicly in June 2022, when it failed to meet margin calls from its lenders—a clear sign of liquidity issues. The firm had made sizable leveraged investments that included significant exposure to the TerraLUNA ecosystem. The implosion of Terra the previous month heavily impacted 3AC's portfolio, but it was the subsequent market-wide crash that exposed the full extent of the fund's vulnerability. This liquidity crisis was exacerbated by the opaque nature of many of its investments and the fund's use of borrowed money to amplify returns, a strategy that looks appealing in a bull market but backfires when markets turn south.

Creditors and partners, including significant players such as Celcius, BlockFi, and Voyager Digital, faced substantial financial losses, with Voyager Digital citing exposure to 3AC as a significant factor in its eventual filing for bankruptcy. The fund's collapse underlined the interconnectedness of the crypto financial system, highlighting systemic risks in a still-maturing market.

In July 2022, a court in the British Virgin Islands ordered the liquidation of 3AC, and its founders faced legal actions and a global hunt for assets to repay creditors. American founders Kyle Davies and Su Zhu fled to Dubai, where they were protected from arrest by the lack of extradition treaties between the US and the UAE (Zhu was subsequently arrested for failure to cooperate with the investigation of the firm when he traveled to Singapore). Their yacht, aptly named *Much Wow*, estimated to be worth over $30 million, was seized by US bankruptcy court liquidators.

While Su Zhu awaits trial, Kyle Davies has launched a new chicken-delivery business for the Dubai market, based on a family recipe. Kyle and Su were in good company in Dubai: they were quickly befriended by Larry, the star of Chapter 7. I can't claim to know whether they have invested in any of each other's latest schemes.

The Third Domino: FTX and Alameda File for Bankruptcy

The domino effect from the collapse of Three Arrows Capital soon found its next victim in FTX.

FTX was perhaps the most dramatic of the crypto collapses, as it was the one none of us saw coming. Founded by the likable Sam Bankman-Fried (widely known by his initials, as "SBF"), a graduate of MIT and the son of two professors at Stanford Law School, FTX was a cryptocurrency exchange created as a spin-out of the hedge fund Alameda Research. FTX offered a seamless and superior derivatives experience to crypto traders that included futures, options, and even digital stocks. At its height, FTX was worth a whopping $32 billion and processed over $10 billion in transactions daily. Top-tier investors in the exchange included Sequoia Capital and Temasek—Singapore's state-funded investment firm, which held a total investment of $275 million.

SBF often made large donations to both Democratic and Republican candidates. In less than 18 months, he contributed over $70 million to various election campaigns, making him one of the largest political donors in the 2022 election cycle. SBF also made sure that the company's optics were always top-notch, employing brand-name celebrities such as Tom Brady, Madonna, Gwyneth Paltrow, and Kevin O'Leary as company mascots.

The unraveling of FTX began with a leak. On November 2, 2022, CoinDesk, a well-known crypto publication, exposed a balance sheet from Alameda Research, FTX's sister company, suggesting that the firm's financial stability was as precarious as a house of cards, based on a valueless FTT token. This revelation prompted Binance's CEO, Changpeng Zhao (publicly known as "CZ'") to announce his intention to liquidate $500 million worth of FTT tokens, inciting panic across the market.

SBF saw his personal net worth shrink by 94%, from an estimated $26 billion to a fraction of that, as both FTX's valuation and his reputation tanked. FTX's bankruptcy filing on November 11, 2022, was the culmination of a rapid descent into financial turmoil.

I was one of those unknowing customers who had trusted FTX more than I trusted any traditional financial institution. Perhaps this was owing to the friendship with SBF that I had struck up during our interview for *Forbes* two years earlier. As a result of our friendly relationship, FTX and Alameda created an open-door policy for any deals I brought them. Maybe, as a young Jewish type-A kid looking to take on the world, I also felt a sense of familiarity around Sam. Or, possibly, I bought into FTX simply because, like so many people, I bought into the hype of the man who was rapidly becoming the great Sam Bankman-Fried.

The Contagion

The turmoil didn't end there. The broader crypto industry faced its Judgment Day as companies disclosed their exposure to FTX: Galaxy Digital, Sequoia Capital, Crypto.com, and Wintermute, among others, came forward with admissions of significant funds tied up in FTX, each firm grappling with the immediate financial implications and the long-term trust deficit in centralized crypto institutions. Brand-name crypto funds, such as Ikigai Capital, were forced to admit that most or all of their holdings were, indeed, on FTX, and locked for the foreseeable future.

And then the hunt for SBF started.

An interview with Sam Bankman-Fried during the *New York Times*'s DealBook conference on November 30, 2022, became a pivotal moment in the unraveling saga of FTX's collapse, casting a spotlight on the complexities and alleged mismanagement within his crypto empire. Throughout the hour-long conversation, led by the *Times*'s Andrew Ross Sorkin, SBF—who participated in the conference from the Bahamas via an online portal—would not acknowledge any connection between his mounting legal difficulties. SBF's alleged crime, to explain it simply, was having used customer funds stored on the FTX exchange for investments made by the related fund Alameda Research, which was run by SBF's on-and-off girlfriend, Caroline Ellison. His acknowledgment of having "screwed up," particularly in aspects of risk management and protective measures for customer assets, revealed the gaps in governance and oversight that had led to FTX's downfall.

Ten days later, SBF was arrested by Bahamian authorities and extradited to the United States on charges of fraud.

By October 2023, things went from bad to worse for SBF. At his criminal trial, the prosecution painted a picture of SBF as a mastermind who siphoned off billions from FTX customers, lavishing the stolen wealth on personal extravagances and political maneuverings aimed at securing influence in the corridors of power. His lawyer, Mark Cohen, counterargued that Bankman-Fried's attempts to navigate the volatile crypto market of 2022, spurred by a surge in customer withdrawal requests, were actions taken in the company's interest, not evidence of fraud: he was a "math nerd," not a criminal mastermind.

Bankman-Fried's portrayal in court as a beleaguered CEO, overwhelmed by the scale of his responsibilities and oblivious to the financial malfeasance occurring under his watch, contrasted sharply with testimony regarding his level of control and influence over the company. Following a damning verdict that found him guilty on all counts of fraud and money laundering, on March 28, 2024, SBF was sentenced to 25 years in prison. Left in his wake were creditors hoping to recover $11 billion in assets in a two-year bankruptcy proceeding, which involved selling off Alameda's venture stakes in an array of companies, including AI darling Anthropic. In a twist of fate, his estate is now claiming nearly all FTX creditors will receive 118% of their funds—stolen and then wisely invested—back in cash. SBF plans to appeal his conviction

Soft Landing in a Pool of Quicksand: Quantitative Tightening

Meanwhile, from the summer of 2022 to 2023, as I was going through my much-needed detox of the body and the mind, America was going through its own detox, but from pandemic monetary policy. As a result of the unprecedented printing of money during the era of quantitative easing, the US was facing a stark inflation crisis.

In 2020, the US government injected a staggering $2.9 trillion in freshly minted dollars into the economy, equivalent to 13% of the nation's GDP. This led to an incredible financial bull run from 2020 to 2022.

Each new generation of investors, it seems, must learn the lessons of interest rates and inflation the hard way, and as the pandemic faded away, our turn came around. Quantitative easing and an era of zero-percent interest rates gave rise to one of the most extraordinary asset price bull markets in history. It was as if you could blindly choose winners across stocks, real estate, commodities, and cryptocurrencies. In an almost comical display of this frenzy, Barstool's Dave Portnoy resorted to picking Scrabble letters out of a bag to select winning stocks. While undoubtedly entertaining, the gag was also a clear sign of peak bull-market absurdity.

By mid-2022, it became painfully clear that the Federal Reserve had made a mistake. In a rapid and forceful response, the central bank executed a series of unprecedented interest-rate hikes to reverse course and decrease inflation. Within a single year, rates catapulted from 0% to 5%, , triggering a dramatic plunge in asset prices across the spectrum. A new era of quantitative tightening dawned, and once again, those who felt the most pain were in the lower and middle classes.

In September of 2022, the Consumer Price Index (CPI) report pegged inflation at 8.3%, ignoring the price inflation in certain consumer categories *precisely because they were key sources of price inflation.* When you dove into the specifics, the figures were stark: Gasoline prices surged by 25.6% while the cost of fuel oil jumped an astonishing 68.8%, and electricity bills went up by 15.8%. Grocery prices rose by 13.5%; meat, poultry, and fish saw an 8.8%; and the price of milk climbed by 17%, while eggs skyrocketed by 39.8%. Airline fares soared by 33.4%.

In response to this persistent inflation, the Federal Reserve implemented a series of aggressive interest-rate hikes. By 2023, the cumulative effect of these rate increases began to ripple through the economy. Mortgage rates climbed to nearly 20-year highs, significantly dampening the housing market. Consumer borrowing costs, including for credit cards and auto loans, climbed, leading to a contraction in consumer spending, a critical engine of economic growth. Businesses, too, faced higher borrowing costs, affecting their expansion plans and hiring capabilities.

The situation presented a delicate dilemma: while higher interest rates helped temper demand and, by extension, inflation, they also heightened the risk of economic slowdown or even a recession. To my generation, federal interest rates of 5% seemed unfathomable, with mortgage rates rising to 7%–8%, putting the cost of a first home out of reach for many. But to the boomer generation, who lived through 18% rates in the 80s, this seemed like only the beginning of a steep hill ahead.

The impact of the Federal Reserve's aggressive monetary tightening has been profound. The S&P 500 index plummeted by nearly a quarter in early 2024, obliterating over $10 trillion in market value. Government bonds, traditionally a haven in turbulent times, have recently turned in their worst performance since 1949. There was nowhere for money to run to—and average consumers continued to get hit the hardest by the rising cost of everyday expenses.

Looking back, we can find numerous instances of prominent investors predicting the very issues we now face. It seems the secret to achieving exceptional returns lies in timing the Fed and interest rates. Despite public opinion, professional investors understand that interest rates are crucial; the saying "Don't fight the Fed" gained popularity for a reason. Hedge fund manager Ray Dalio is well known for having stated, "It all comes down to interest rates. As an investor, all you're is putting up a lump-sum payment for a future cash flow." The name of the game, then, is cashing out in time, before interest rates begin to rise.

Similarly, in 1996, President Bill Clinton once observed, "You know what higher interest rates mean. To you, it means a higher mortgage payment, a higher car payment, and a higher credit card payment. To our economy, it means business people will not borrow as much money, invest as much money, create as many new jobs, create as much wealth, raise as many wages."

The New American Banking Crisis

By March 2023, the effects of peak interest rates in major economies reached developing nations, with the IMF urging the Federal Reserve to consider what its contractionary policies were doing to weaker economies. Rumors of recession and economic collapse rippled throughout the globe. But then the ripple hit back home. And something truly astonishing happened: American banks started to fail.

During the first week of March, VCs and start-up founders in Silicon Valley started to hear rumors that Silicon Valley Bank (SVB) might be insolvent. As interest rates spiked in an aggressive move by central banks to quell inflation, SVB's vulnerabilities had been exposed, leading to a crisis of confidence and liquidity. Like wildfire from savvy fingertips, texted warnings spread from company to company. SVB clients, most of whom were founders of tech companies, began to pull their funds from the bank.

At the heart of SVB's failure was a fundamental misalignment in asset-liability management, exacerbated by the "fractional banking" practices that permit banks to maintain only a small percentage of deposits on hand. Most people forget that banks aren't actually there to serve you. They are businesses, just like any other.

In 2020 and 2021, SVB (like all banks) was highly encouraged by the government to purchase federally-backed mortgage securities yielding 1.5% to 1.8% interest. Theoretically, these securities carried very little risk. But SVB made an error by investing in mortgage securities with a maturity period of 10 years, instead of opting for shorter-maturity Treasuries or mortgage bonds with a maturity period of less than five years. This would have been fine, provided that interest rates stayed relatively stable over the next 10 years, but of course, that's not what happened.

In 2022, when interest rates surged and the bond market plummeted (since bond prices move opposite yields), SVB's bond portfolio suffered significant losses. The risk could have been hedged, but basically wasn't. As a result, by the end of 2022, SVB had $211 billion in assets, with $117 billion of that amount invested in securities. But due to the drop in bond prices, $91 billion of the bank's bond portfolio, classified as "held-to-maturity" securities for accounting purposes, was now worth just $76 billion.

Even though these securities were facing 20% to 30% losses on paper, the accounting rules for these assets allowed the bank to report them at their value at maturity and not mark them down.

As rumors of insolvency began to spread, customers lined up to withdraw capital as quickly as possible. Ultimately, to prevent a systemic crisis, the government was forced to seize the bank, guarantee all of its customer deposits, and then wind down the business. It was the most significant bank failure since the 2008 financial crisis. The sudden downfall of SVB sent shock waves through the tech and venture capital communities, marking a pivotal shift in the landscape of financial institutions supporting innovation. The bank's collapse not only instigated a reassessment of risk within the banking sector but also ignited fears of a broader impact on the economy, especially within the innovation-driven sectors that heavily relied on SVB and banks like it for financial support.

Meanwhile, just over a month later, regional favorite First Republic Bank—the bank of record for many small and medium-sized businesses—started to also face a crisis of confidence among investors and customers. To protect its depositors, it received a lifeline of $30 billion from a consortium of the largest banks in the US, including JPMorgan Chase, Bank of America, Wells Fargo, Citigroup, and Truist, and most of its assets were eventually sold to Chase.

And then, just as we thought the crisis was over, word began to spread about a new report from the Stanford Institute for Economic Policy Research, titled "Monetary Tightening and US Bank Fragility in 2023: Mark-to-Market Losses and Uninsured Depositor Runs?" The report estimated the market value loss of assets held by individual banks during the Federal Reserve's rate-hike campaign. It also examined the percentage of funding at each bank from depositors with accounts valued over $250,000 (and therefore uninsured by the FDIC). The report concluded that a whopping 186 banks in the US are at risk of failure due to increasing interest rates and a high percentage of uninsured deposits.

As I sat there absorbing this news, I couldn't help but reflect back on my childhood, when my family lost all of its wealth during a 1998 bank run in the newly independent Russia. Throughout my financial education, I would read stories about bank runs in places including Argentina and Lebanon, but, as it did for many of my peers, the American banking system always felt safe to me. This new spate of bank failures was a wake-up call for me and my entire generation, as we collectively asked ourselves, "When did depositing your money in an American bank become a high-risk activity?"

Behind the Vault Door: There Is Less than You Think

America (and most of the world) runs on fractional reserve banking.

Established as government policy in 1913 by the Federal Reserve, fractional reserve banking is a system wherein banks keep only a small portion of their deposits in reserve and loan out the rest in order to make a profit. Fractional reserve banking can lead to the rapid expansion of the money supply, which can be good for economic growth. However, it also creates the risk of bank runs. When at risk, a bank may need to borrow from other banks or from the central bank in order to meet its reserve requirement. Most banks are required to hold 5% to 10% of deposits in reserve, but this requirement was dropped temporarily to nearly 0% during COVID-19, creating further risk in the system.

How Does Fractional Reserve Banking Work?

Banks hold only a fraction of the deposits they receive as reserves. This practice allows them to use the rest of the deposits to make loans and generate profits through interest. Here's a breakdown of how this system works:

Deposit and reserve requirements: When customers deposit money into their bank accounts, the bank doesn't just hold onto all that money. Instead, it is required by regulation to keep a certain percentage of total deposits in reserve. This reserve ratio is set by the central bank or financial regulatory authority of the country.

Creating loans: Banks can lend out a portion of the deposits they receive. This lending is how banks primarily make money, through the interest charged on these loans.

Money multiplication effect: When a bank lends out money, that money doesn't disappear; instead, it typically ends up deposited in other banks. These banks can then lend out a fraction of these deposits. For example, a bank might receive a deposit of $100, keep $10 in reserve, and loan out $90. The borrower then deposits the $90 in another bank, which keeps $9 in reserve and lends out $81—and so on. This process can multiply the initial deposit across the banking system, increasing the money supply.

Interest rates: Banks pay interest on deposits to attract customers and charge interest on loans to make a profit.

Liquidity and risk management: Banks must carefully manage their liquidity to ensure they can meet the withdrawal demands of depositors while also earning a return on loans and investments. They also need to manage the risk of loan defaults, which could lead to financial instability.

Central bank's role: The central bank uses monetary policy tools to influence lending, interest rates, and inflation. For instance, by adjusting the reserve ratio, the central bank can directly influence the amount of money banks can lend.

Fractional reserve banking is a double-edged sword. It allows for the expansion of the economy by enabling banks to lend money and invest, promoting business growth and consumer spending. However, it also introduces risks, particularly if banks lend irresponsibly or if too many depositors decide to withdraw their money simultaneously.

The collapse of Silicon Valley Bank exposed the federal government's complicity in the instability of the nation's financial system. Increasing evidence appeared that the Federal Reserve was aware of the potential consequences of its actions at the time it made its decisions. Reports suggested that as early as September 2022, the Fed understood that its aggressive interest-rate increases were jeopardizing the solvency of more than 300 community banks.

On September 8, 2022, the Federal Reserve of Kansas City published a "Community Banking BULLETIN," which offered the following warning:

On June 30, 2022, the Tangible Equity Capital Ratio at CBOs fell to 8.7 percent as a result of mounting unrealized losses on AFS securities, which totaled 1.5 percent of average assets. At year-end 2021, only 4 community banks had tangible equity capital ratios below 5 percent; that number increased to 333 on June 30, 2022, indicating less ability to sustain economic shocks.

The Fed, however, chose not to alert the depositors at these banks to the situation, leaving them to discover the precariousness of their financial positions through tumultuous bank runs.

The post-pandemic bank failures, and the federal government's failure to either lessen the odds of these collapses or inform depositors that their money was at risk, points to another failure in the federal government's management of the US financial system: the insufficiency of the Federal Deposit Insurance Corporation (FDIC) system. Currently, FDIC insurance safeguards deposits up to $250,000 per account holder, a ceiling that hasn't seen an adjustment since 2008. (As of this writing, rumors are swirling that an increase might be on the horizon.)

Yet, a pressing question looms: Could the FDIC's funds be depleted? Investment banker Caitlin Long has warned that the FDIC's reserves are far from sufficient to cover a widespread bank run, noting, "The FDIC insurance fund only has $128 billion, yet total deposits in U.S. commercial banks amount to $17.6 trillion, and money itself is fundamentally a confidence game."

Neither banks nor the regulators who oversee them seem especially motivated to protect their depositors. The $250,000 insurance limit, while sufficient for most families, falls short for medium-sized businesses, which must juggle funds across several accounts to ensure full coverage. But more to the point, why aren't all bank deposits fully guaranteed? Opening a checking account should not be akin to a high-stakes gamble.

Amid growing public outcry over the 2023 bank failures and the government's role in allowing them to happen, a joint statement from the Fed, the US Treasury, and the FDIC reassured the public by pledging to cover any deposit shortfalls, though the statement also made it clear that this would not extend to bailing out the failing banks themselves. This announcement was initially met with relief, but the realization quickly set in that this means reigniting the proverbial money printer—signaling that inflation is likely to remain a persistent issue.

Protect Yourself from Economic Turbulence

As of April 2024, the annualized three-month Consumer Price Index rate, a proxy of inflation, hovers around 3.5%, significantly exceeding the Fed's 2% target despite two years' worth of effort across multiple tightening actions. As most of us would expect quantitative tightening to continue to thwart sky-high fuel, food, and shelter prices (especially ahead of an impending presidential election), the current tightening approach via interest-rate hikes may turn out to be superficial. To avert a financial crisis and prevent widespread bank runs caused by its own interest-rate policies, the government may again be compelled to print new money, which could, ironically, fuel further inflation.

So how do we invest effectively in a high-inflation environment?

In 2020, when the government initiated its program of money printing in response to COVID-19, renowned hedge fund manager Paul Tudor Jones penned a compelling investor letter, widely regarded as the rational case for hedging one's portfolio against inflation with Bitcoin.

In the letter, PTJ wrote:

Below is a list of inflation hedges, rank-ordered in what we call the Inflation Race. While some of this list will track inflation in the classic sense, other instruments have been added to pick up the assets that will respond best to an acceleration in monetary growth not just consumer goods and service price inflation. So, it includes a host of assets that at one time or another have worked well in reflationary periods.

The list included gold, the yield curve, the NASDAQ 100, and several other well-known financial products. But, perhaps surprisingly for many in PTJ's habitual audience, product number four on this rank-ordered list was Bitcoin. The letter went on:

At the end of the day, the best profit-maximizing strategy is to own the fastest horse. Just own the best performer and not get wed to an intellectual side that might leave you weeping in the performance dust because you thought you were smarter than the market. If I am forced to forecast, my bet is it will be Bitcoin.

PTJ then proceeded to outline four metrics by which to analyze inflation hedges:

1. *Purchasing Power – How does this asset retain its value over time?*
2. *Trustworthiness – How is it perceived through time and universally as a store of value?*
3. *Liquidity – How quickly can the asset be monetized into a transactional currency?*
4. *Portability – Can you geographically move this asset if you had to for an unforeseen reason?*

His analysis led him to identify Bitcoin as the top candidate for an inflation hedge, due to its ability to retain purchasing power (as the best-performing institutional asset of all time), trustworthiness (backed by cryptography), liquidity (tradable 24/7), and most importantly, its portability.

The SVB bank run highlighted the nascent power of digital finance, as VCs managed to bring down a bank using smartphones in a matter of hours. When you no longer need to physically walk into a bank in order to remove your money from it, a bank run can occur on an exponentially faster timescale. Similarly, just as in times of economic upheaval, in times of political upheaval—such as wars, pandemics, or governmental changes—digital portability of assets is key. After all, no one is likely to carry gold or paper bonds across borders. I have personally interviewed several refugees from Lebanon and Ukraine who credit Bitcoin as the reason they were able to flee conflict zones with anything at all.

Many crypto advocates would argue that Bitcoin was made for this historical moment.

The Bitcoin network was created as a direct response to the Great Financial Crisis in 2008, during a period when many hardworking people felt that both the government and the financial system were working against them.

Bitcoin's beauty lies in its ability to store value in a decentralized manner backed by math, without requiring humans to validate or support it. If you own and hold Bitcoin in a cold wallet, no one lends out 90% of your deposits to make a profit, there is no possibility of a bank run, and no one gambles on bonds or other financial products with your hard-earned money. In the words of Satoshi Nakamoto: "*The root problem with conventional currency is all the trust that's required to make it work. The central bank must be trusted not to debase the currency, but the history of fiat currencies is full of breaches of that trust.*"

MONEY MYTH #9: Getting rich quickly is easy.

"Get rich quick"? That's the oldest and shortest fairy tale in the book— and yet, even as otherwise sensible and financially literate adults, we keep falling for it. The allure of quick riches often leads people down risky paths, and history is littered with examples of spectacular financial collapses that prove this point. If something sounds too good to be true, it probably is. The reality is that wealth takes time, effort, and a hefty dose of skepticism to build. And in today's economy, increasingly, if you're not thinking straight, the wealth you've built over a lifetime can be lost in the press of one button.

A macro view of the cyclical bear and bull markets in the crypto and traditional financial worlds shatters the myth of easy money. People rush into these markets, caught up in the excitement of the moment and a false sense of urgency, only to see their investments evaporate overnight.

Market volatility is a brutal teacher, reminding us that there are no short-cuts to financial stability. Quick gains can vanish just as swiftly, leaving you worse off than before.

Underpinning these cautions to protect your wallet is one to protect something even more important: your mental and physical health. Stress, burnout, and perpetual anxiety are the real costs of chasing unrealistic financial goals. Balancing ambition with well-being is crucial. Grinding yourself into the ground for money, *especially* to make money for somebody else, isn't just unwise; it's unhealthy. At the end of the day, even more than your bank account, your body keeps the receipts.

Instead of falling for schemes and shortcuts, focus on sustainable wealth-building. Invest wisely, keep learning, and plan meticulously. True financial success isn't just about money; it's about the freedom to live a happy and healthy life.

If you do choose to invest in crypto, here are a few pointers to keep in mind.

Exchanges, staking services, and custodial wallets encourage or mandate that they hold the private keys to your crypto while they invest assets for you. This is no different than a bank pretending to act for your benefit. It is worse, as these services are not FDIC insured.

"Not your keys, not your coins" is a harsh truth in the crypto world. Third parties can get hacked, go bankrupt, or simply disappear, leaving you with nothing. The only way to ensure your investments are safe is by keeping control of your private keys, preferably in a cold wallet. It's a simple rule, but ignoring it can mean losing everything.

10

Waking Up from the American Dream

Democracy is the worst form of government, except for all those others that have been tried.

—Winston Churchill

In the spring of 2024, I received my green card based on extraordinary ability (given to a handful of experts in their fields), capping off a decade of life in America pieced together on a string of work permits and business visas. I reflected on the journey that took me as a child from the Soviet Union to Canada before I arrived in the United States, and the various adventures to Europe, Asia, Africa, and the Middle East, shaping my perspective of what a society should be.

Despite its challenges and the existential risks it faces, I join many in believing that the West, and particularly America, represents a paragon of societal virtues. Here, the freedom to live as one chooses and to voice one's opinions, even when they diverge sharply from those of the majority, stands as a testament to what makes America a leading light among nations. America's elevated position as the issuer of the world's reserve currency, its influential culture of film and music, and its foundational principles of freedom and opportunity are still coveted worldwide.

I first became aware of America in 1991, at the age of four, as I watched the Soviet Union disintegrate on my television screen. This pivotal moment represented not just the collapse of a superpower but also the climax of a fierce geopolitical rivalry that had stretched across decades. The US and the USSR had long been locked in a global struggle for dominance, marked by economic pressures and ideological confrontations that ultimately led to the dissolution of the Soviet state. The Cold War, with its proxy wars, relentless nuclear arms race, and clash of economic and political ideologies, had laid the groundwork for this dramatic unraveling.

From the late 1940s onward, America had pursued a policy of containment aimed at curbing Soviet expansion following World War II. The Truman Doctrine and the Marshall Plan bolstered Western Europe's economies and reinforced military alliances such as NATO that served to stanch the flow of communism westward from Russia's borders. The ensuing costly arms race with the USSR, which largely continued for the next 40 years, pushed the Soviet economy into unsustainable military expenditures at the expense of much-needed domestic investment.

In the 1980s, the Reagan administration introduced measures that intensified the economic challenges facing the Soviet Union. The Strategic Defense Initiative, though never fully actualized, pressured the Soviets into further heavy defense spending. The US also managed to restrict the USSR's access to vital technology and manipulated oil prices, cutting off significant revenue sources for the Soviet state. In addition to these measures, the US supported dissident movements within the Soviet Union and its satellite states, advocating for human rights and democratic ideals. Western cultural and economic ideals were spread through media and personal contacts, undermining the Soviet narrative and highlighting the advantages of a more open and economically liberal society.

Earlier, in Chapter 2, we discussed the "veil of ignorance" theory put forth by liberal philosopher John Rawls, which posits that while participants in society may have different advantages and disadvantages in life, all should have the same equality of opportunity—a fair shot to rise above their circumstances. This, in its essence, is the American dream. The American dream, a foundational ethos of the United States, represents the belief that individuals, regardless of their background, have the opportunity to achieve success and prosperity through hard work, determination, and initiative. This dream inspires the notion that the freedom afforded by the American socioeconomic landscape allows anyone to rise above their original circumstances and reach a higher standard of living. Historically, it has motivated countless immigrants to venture to America in pursuit of better lives, influencing global perceptions of the US as a land of opportunity.

Today, for many, the American dream remains intact. Immigrants from around the world wish to live here despite challenges, and millions queue up at the nation's southern border to seek asylum each year, while still more cross into the country illegally. In December 2023, a staggering 249,785 arrests of migrants crossing the border illegally were made by the US Border Patrol, the highest monthly total on record. Texas has resorted to taking unilateral action to deter migrants, installing razor wire and other barriers.

The ascent of the United States to the pinnacle of global dominance is attributed to its vast economic influence, formidable military presence, and web of strategic alliances worldwide. Cutting-edge innovation over the last 100 years, most recently from tech giants such as Apple, Amazon, and Google, allowed it to command a significant share of international markets and shape international trade and economic flows. The US dollar's current role as the world's foremost reserve currency further secures America's position in international finance. Abundant natural resources and a willingness to exploit them contribute to its riches.

The cultural outputs of the United States in technology, entertainment, and consumer trends perpetuate its soft power, spreading the pursuit of the "American dream" to the furthest reaches of the globe. (Recall that as a young girl on the other side of the world, eating McDonald's was one of my earliest and strongest happy memories.)

These elements, coupled with the country's geographical positioning that serves to isolate it from major threats, have allowed the US to industrialize rapidly and project power globally in the vacuum created by the fall of the British and Soviet empires.

The Beginning of the End

But even the strongest of empires do not last forever.

The Trump presidency, from 2017 to 2021, was riddled with myriad ups and downs, from racist uprisings and loose monetary policy to significant efforts at peace worldwide with the Abraham Accords, which ended decades of staunch Arab solidarity against formal recognition of Israel.

At the turn of the presidency, the unthinkable happened: On Wednesday, January 6, 2021, a few days before President Trump was set to turn over the presidency to President-elect Joe Biden, a mob of Trump supporters broke into the Capitol Building with the intent to disrupt certification of the election results, entering offices and chambers, vandalizing government property, and chanting "Hang Pence." Mike Pence, Trump's vice president, had refused to stand behind Trump's narrative that the 2020 presidential election was rigged, so Trump had aimed the mob directly at him, as well as Congressional Democrats. Trump supporters even erected a wooden gallows, to make good on their chant.

Trump's "Stop the Steal" narrative, which claimed the 2020 election was stolen from him, was championed by right-wing media outlets such as Newsmax, which continued to spread misinformation about the election even after the attacks. Such misinformation has been as effective as it is pervasive: a *Washington Post*–University of Maryland poll in 2024 found that nearly a quarter of Americans believe that the FBI instigated the attack.

Although the attack was eventually quelled once Trump asked the rioters to "go home" (although he also told them he loved them), the events of the day shook up many and forced some of us to finally ask: Could this be the beginning of the fall of the American Empire?

Empires throughout History

A quick review shows at least 20 major empires across human history. An empire refers to a large, centralized political entity where a single sovereign authority governs diverse territories and populations, often through conquest or colonization. Here is a snippet view of five.

The Achaemenid Persian Empire (550–330 BCE) settled, civilized, and populated the world, dominating the Middle East, North Africa, Central Asia, India, and Europe, ruling over a greater percentage of the world (44% greater than any empire in history at the time. The Persian Empire's legacy to the world includes the use of a network of roads, a postal system, a single language for administration, autonomy for various ethnicities, and a bureaucracy.

The Roman Empire (264 BCE–476 CE), regarded as one of the greatest global empires, was not held together by brute force alone—people aspired to become Roman, which meant participating in a sophisticated, urbane classical culture. Roman law influenced all subsequent legal and governance systems in the West.

The Caliphate (Arab Empire) (632–1258) encompassed most of Arabia by the time of the Prophet Muhammad's death in 632 CE. The Arab Empire was extraordinary: a loosely organized, tribal people on the fringes of world civilization defeated the Byzantine Empire and overthrew the Persian Empire, both of whose populations and resources dwarfed those to be found in the Arabian Desert. The Arab conquests are a good example of how ideological zeal can make up for technological and organizational deficiencies.

The Mongol Empire (1206–1405) was the world's largest contiguous land empire, one that struck terror into its enemies. Although there were only about two million Mongols in the whole world, they subsequently conquered most of the Middle East, Russia, and China under Genghis Khan's descendants. In the long run, however, the Mongols proved inefficient at administering their empire, which eventually split into four khanates before each one eventually fell apart or further split.

The British Empire (1607–1980) essentially made the modern world. The main characteristics of the United States—a commitment to liberalism, the rule of law, civil rights, and trade—were inherited from the British and spread throughout the world. This feat was made possible more because of England's organizational and financial prowess rather than through military might. For example, the British conquest of India was mostly undertaken by Indian troops who chose to serve the British because of the regular salaries and benefits they offered. Approximately 60 countries were, at one point in their histories, ruled by the British.

Today, we are living in the age of the American empire.

The United States is the world's most militarily powerful nation, ever. It combines the British ingenuity for trade with a more deeply held liberalism and continent-sized resources. Like the Romans, it has an attractive culture. Like the Mongols, it can wield total destruction against its enemies. Like the Arabs, it has spread a universal ideology across the globe. Like the Persians, America combines different cultures and links together regions.

Yet, internal divisions and squabbling can kill even the most power-ful empires. Despite its overwhelmingly strong military, Rome fell. The Persians were conquered not because they were weak but because their leadership failed. Although the Mongols could win wars, they could not win the peace, and ultimately they failed to establish themselves per-manently anywhere. The Arabs spawned a successful civilization, but its positive aspects were overtaken by newcomers. The British Empire was exhausted by attempting to uphold its own interests, global order, and the European system, trying to do too many things at once, all while recovering from the devastating economic costs of the war.

America is facing all of these challenges and more. Meanwhile, China is actively vying to become the next world-dominating empire, with a highly organized and educated population, superior technology and infrastructure, climate change initiatives, deliberate expansion into emerging markets, and even the launch of its own digital currency.

And yet, there is another potential empire candidate brewing: the modern Middle East. A decade after the Arab Spring, the region is mov-ing forward with a new message of unity and innovation-focused think-ing, including the UAE's newly established peace with Israel and, most recently, with Qatar. The UAE is attracting businesses and new residents from all over the globe who are seeking greater opportunities. Diversify-ing away from the oil trade, the UAE has become the "new Monaco," a 0% income tax haven for the rich, particularly those running from con-flict during the recent Russia-Ukraine war and those seeking to conduct businesses in the cryptocurrency sphere away from the cumbersome regulatory regime of the US.

What does this mean for America? The fact is, no one empire has ruled human history forever. Even though Trump's term ended in 2020, he is up for reelection this year. Although I am not going to take a pub-lic stance on his viability as president, I will posit that the cracks Trump's presidency created in America are long-lasting.

Not only did Trump seem to embrace the underbelly of divisiveness and racism within our country, but he also gave a green light to radi-cal conservatives and revolutionaries. With over seventy million support-ers behind him, what we saw during the attack on the Capitol is only a symptom of a much larger disease: a distrust in the system, a desire for something different, and rumblings of a revolution.

The American Debt: A Downward Spiral

One of the elements driving a high level of distrust in the system is the nation's debt problem. The heightened interest rates employed by the Fed since the pandemic have had negative effects on businesses and on prospective homeowners, but many of us have not considered the effects on the biggest borrower of them all: the US government itself.

The national debt is a tool used by governments to fund projects, such as infrastructure, that promise long-term economic benefits without immediately raising taxes. Governments issue bonds to finance these projects, betting on their future economic returns to justify the initial outlay. For example, if a hydroelectric dam is projected to boost the regional economy by 10% over a decade, the government might issue bonds with a yield close to this rate, hoping the project's economic impact will offset the cost of borrowing.

When governments want to fuel growth through deficits, they should, ideally, offer bond yields that match or exceed the nominal GDP growth rate. Doing so aligns investor returns with economic expansion. However, in practice we find that politicians often prefer to pay lower yields to reduce the cost of borrowing; if politicians can create a situation where government debt yields are less than the nominal GDP growth rate, they can spend money faster. How does a politician create such a utopia? They financially repress savers with the help of the traditional finance (TradFi) banking system. The easiest way to ensure government bond yields are less than nominal GDP growth is to instruct the central bank to print money, buy government bonds, and artificially reduce government bond yields. Then, the banks are instructed that government bonds are the only "suitable" investments for the public. In that way, the public's savings are surreptitiously funneled into low-yielding government debt. The people are convinced to lend their money back to the government without raising taxes. This makes government bonds a "safe" investment but at the expense of savers, who are pushed into accepting lower returns on their investments.

This approach can lead to malinvestment, whereby funds are misallocated to less economically viable projects as political objectives overshadow sound economic planning. Early investments might be justifiable, but over time, as the focus shifts from quality to quantity of projects in order to achieve electoral gains, economic output fails to keep up with debt levels. The repercussions of such financial strategies become evident during economic downturns, when central banks may double down on their efforts to suppress bond yields, further distorting the economic landscape. This scenario typically results in prolonged periods of economic stagnation or mild growth, as governments choose to inflate away their debt rather than confront underlying economic challenges directly.

Monetizing the Debt

As of April 2024, the gross federal debt is $34 trillion, while the nation's GDP (or the value of all domestically produced goods and services) is estimated at $27.36 trillion as of 2023. Meanwhile, the annual interest payment on the national debt in 2023 was $658 billion, or 2.4% of GDP, and is estimated to rise to $870 billion in 2024, or 3.2%. The federal government spends more on interest-rate payments than on Medicaid, income security, veterans' benefits, and many other necessary social security programs. (For a visual aid, picture this: last year's debt payment of $658 billion, in $20 bills, would fill approximately 15 Olympic-sized pools.)

The primary holders of US government bonds include a diverse group of entities. Within the US, various government departments, such as the Social Security Trust Fund, are significant holders, essentially marking a scenario where the government owes money to itself. Internationally, foreign governments and investors, notably Japan and China, hold substantial amounts of US Treasuries, drawn by their reputation as safe investments. The Federal Reserve is another major holder, at nearly 20%, purchasing these bonds as part of monetary measures such as quantitative easing to stimulate the economy. Additionally, US Treasuries are popular among mutual funds, pension funds, and private investors due to their safety and liquidity. Banks and financial institutions also purchase substantial amounts of government debt, partly to meet regulatory requirements that mandate holding secure and liquid assets. These groups collectively finance the US government's operations and play a crucial role in the global financial system.

Yet, as interest rates increase or stay elevated, the government finds itself in a position where it owes large interest payments on its debt, much of it going to the Federal Reserve or other government-related institutions. And so it borrows more to service this debt to, essentially, itself.

How does the government get out of this spiral?

One way is to radically increase overall production in the economy. There's no easy way to do that, although the advent of artificial intelligence offers some hope. The other is to "monetize" the debt. Monetizing debt is the act of borrowing from the central bank rather than issuing more bonds to private investors. In this process, central banks create new money by purchasing government debt, aka, they print more money. This practice is prohibited in several countries, as it is deemed risky due to the possibility of triggering uncontrollable inflation. And yet, as the US national debt spirals out of control, it seems it is the most likely of options.

Global De-Dollarization

The main driver of America's elevated status as the leading empire on the contemporary global stage is the US dollar's status as the global reserve currency.

Following the end of the gold standard, in order to ensure the continued acceptance of the US dollar as a global currency, a significant new mandate was needed to drive demand for dollars. In 1973, the Nixon administration struck an agreement with Saudi Arabia, the world's largest oil producer at the time. The deal stipulated that Saudi Arabia would sell its oil exclusively in dollars, and in return, the US would guarantee the security of Saudi Arabia, particularly against Iran. As a result of this agreement, the dollar became the standard currency for buying and selling oil and natural gas worldwide; this new system became known as the "petrodollar regime." Any leader of a nation, such as Saddam Hussein in Iraq and Muammar Gaddafi in Libya, who attempted to sell their oil or gas in currencies other than the US dollar faced harsh consequences for themselves and their countries.

Thanks to the petrodollar regime, the US dollar became the most widely used currency in the world. There are approximately 2.3 trillion physical US dollars in circulation, with around 80% of these dollars being held outside of the United States. The US dollar is used as the official currency in several non-US countries, including Panama, Ecuador, and El Salvador. Furthermore, the US dollar is the currency of choice for international transactions, with around 88% of all foreign exchange transactions involving US dollars.

Yet gradually, the global ubiquity of the US dollar is being challenged through de-dollarization. "De-dollarization" refers to the process of reducing or eliminating the dominance of the US dollar in the global economy. It can take various forms; countries may choose to diversify their foreign exchange reserves, reduce their dependence on dollar-denominated trade and financial transactions, and/or create alternative payment systems. The trend has gained momentum in recent years due to concerns about the US government's increasing use of economic sanctions as a foreign policy tool, dollar volatility, and the rise of other economic superpowers. If the dollar loses its predominant global status, the US could face higher borrowing costs and greater difficulty in financing its deficits.

Evidence of this shift is appearing, for instance, in countries eager to trade with China, with China and France executing their first liquefied natural gas transaction using the Chinese yuan, China and Brazil agreeing to conduct their trade using their respective currencies, and China and Saudi Arabia constructing an 83.7 billion yuan ($12.2 billion) oil refinery priced in yuan. Elsewhere in Asia, the Association of Southeast Asian Nations is also considering abandoning major Western currencies in favor of local settlements; India has announced plans to settle its international trades with certain countries in rupees.

In Russia, Vladimir Putin has signed an order forbidding "non-friendly" countries (including the EU, the US, and Japan) from buying Russian gas in any currency besides the ruble. Forced by US sanctions, Iran has begun denominating oil sales in non-dollar currencies and developing alternative payment channels with India and China. In Africa, Kenya has shifted toward using its own currency for oil purchases from Saudi Arabia and the UAE, and its president has urged citizens to move away from holding US dollars. These global developments mark significant steps in the move away from dollar-centric trade and reserves, illustrating a broader pattern of economic diversification and regional cooperation.

Recently, more than 30 nations have expressed interest in joining the BRICS bloc (Brazil, Russia, India, China, and South Africa) and embracing its proposed new currency for international trade, signaling a collective move by this large group of countries towards de-dollarization. This expanding consortium, now potentially including diverse economies from Afghanistan to Argentina and from Saudi Arabia to Zimbabwe, illustrates a growing disillusionment with Western financial institutions and a readiness to adopt alternatives that could challenge the US dollar's hegemony in global trade. The inclusion of significant oil-producing countries in this alliance could further set the stage for a redefined global financial order.

So, what does de-dollarization mean for inflation? Traditionally, inflation in the US is measured using the Consumer Price Index (CPI), which assesses a basket of goods to gauge price changes. However, an alternative perspective, provided by the quantity theory of money, suggests that inflation can also be assessed more simply by the formula: Inflation rate = (GDP / Money Supply) – 1. According to this theory, if the money supply grows more rapidly than economic output, the currency tends to devalue and lose purchasing power.

International demand has historically helped stabilize the dollar's value despite fluctuations in domestic monetary policy. However, a shift towards de-dollarization could diminish this demand, leading to potential depreciation of the dollar relative to other currencies. Such a scenario could increase the cost of imports, contributing to higher inflation rates domestically. Moreover, the current climate of high interest rates has disproportionately affected emerging markets, sparking discussions among some nations about reducing their reliance on the US dollar in order to regain monetary sovereignty.

As the Federal Reserve intensifies its efforts to tame inflation by manipulating interest rates and other economic instruments, the growing trend towards de-dollarization could undermine these measures. If global reliance on the US dollar continues to diminish, sending more dollars back to the US, it would increase the domestic monetary supply. Without a proportional increase in domestic production, such an influx could sharply escalate inflation, making the Fed's efforts resemble trying to bail out a sinking boat with a bucket while ignoring a gaping hole in the hull.

China's Digital Money: Pioneering the Digital Yuan

Over the past few decades, China has embarked on a transformative economic journey that has not only bolstered its domestic capabilities but has also significantly increased its influence across the globe.

In 2018, China took a significant step toward reducing its dependence on the unlimited US dollar by introducing yuan futures oil contracts. Under the new model, China, being the world's largest importer of oil and gas, would use its own currency, the yuan, to pay for them. Meanwhile, sellers such as Iran and Russia were guaranteed to convert their yuan into gold on China's Shanghai Stock Exchange. With this move, the Chinese government reestablished a link between gold and money, taking a step back from the fiat model.

On December 17, 2019, I published an article in *Forbes* titled "How China Will Take Over the World." In it, I discussed the most recent development in China's efforts at economic expansion and global de-dollarization—the impending launch, by the People's Bank of China (PBOC) of the digital Chinese yuan, making China the first country in the world to have a digital central bank currency.

China has been experimenting with innovative monetary policy for decades, having started working on its currency ascension plan to stimulate trade and economic growth between 1994 and 2005, when it pegged the yuan to the US dollar. In the years that followed, China averaged annual GDP growth of 10% and lifted half of its 1.3 billion people out of poverty, widely regarded as an economic miracle. In the next decade, China is projected to surpass the United States as the world's largest economy. Still, the next cold war will be fought by exerting dominance not in the physical world but in the digital one. Data has become more valuable than oil and is now the economic fuel of modern societies. Companies such as Google, Facebook, and Palantir have more knowledge and power than governments have ever had, yet without the same level of accountability to their "digital citizens"—we are their product, not their customers.

Yet while our government increasingly attempts to regulate data collection, it has made no such progress in figuring out how to live with digital currency. In the physical world, the US is known for weaponizing its currency through economic sanctions. But in the digital world, it wages war on its own tech companies with regulations, disabling the very tools that could help it sustain global dominance. For example, the proposed Keep Big Tech Out of Finance Act aims to prevent companies such as Facebook, Amazon, and Google from creating their own "corpo-currencies." (A similar effort to fight US Big Tech was undertaken in Europe with the GDPR.) Meanwhile, the popular Chinese chat and peer-to-peer payment app WeChat has more than 1 billion users, both in China and in other parts of Asia and Africa. Consumers can use the app, which accounts for 34% of China's total mobile traffic, to pay for their everyday expenses. The app is so ubiquitous that it is already accepted by most merchants, with paper bills rarely used; even homeless citizens proudly display their QR codes in the streets.

China already manufactures the majority of the world's consumer products. What happens if, due to the hesitation of Western governments to allow their tech companies to enter the financial sector, China also becomes the owner of the most efficient payment system in the world and forces us to use it when buying its goods? In such a case, the US faces a real threat of no longer being, for the first time in almost a century, the world's reserve currency.

While the renminbi (RMB), as China's currency is known domestically, continues to evolve in its role on the global stage, its integration into international trade reflects its growing status as a potential reserve currency. Historically, currencies have first become integral to trade transactions before ascending to reserve-currency status. The RMB is on a similar trajectory, bolstered by China's extensive trade networks; statistical data reveals a significant link between the extent of a country's trade with China and its accumulation of RMB reserves. This trend is supported by the widespread acceptance of the RMB for invoicing and payments, which facilitates and encourages commerce between Chinese businesses and international partners. Remarkably, the proportion of RMB reserves relative to RMB-denominated trade is comparable to the relationship between Euro reserves and Euro-denominated trade, underscoring the RMB's potential despite China's relatively restricted capital account.

China's strategic use of various financial tools—such as import financing, debt payments, and currency swaps—could continue to elevate the RMB's in the global economy. While holding US dollars has its advantages, it also ties China to mutual dependency with the US, making the evolution of the RMB as a reserve currency a complex but strategic endeavor to diversify economic influence and mitigate reliance on the dollar. The critical question remains: How much US currency does China need to support its economic growth and encourage international use of the RMB? This delicately balanced economic strategy defines the nuanced relationship between the world's leading economies and their currencies.

Behind the Battlefield: The Economics of War

The coming currency battles between China and the United States will be a critical factor in the shape of the world by the end of the 21st century. But the wars the United States will fight in those decades will not, regrettably, be limited to the conceptual. In thinking about the future of the American empire, there is one fact of history that we must never forget: the United States and its currency ascended to global dominance as a result of an almost universally devastating—and wholly physical—world war. The economics of war is at times taboo to discuss, but it is nonetheless an important concept to understand as a motivator behind geopolitical strife.

War can be a unifying cause for a country that wants to divert the attention of its populace attention from internal problems. Governments often use war to unite a divided country, distract from domestic issues, or bolster national pride. The rallying-around-the-flag effect can temporarily boost government popularity and suppress dissent, which can be particularly appealing for leaders facing low approval ratings or internal unrest.

War can also be a mechanism to stimulate economies, especially those that are heavily industrialized or have significant military-industrial sectors. During periods of economic downturn, wars can stimulate economic activity by increasing government spending, notably in defense and infrastructure, leading to higher employment and manufacturing output. This idea is somewhat reflected in Keynesian economics, which advocates for increased government expenditure and lower taxes to stimulate demand and pull the global economy out of depression; a prime example is the increase in production and employment during World War II, which is often credited with helping the United States recover from the Great Depression. Wars also often grant access to resources. This can be a significant incentive for countries that depend on specific strategic resources such as oil, minerals, or territory; control over oil-rich regions has frequently been cited as a driving factor behind numerous 20th- and 21st-century conflicts in the Middle East.

Examples of Wars Fought for Economic Gain

Whether internal—such as the US Civil War, rooted in the economics of slavery—or multilateral, wars have long been fought to settle economic questions or remediate economic issues. Here are just a few prominent historical examples.

The **Anglo-Dutch Wars** (1652–1674) were a series of conflicts between England and the Dutch Republic, largely driven by commercial and maritime rivalries as the two nations competed for trade supremacy.

The **Opium Wars** (1839–1842, 1856–1860) were fought by Britain against China to force open Chinese markets for British opium and other trade. In these wars, Britain sought to improve its trade deficit with China and gain economic concessions.

The **Banana Wars** (1898–1934) refer to the various military interventions by the United States in Latin America and the Caribbean aimed at protecting American commercial interests, especially the United Fruit Company's banana plantations.

World War II (1939–1945) had economic dimensions, with Japan's invasion of East Asia partly motivated by its need for raw materials and resources to fuel its industrial economy. Nazi Germany also sought to conquer territory and resources through *lebensraum* ("living space" for economic exploitation).

The **Six-Day War** (1967) between Israel and several Arab states (especially Egypt, Syria, and Jordan) was partly driven by tensions over control of the Strait of Tiran, a key shipping lane for Israeli trade.

The **Boer War** (1899–1902) was fought between Great Britain and the Boer Republics in modern-day South Africa over control of the Witwatersrand gold mines, which were the largest gold-mining complex in the world at the time.

The **Gulf War** (1990–1991) between the United States and Iraq was triggered by Iraq's invasion of Kuwait, which was seen as an attempt by Saddam Hussein to control Kuwait's oil, wealth, and resources.

In his farewell speech to the nation in 1961, President Dwight Eisenhower, who rose to national prominence as the Supreme Allied Commander in the European theater in World War II, famously warned of the rise of the "military-industrial complex"—a coalition of armed forces and defense industries that have a vested interest in the maintenance of high military spending. This sector benefits directly from wars and prolonged military engagements, and its influence on policy can be a powerful driver for entering or continuing conflicts.

The incentives for war often involve a combination of economic, political, and social factors, making it a tool that can be exploited for multiple ends. However, the costs of war are also very high—in terms of loss of life, resource expenditures, and long-term social impacts—which makes the calculus of war a subject of intense debate and ethical consideration. Recent wars in which the United States has significant involvement, despite a total lack of US troops on the ground, constitute prominent displays of these competing incentives at work in American politics.

Ukraine vs. Russia

The genesis of the recent conflict between Ukraine and Russia, which escalated significantly in 2022 with Russia's invasion of Ukraine, arguably has a strong economic undercurrent.

When I was born in the Soviet Union, I was technically born on the Ukrainian side of the border between the two Soviet republics, moving to the Russian side shortly afterward. At the age of four, on New Year's Eve 1991, I saw the two become fully separate countries. Yet for my family, which had heritage from both sides, there remained very little difference. Travel between the two countries was virtually unrestricted, and they shared similar cultures, from food to music to humor. Although Ukrainian is a distinct language, it shares roots with Russian, and the vast majority of Ukrainian citizens still speak Russian fluently.

The two nations' economies were also historically incredibly intertwined, with many Ukrainians choosing to attend Russian universities and seek employment in other countries. The countries were also intertwined in terms of natural resources, with Ukraine being a large food supplier to Russia and the rest of Europe, and Russia supplying natural gas and oil to Europe through pipelines under Ukrainian soil. Ukraine is a major global supplier of grains and is the EU's fourth-biggest external food supplier, providing about a quarter of its cereal and vegetable oil imports. Before the war, more than 400 million people globally relied on foodstuffs from Ukraine, which has over one-third of the world's most fertile soil, known as *chernozem*, or black soil.

The situation escalated in 2014, leading to the annexation of Crimea by Russian forces (which Putin claimed, at the time, were domestic Ukrainian operatives, though this assertion was never widely taken seriously) and, eventually, a full-scale invasion of Ukraine by Russia in February 2022. This essentially open declaration of war by Putin, largely viewed as Russia's attempt to reassert its influence over Ukraine and prevent its further integration with Western political and military structures, has led to international condemnation, severe economic sanctions against Russia, and a humanitarian crisis.

But many other factors were also at play here.

Globally, the war resulted in temporary fuel shortages in Europe, as Russia cut off the supply of natural gas to Germany and other European countries that refused to pay in rubles, jump-starting a European energy crisis. Most of Europe is natural gas dependent, using it to run factories, generate electricity, and heat homes. In some areas, the plunging supply caused natural gas costs to increase tenfold. As usual, those who suffered the most were the working class, as they struggled to pay their utility bills. Many government leaders feared political unrest. Rising fuel costs also led to rampant inflation. In the weeks and months following the invasion, the ruble, the euro, and currencies of Central and Eastern European nations such as Poland, Hungary, and the Czech Republic hit multiyear or record lows against the US dollar.

Meanwhile, America is fighting its own inflationary pressures exacerbated by helping to foot the bill for Ukraine to fight this war. According to the Kiel Institute for the World Economy, from January 24, 2022, to February 29, 2024, the US allocated $72.3 billion to Ukrainian aid following the invasion. In April 2024, after months of deliberation and deadlock, the US Senate approved an additional $61 billion. About one-third of this money will be spent replenishing the US military with more modern and advanced weaponry to replace the old and, as a result, used machinery that is by some accounts inoperable being sent over to the Ukrainian army. So the assistance is in reality serving many purposes, among them continuing to fuel the military-industrial complex warned of by President Eisenhower some 60 years ago.

Israel vs. Hamas

On October 7, 2023, Palestinian Hamas militants based in Gaza organized a large-scale incursion into Israel, killing at least 1,163 Israeli men, women, and children. This was the deadliest attack against Israel since its founding in 1948, and the unprecedented scale of the violence left the country and its people deeply scarred. The day marked an intense and irreversible escalation in tensions between Israel and the anti-Israeli Arab world.

Israel's retaliation against these terrorists, thought to be hiding in Gaza, has been swift and deadly: as of May 2024, the estimated death count in Gaza is over 31,000. The US initially signaled it would stand with Israel, with President Biden condemning the attack in the strongest possible terms, promising American support would be "rock solid and unwavering." (Even before the Hamas attack, the United States provided between $3 billion and $4 billion to Israel annually, primarily for the maintenance of its military capabilities; since its founding in 1948, Israel has received almost $300 billion in US aid, nearly twice as much as any other nation.) In the months that followed, however, the strain between the US and its fiercest ally began to show, with American public support for the war waning in the face of the mounting death toll.

By mid-April 2024, protests against US involvement in the conflict overtook college campuses across the country in a stunning display of civil unrest, especially at Columbia University, in New York; the University of California, Los Angeles; and Northwestern University, in Illinois. Students set up tent encampments at more than 80 schools across the country, calling for their institutions to divest from and cut ties with companies and entities linked to Israel or endorsing Israel's retaliatory actions in Palestine.

During these protests, students and administrators often pitted competing civil rights against each other. Suppression by police forces—over 2,000 students arrested at around 30 campuses to date—led to accusations of First Amendment violations. Jewish students and staff accused both protesters and college administrations of anti-Semitism and failing to maintain a safe environment. Clashes between pro-Palestinian protesters and pro-Israeli counter-protesters have resulted in vandalism and violence on both sides.

In a May 9 speech addressing the protesters, President Biden said, "We are a civil society, and order must prevail.... Dissent is essential for democracy. But dissent must never lead to disorder." Of course, such a speech—attempting, in a critical presidential election year, to thread the needle between an older generation of voters that predominantly approves of US military support for Israeli in Gaza and a rising generation of voters that frequently does not—fails to take account of the fact that dissent without disorder rarely brings about major policy change. So which is it—order or freedom to dissent?

These ongoing geopolitical conflicts, and America's continued need to both lead and fund them, are resulting in a loss of national pride and, more importantly, a loss of faith in the superiority of the American way. Most empires fall when their citizens lose faith in the empire's superior status and, thus, its right to benevolently lead the world in a productive direction.

Increasingly, our beliefs about whether or not the American empire is benevolent are shaped by our interactions with social media. Six years ago, the Cambridge Analytica scandal exploded across our smartphone screens, revealing the extent to which big data and social media giants have graduated from reflecting to *shaping* political outcomes. The scandal hit very close to home for every Facebook user in America, whose data was specifically mined and who were sent targeted ads designed to sway or reinforce their political leanings; Cambridge Analytica bragged that it had up to 5,000 data points on every US voter.

Experts have warned that this is just the tip of the iceberg. Far from an outlier event, this is the business model that academic Shoshana Zuboff dubs "surveillance capitalism." "Microtargeting" social media users involves data-driven service providers analyzing harvested data for political campaigns, allowing their clients to better target political messages to people most likely to be influenced by them. The pioneers of surveillance capitalism—Google and Meta, Facebook's parent company—control the primary means by which people outside China access the online world. In a harbinger of much worse to come, in May 2024, OpenAI announced the removal of influence operations tied to Russia, China, and Israel that used its generative artificial intelligence to create social media content advancing political agendas.

For the US, what is coming from China poses yet another threat altogether.

Recently, the US has passed legislation giving ByteDance, the parent company of the overwhelmingly popular social video app TikTok, up to one year to sell the app to a US buyer or face a nationwide ban on its flagship product, citing the app's potential for harvesting data that could be made accessible to the Chinese government for purposes, among other things, of spreading misinformation and propaganda. (Of course, savvy social media users will note that Facebook, Google, and other US tech giants have already been shown to share user data with US intelligence agencies and moderate content at their request, as evidenced by the "Twitter Files.")

While data privacy and concerns over the accuracy of online media consumed by American youth is the stated reason for the proposed ban, it may in fact be driven more by geopolitical tensions with Beijing. More than two-thirds of Americans aged 18 to 29 are TikTok users (about 150 million Americans, almost half the nation's population, over-all), and a 2023 Pew survey found that 32% of TikTok users in that age cohort said they regularly get their news on TikTok—which (again, like all social media) is fueled by algorithms that favor confirmation bias and echo chambers. This makes TikTok potentially one of the most danger-ous weapons against American global hegemony.

And if our youth no longer believe in the American dream, who will defend the American empire?

Bitcoin Is a Silent Protest

So how does Bitcoin fit into this global shift? Increasingly, Americans of all political stripes (as well as citizens of the world) are finding that Bitcoin offers a way to opt out of or hedge against the risks of political and financial systems you may no longer believe in. If American financial hegemony is in fact at risk, Bitcoin offers a store of value outside the US dollar, a truly borderless and independent asset class that will continue to keep its value, regardless of global political and economic transitions. Notably, it tends to be much easier to convince those who grew up in unstable and/or inflation-prone countries to believe in the value of Bitcoin, than to convince those in the West who have experienced life-times of relative stability. Unlike those in many developing countries, Western systems have not yet fully broken. Yet those of us who have seen what a collapsing empire looks like cannot unsee it.

America is not immune to a financial revolution.

America is unique in that it has not experienced major economic upheaval besides the Great Depression and the financial crisis in 2008, creating a widespread base of trust in the system. But America's fiat cur-rency is only about 50 years old, a relatively unproven experiment. By contrast, Sterling, the British pound (GBP), is the world's oldest cur-rency still in use and is around 1,200 years old. In other nation-states, such as Venezuela and Zimbabwe, fiat currency has already failed.

Increasingly, many everyday people who are dissatisfied with the ways that government-run and highly centralized financial systems have failed to support their basic survival needs argue that money should not be politicized. The wealth you work so hard to create should remain intact regardless of the decisions of your government, whether that's to start a war, issue a corporate bailout, or make a bad trade agreement. The value of money that is backed only by the authority of governments is constantly in jeopardy from the actions of those same governments. In fact, the entire thesis behind the traditional investment industry is a grand attempt to prevent the erosion of value through inflation. Bitcoin allows us the opportunity to opt out of the current financial system, all without lifting a weapon or raising our voices. It is a silent, but effective, protest.

Experts have long foreseen the emergence of a revolutionary financial system. Nobel Prize–winning economist Friedrich Hayek said, in 1984, "I don't believe we shall ever have good money again before we take the thing out of the hands of government, that is, we can't take it violently out of the hands of government: all we can do is, by some sly roundabout way, introduce something they can't stop." In 2008, that unstoppable thing was introduced, as a protest against the financial system in general and monetary stimulus in particular. Bitcoin is money for people, not governments; since its creation more than fifteen years ago, a growing number of individuals have chosen to opt out, at least to some degree, of the traditional financial system, the central source of government's power. They are turning instead to a new monetary system, one that is not controlled by any single authority but is decentralized and run by a network of computers.

Bitcoin was born out of protest against the financial system in 2008.

And for the first time in thousands of years, Bitcoin has created a world that envisions a separation of money and state.

MONEY MYTH #10: The US dollar is different.

The US dollar has been the world's reserve currency for so long that it has acquired an air of permanence and invulnerability—an illusion that American financial companies and politicians are more than happy to promote. However, the notion that US dollar hegemony will last forever is not just misguided but increasingly unlikely. Firstly, it's crucial to understand that no empire lasts forever. The United States, despite its unprecedented power and influence, is not immune to the cyclical nature of history. Signs of the American empire's decline are evident in the nation's political polarization, rampant economic inequality, and overstretched military commitments. These issues weaken the foundations upon which the dollar's dominance was built.

Moreover, de-dollarization is a growing trend in the world economy. Countries such as China and Russia are actively reducing their dependence on the dollar by promoting their own currencies in international trade. The emergence of digital currencies and blockchain technology further threatens the dollar's supremacy by providing alternative means of transaction that bypass traditional financial systems. As more nations seek to insulate themselves from US economic policies and sanctions, global reliance on the dollar diminishes.

The American dream, once a symbol of opportunity and prosperity, is also under threat. Economic inequality in the United States has reached alarming levels, with the middle-class shrinking and wealth increasingly concentrated at the top. The cost of living continues to rise, making homeownership and higher education unattainable for many. Health care remains prohibitively expensive. These factors contribute to a growing disillusionment with the idea that anyone in America can achieve success through hard work alone.

In light of these realities, assuming that assets denominated in USD are untouchable is a dangerous misconception. The dollar, like any currency, is subject to geopolitical and macroeconomic forces that can devalue it. Inflation, national debt, and global shifts in power all play roles in undermining its value. Believing in the dollar's perpetual dominance ignores the lessons of history and the current global economic landscape. To safeguard one's financial future, it's essential to recognize these vulnerabilities and adapt accordingly. The dollar's reign may yet endure a while, but there are always competitors with their eyes on the throne.

A Path Forward

If it's not #bitcoin, your money is melting.
— Michael Saylor (@saylor) May 17, 2024

I sit down to write the concluding remarks of this book in June of 2024, a pivotal election year in the United States. The outcome of this election will be important not only for the future of the American empire but also for the financial future of the American people. The events that unfold over the next few months will have a dramatic impact on America's fiscal and monetary policy, the status of the US dollar, and the well-being of those in the West and abroad.

Regardless of the outcome, however, it is important to note that the conventional wisdom about finances that governed previous generations has become obsolete. The principles that once underpinned our governmental currency systems were largely discredited with the abandonment of the gold standard in the 1970s. Since then, an entire investment industry has been created with the goal of preserving our capital in an environment where the target rate of inflation is 2.4%. Yet the investment-banking models created for this purpose, and that defined the 90s and early 2000s, began to crumble in the wake of the 2008 financial crisis. Even the once-sacrosanct belief that homeowner-ship is the pinnacle of financial success, and perhaps the best savings tool available, is being reevaluated in a world where such milestones are increasingly elusive due to unreachable prices and rising interest rates. Meanwhile, over the last few years, aggressive monetary policy in the US has revealed that our current financial system often does more harm than good to its citizens. The entire financial system feels like a game of hot potato where so many investments, including fiat currency itself, seem increasingly risky. This pattern is unsustainable.

In an era marked by rapid globalization and technological advancement, the pressing question remains: How can we ensure that our financial system serves us, rather than us serving it? How do we create a reality where we can engage with the world, pursue our passions, and maintain a sense of groundedness, knowing our finances are secure and our assets are appreciating in value, rather than diminishing through inflation?

Throughout this book, you have heard the story of how I learned the ins and outs of money—its realities and its myths—firsthand. Most importantly, you have read about the challenges we all face in preserving the value of what we earn within a fiat system inherently skewed toward perpetual inflation. As I close this narrative, my focus will shift toward practical strategies and innovative approaches to harness financial tools that empower us, ensuring our money endures and enhances our lives in a rapidly inflationary landscape.

Before we understand how to preserve it, we must understand what money and value actually are, and how they differ from each other. We have already discussed, in Chapter 6, the classic definition of money and its intended functionalities. To recap, economists define money as a medium of exchange, a unit of account, and a store of value. Most economists also believe that the modern system of fiat currency meets all three of these requirements.

At the Abundance Summit in April 2024, I attended a fireside chat led by Peter Diamandis, founder of X Prize, and Michael Saylor, CEO of Microstrategy and one of Bitcoin's biggest proponents. In Michael's comments, he pointed out that the above definition of money is actually incredibly flawed, as many of the things we currently consider money do not satisfy all of its conditions.

The world has hundreds of fiat currencies in use, and there are many mediums of exchange, as any nation can designate its currency as legal tender—such as the Zimbabwean dollar, the Argentinian peso, or the Lebanese lira. However, many of these currencies suffer from hyperinflation and thus fail as a stable medium of exchange.

Saylor further highlighted that only three currencies are globally recognized as principal units of account: the US dollar, the euro, and the Chinese yuan. He posited that Bitcoin is on track to become the fourth, as people in countries with volatile currencies will logically begin to reject their local currency for purposes of keeping savings or pricing significant assets, opting instead for more stable alternatives. This shift underscores the crucial role of stability in the world's acceptance of a currency as a valid unit of account.

What about money as a store of value? We've observed that the wealthiest echelons of society rarely maintain their wealth exclusively in standard currencies such as US dollars. Instead, their portfolios are diversified into assets such as real estate, businesses, art, and even sports teams. For instance, billionaire Mark Cuban not only owns the Dallas Mavericks, of the NBA, but he also holds investments in a multitude of other ventures. Similarly, affluent celebrities often own multiple properties in sought-after locations with staggering price tags: in May 2023, Beyoncé and Jay-Z bought a house in Malibu for $200 million. The Toronto and Vancouver real estate markets have seen dramatic increases in value over the past decade, fueled in part by wealthy Asian investors seeking long-term opportunities in politically and economically stable Western markets. In 2015, Canada's National Bank Financial estimated purchases of real estate in Vancouver by Chinese nationals over the preceding year amounted to nearly one-third ($10 billion USD) of total real estate transactions in the city, causing the median price for a single-family home to jump 40%.

In regions where local economic systems are less stable, individuals who seek to use real estate as a store of value face significant risks, such as sudden changes in taxation, zoning laws, or even the imposition of eminent domain (a government's power to seize private property for public use). Business ventures in these areas can likewise be fraught with instability, and the resultant volatility of the local currency means that financial institutions might be vulnerable to bank runs. In this context, Bitcoin emerges as a compelling alternative. It provides a borderless, accessible method to safeguard wealth, offering not just a store of value but also remarkable growth, with an average annualized return of 67.4% in the 15 years since its creation. This positions Bitcoin not merely as an alternative investment but as the premier technology for savings in an increasingly uncertain global economy.

Critics often argue that Bitcoin is impractical as a medium of exchange, due to the high costs and complexities associated with small transactions. This challenge, however, has been largely mitigated by innovations such as the Lightning Network, a topic we explored in depth during our visit to El Salvador in Chapter 5. Even so, Bitcoin maximalists (those who believe that Bitcoin is the only digital asset that will be needed in the future and the only cryptocurrency that embodies the ideals of creator Satoshi Nakamoto) contend that Bitcoin should not be compared to traditional money but should be viewed as digital property. Just as one wouldn't chip off a piece of a Monet painting or a Mies van der Rohe building to pay for lunch, they assert, we shouldn't expect to use Bitcoin in the same way for everyday purchases.

Wealthy individuals often leverage their assets for liquidity by taking out loans against them. As the Bitcoin ecosystem matures, Bitcoin is also becoming an asset against which one can borrow. This capability extends to everyday spending and even securing mortgages. Additionally, Bitcoin's acceptance by regulators has grown, enhancing its accessibility for those looking to capitalize on its potential for appreciation. While I advocate for storing coins in hardware wallets—a precaution emphasized by the maxim "Not your keys, not your crypto" discussed in Chapter 9—new solutions are emerging that are easier to use for traditional investors.

A significant recent development in the crypto investing world was the regulatory approval of Bitcoin ETFs in the US in January 2024. Among these were ETFs structured by renowned financial institutions such as Blackrock, Franklin Templeton, and Fidelity, with management fees ranging from 0.19% to 0.90%. This milestone serves to mainstream Bitcoin investment, offering a more accessible platform for traditional investors to engage with digital assets.

The SEC's recent approval of the listing and trading of 11 spot Bitcoin exchange-traded product shares marks a pivotal moment, potentially easing some of the concerns surrounding investments in the cryptocurrency space. This regulatory nod introduces more robust safeguards, paving the way for investments through well-established financial entities. Previously, options for retail investors to delve into cryptocurrency were somewhat limited, confined to direct purchases or investments in ETFs tied to crypto futures. The introduction of a spot Bitcoin ETF allows investors, especially at the retail level, to access Bitcoin through standard investment accounts such as brokerage and retirement accounts without directly managing a Bitcoin wallet. This simplification of access is likely to broaden the asset's appeal to a wider investor base. Although Bitcoin ETFs do not provide in full the decentralization, liquidity, and portability of Bitcoin itself, they offer more traditional investors an opportunity to dip their toes into the waters of Bitcoin's value proposition.

This significant shift in the regulatory landscape enhances Bitcoin's accessibility and cements its status as the modern "digital gold," especially amid escalating geopolitical uncertainties. It encourages major investors such as college endowments, pension funds, sovereign wealth funds, and treasuries of S&P 500 companies to consider hedging part of their cash holdings in Bitcoin. In April 2024, Cathie Wood, the CEO of ARK Invest, speculated that Bitcoin's value could soar to as much as $3.8 million by 2030 if institutional investors allocated just 5% of their portfolios to it.

Thus, Bitcoin stands out not only as a promising avenue for retail investors to secure and potentially enhance their financial futures but also poses a stark contrast to traditional investment vehicles such as government bonds and treasuries, which currently offer returns of 4% to 5% hardly keeping pace with an inflation rate exceeding 3%.

Meanwhile, the venture capital sector faces challenges from overvaluation in sectors of questionable necessity, mirroring similar corrections in the public stock market, with the notable exception of the burgeoning deep tech sector. "Deep tech" encompasses a range of industries that involve significant scientific advances and high-tech engineering innovation. These sectors typically focus on profound technology breakthroughs, which are often based on tangible engineering innovations or scientific discoveries. One can invest in these themes in both public stock and private venture capital markets.

Here are some of the key verticals that are positioned for success in the deep tech sector:

1. **Artificial intelligence and, in particular, machine learning** encompass technologies that enable machines to learn from experience and perform humanlike tasks. With the advent of OpenAI's ChatGPT, this is currently one of the hottest sectors in Silicon Valley. There are thousands of companies involved in the sector, from small AI start-ups to large publicly traded giants such as NVIDIA.

2. **Robotics** entails the design and manufacturing of robots that can automate tasks traditionally done by humans, often used in manufacturing, health care, and services. A couple of notable public companies in this sector are iRobot and Boston Dynamics.

3. **Biotechnology and pharmaceuticals** include the use of biological processes, organisms, or systems to develop products that improve the quality of human life, including genetic engineering, cell therapy, and regenerative medicine. This is an incredibly dense sector that requires a deep understanding of the subject matter. Although I personally have a couple of early-stage investments here, I often refer folks to ARK Invest's Biotech ETF, which is available on the stock market and invests in a basket of some of the best companies in the sector.

4. **Quantum computing** involves leveraging the principles of quantum mechanics to process information in fundamentally different ways than classical computers. Microsoft and Google are just some of the possible investments in this sector.

5. **Energy** encompasses innovations in clean-energy production, storage, and consumption, including solar, wind, and other renewable energy technologies. A popular investment in this category is electric cars, especially Tesla, one of the best-performing stocks of all time.

6. **Space technology** includes all development related to spacecraft, satellites, and other technology used for space exploration and commercialization. Space tech is a bit more difficult to find on the public markets, with Elon Musk's SpaceX and Jeff Bezos's Blue Origin being private-sector leaders. Richard Branson's Virgin Galactic was taken public by Chamath Palihapitiya and is available to retail investors, although historically the stock has underperformed.

7. **Neurotechnology** entails technologies that enhance our under-standing of the brain and can treat or manipulate brain function, including brain-computer interfaces. Elon Musk's Neuralink comes to mind.

All of these sectors are characterized by their high capital intensity, long research and development cycles, and significant technological risks. They often require substantial investments in both time and money and typically aim to address or transform large-scale global issues or industries. But they are also the sectors that are best positioned to outperform over the next two decades.

An additional trend to keep in mind when looking at these sectors as potential investments is a push for investment in American dynamism.

"American dynamism" refers to a concerted effort to keep the American empire as a technological leader on a global stage. Though the Manhattan Project and the moon landing happened when America was arguably at her most dynamic, the technology sector is the only sector of the American economy that has maintained its vibrancy, vigor, and growth through innovation over the last 25 years. The top six companies by market capitalization in the US are now technology companies, two of which were founded in the 2000s. Indeed, tech has been propping up all other sectors, including the financial institutions that have lost all civic and public trust. In 2020, this fact became so obvious that there isn't much of a counterargument: from the Moderna vaccine to the uninterrupted services of Amazon Prime, Zoom, and Netflix, the scientific and operational excellence of consequential technology companies made up for the shortfalls of our flailing governmental institutions. American dynamism is rooted in the United States' history of embracing change, fostering technological advancements, and maintaining a competitive, free-market economy that encourages individuals and businesses to innovate and take risks.

The Biden administration's strategic maneuvers to bolster the US as a global technological powerhouse have been evident through a series of decisive actions. One of the administration's most foresighted initiatives has been the re-onshoring of semiconductor manufacturing. By blacklisting 21 key Chinese manufacturers, the administration has made a significant move to enhance domestic chip production, signaling a stronger future for America's technological sovereignty. Additionally, the push to diminish the influence of Chinese social media apps such as TikTok in favor of US-based alternatives such as Instagram exemplifies this drive toward technological independence.

In a bold step to safeguard American industries from foreign competition, in May 2024, President Biden announced substantial increases in tariffs on a swath of Chinese imports. This includes a dramatic rise in tariffs on Chinese electric vehicles—from 25% to 100%—and on solar cells, with the tariffs doubling from 25% to 50%. Tariffs on certain Chinese steel and aluminum imports are set to escalate from 7.5% to 25%. The administration has also planned to significantly increase tariffs on lithium–ion batteries for electric vehicles and other uses, and by 2025. Tariffs on Chinese semiconductors will also see a substantial change, from 25% to 50%. These measures, led by US Trade Representative Katherine Tai, are designed to fortify domestic industries and reclaim technological leadership.

The final investment trend to be aware of when preserving (and accumulating) wealth is the concept of financial nihilism. Financial nihilism is a philosophy that questions the traditional financial system and its mechanisms; people with this view doubt the fairness and efficacy of modern financial architecture, from its instruments to its institutions. They feel the system is rigged against them, leading to what is seen as risky, spontaneous, or poorly informed financial decisions. Perhaps the most interesting aspect of financial nihilism as a philosophy, from my perspective, is that it is seen to be dangerous, as it undermines the trust that is essential for the existing financial system to continue to operate as the status quo.

Financial nihilism encapsulates the terrible truth that upward mobility and trickle–down wealth are evaporating dreams for many Americans and that the American dream as an ideal is increasingly untenable. The ratio of median home prices to median income has soared, making both the millennial and Gen-Z generators less likely to be homeowners. Inflation and rising interest rates mean the traditional value of saving currency and investing in government bonds are no longer viable means to secure your financial future. These grim realities have laid the groundwork for a radical shift in attitudes among young earners: witnessing minimal growth in their share of household income, more young Americans are falling for the allure of high–risk, high–reward investments such as meme stocks and cryptocurrencies. From GameStop to crypto meme coins such as $PEPE, as the rich grow richer and economic disparity deepens, those left behind or underserved by the financial system are finding themselves compelled to take more significant risks.

The link between poverty and a rise in problem gambling is well documented, though complex (especially if you consider Wall Street investments to be bets; at some level of analysis the link muddies), but America's poorest households spend 33 times more of their income on lottery tickets than the rich. Many Americans are essentially attempting to buy their way out of a system that wasn't made for them and doesn't work for them, yet even as they attempt to buy hope with what they have, they're *still* playing a game where the house always wins. This phenomenon is widespread both domestically and abroad.

Throughout my journey, discovering the myths of money the hard way, I have learned that wealth for the youngest generations is often created by a different set of rules from those of our forebears. Whether we are buying Bitcoin or meme coins or a futuristic tech investment, we are no longer in it for an 8% return. And so, dear reader, as we conclude the story of my personal journey through the financial world, I will leave you with one final thought: The world is changing at an unprecedented pace. In this new landscape, your teacher, your banker, your friends, and even your parents do not necessarily know the correct course of action for your career or your financial well-being. Stay curious, ask questions, and chart your own path. Now more than ever, your financial future is up to you.

For up to date market tips and news, follow our weekly newsletter at www.MythOfMoney.com.

About the Author

Tatiana Koffman is a globally recognized investor, writer, and speaker with over a decade of experience across investment banking, derivatives, venture capital, and digital assets. She's widely recognized for her finance and technology expertise, frequently sharing her insights in prominent publications such as *Forbes*, CoinDesk, CoinTelegraph, CNBC, the *Economist*, Business Insider, and TechCrunch.

Koffman is the General Partner of the investment firm Moonwalker Capital and is the author of the popular financial newsletter MythOfMoney.com.

Koffman holds a JD/MBA from York University and is a member of the New York State Bar. Koffman started her career in derivatives trading at TD Bank in Toronto. Previously, Koffman wrote a popular

Forbes column and worked on venture capital investments for Grammy Award-winning artists such as the Chainsmokers and Linkin Park in Los Angeles.

Additionally, Koffman contributes to academia as a visiting lecturer on blockchain at UCLA and Pepperdine. Her work has been academically cited at prestigious institutions including UCLA, Sorbonne University, and in the *Michigan Law Review*.

Index